Building Reading Skills

Revised Edition

Level 1

LEVEL 2

Level 3

Level 4

Building Reading Skills

Revised Edition
LEVEL 2

Gerald G. Duffy
Professor of Education, Michigan State University

Laura R. Roehler
Associate Professor of Education, Michigan State University

McDougal, Littell & Company
Evanston, Illinois
New York   Sacramento

About the Authors

Dr. Gerald G. Duffy, a professor in the Department of Elementary and Special Education, Michigan State University at Lansing, spent ten years as an elementary and middle school teacher and regularly returns to the classroom during his sabbaticals. He received his doctorate in June of 1966 from Northern Illinois University. His pre-service and in-service workshops, field work, and research all center on his continuing interest in teaching reading in the classroom.

Dr. Laura R. Roehler, an associate professor and co-ordinator of the Language Arts Project of the Institute for Research on Teaching at Michigan State University, has wide experience in training teachers of reading and in developing materials for their use, both within the university program and in a public school setting. She taught middle grades and junior high school for five years before receiving her Ph.D. in 1972 from Michigan State University.

Acknowledgments

"Airline Schedule," adapted from *American Airlines Quick Reference Timetable*, effective September 16, 1978. "The Ballplayer" by Amy Love; adapted from *GirlSports* by Karen Folger Jacobs; copyright © 1978 by Karen Folger Jacobs; reprinted by permission of Bantam Books, Inc., New York; all rights reserved. "Before the Big Trouble Came," an adaptation of pages 21–23 from *Boy and Girl Tramps of America* by Thomas Minehan; copyright © 1934, © 1962 by Thomas Minehan; reprinted by permission of Holt, Rinehart and Winston, New York. An excerpt from pages 23–30 of *Ben and Me* by Robert Lawson; copyright 1939 by Robert Lawson, renewed © 1967 by John W. Boyd; reprinted by permission of Little, Brown and Company, Boston. An adaptation of "Benjamin Banneker" by Charles E. Anderson from *Boys' Life* Magazine, July 1976; copyright © 1976 by the Boy Scouts of America, North Brunswick, New Jersey; reprinted by permission of Charles E. Anderson, attorney-at-law, Washington, D.C. "The Blackbird and the Worm" from *Woodland Crossings* by Stephen Krensky; copyright © 1978 by Stephen Krensky; originally adapted by *Cricket* Magazine, March 1978; reprinted by permission of Atheneum Publishers, Inc., New York. "Breaking into TV" by Susan Collins; an adaptation from *Who Puts the News on Television?—Adventures in the World of Work*, by Barbara Steinberg; copyright © 1976 by Random House, Inc.; reprinted by permission of Random House, Inc., New York. An adaptation of pages 68–73 from *Breakthrough to the Big League, The Story of Jackie Robinson*, by Jackie Robinson and Alfred Duckett; copyright ©
(continued on page 481)

ISBN: 0-88343-807-0

Contents

Section 2 Comprehension Skills

Unit 8   Reactions to Fear   202

Learn About the Skills

Apply the Comprehension Skills You Have Learned

Section 3   Study and Research Skills

Unit 9   Ways and Means   234

Learn About the Skills

Apply the Literary Appreciation Skills You Have Learned

About This Book

This is a book about reading. It will help you to read with ease, understanding, and pleasure. You will learn how to apply your skills to the reading you do for your other school subjects. You will also learn how to apply your skills to your reading outside of school.

The Organization of This Book

This book is divided into four Sections. Each Section emphasizes a major reading skill:

Vocabulary Development Skills: pages 2–115. These pages have blue tabs in the bottom outside corners.

Comprehension Skills: pages 117–231. These pages have red tabs.

Study and Research Skills: pages 233–347. These pages have green tabs.

Literary Appreciation Skills: pages 349–463. These pages have yellow tabs.

Each Section is made up of four units. Each unit contains:

- ## Four Skills Teaching Pages

  Overview and Purposes for Reading. This page introduces the theme of the unit and defines your purpose for reading the unit. For example, see page 2.
  Learn About the Skills. The next two pages teach the major skill covered in the section. The fourth page discusses another type of reading skill. See pages 3–5, for example.

- ## Five Reading Selections

  These center around the theme of the unit. Each selection is preceded by a Use the Skills page and followed by questions that Check the Skills.

- ## Apply What You Learned in the Unit

  These pages summarize the theme of the unit and offer further questions to help you check your understanding of the skills.

  At the end of each Section, there are several pages that help you to Apply the Skills You Have Learned. These pages provide questions and further discussion about the skills and show how these skills relate to your schoolwork and to your life.

Additional Help for the Student

Context Clues. Some words in the selections may be unfamiliar to you. Many of these have hints to their meanings in other words and sentences around them. These hints are called *context clues*. A word for which there are context clues is followed by a small letter *c*, like this.c

Glossary. Some words in the selections are included in the glossary at the back of the book. A small *g* after a word means the word is in the glossary.

A list of the context clue words and glossary words begins on page 475.

Section 1 Vocabulary Development Skills

Unit 1

Accomplishments

Overview and Purposes for Reading

The Theme

Accomplishments

1. An accomplishment is something done or achieved because of special knowledge, skill, or talent. How do people's interests and abilities influence what they choose to accomplish?

The Skills

Vocabulary Development Skills Word Structure

2. Can knowing something about suffixes help you when you read? How?

3. How can you combine the meaning of the base word with the meaning of the suffix to figure out the meaning of a word?

Study and Research Skills Reading Techniques

4. Why is it important to adjust your reading rate to the type of material you are reading and to your purpose for reading the material?

Learn About the Skills

Vocabulary Development Skills Word Structure

You probably recognize the words *sight* and *thank*. But can you figure out *sightless* and *thankful?* These may look like long, hard words. But you can easily figure them out if you know something about suffixes. A suffix is one or more syllables added to the end of a word.

In the English language a new word is often made by adding a suffix to the end of another word. In fact, several suffixes may be added in a row, as in *sightlessness* and *thankfully.* Suffixes usually give you a good clue to how the word is used in the sentence. Many suffixes also have their own special meaning.

You already know most of the common suffixes. You use them when you talk and you understand them when you hear them. But you may have difficulty figuring out words with suffixes when you meet them in your reading.

To figure out a word that includes one or more suffixes, follow these steps:

Reading Suffixes

1. Drop all the suffixes so you can identify the base word. The base word is sometimes called the root word. It is the smallest real word left after all prefixes and suffixes are taken away.

2. Decide on the meaning of the base word.

3. Think about the meaning of the suffix. But remember that not all suffixes have clear meanings.

4. In your mind, add the meaning of the suffix to the meaning of the base word.

Try the Skill. Let's see how this works with *sightlessness*. Drop the suffixes *-less* and *-ness* to find the base word *sight*. You know that *-less* usually has a clear meaning of "without" or "not having." So *sightless* means "without sight." Go through the same steps with *-ness*. You'll figure out that *-ness* often means "having the quality of" or "the condition of being." So *sightlessness* is the condition of being without sight.

What does *thoughtfully* mean? See if you can figure it out. You can find *-ful*, *-ly*, and some other common suffixes in most dictionaries. Look them up if you need to. You're right if you decided that *thoughtfully* means "in a manner showing thought."

The trick is to make sure a real base word remains after taking off what seems to be a suffix. If you don't find a base word you recognize, then the suffix strategy won't help you figure out the word! The *-able* in *cable* and *constable* is not the suffix you see in *laughable*. Why not?

As you read this unit, you'll have more chances to use your skill with suffixes.

Study and Research Skills Reading Techniques

Many people think that good readers always read as fast as possible. That is not true. Good readers adjust their reading rate to suit their purpose for reading and the type of material they are reading. You can, too. Look at this chart:

Purpose for Reading	Type of Material	Reading Rate
Fun, general interest	Library book, paperback, magazine	Quick and easy. You don't have to read every word. No need to remember everything.
Information	Encyclopedia, dictionary, newspaper, other reference materials	Skim, or glance quickly, to locate what you need. Then change your rate to slow and careful. Read only the part you need.
How to do something	Directions for making, building, or repairing something	Skim first to get a general idea. Then change your rate to very slow. Read every word. Reread each step as you follow it.
Study	Textbooks, materials assigned in school	Quickly survey by reading titles and looking at illustrations. Use that information to decide what questions the material will probably answer. Then read slowly. Think about the questions and recite the answers to yourself. Review and reread if necessary.

Whatever you read, think about why you are reading. Use the rate that suits that purpose. You'll get a chance to practice as you read the selections in this unit.

Use the Skills

Understanding the Selection

Cathy Rigby became interested in gymnastics when she was very young. She entered the Olympics at age fifteen. Her presence on the team inspired worldwide respect for American women gymnasts.

1. Read this selection to find out how Cathy Rigby developed her athletic ability.

2. Discover what she was able to accomplish because of her talent and interest.

Vocabulary Development Skills Word Structure

3. Use your knowledge of suffixes to figure out several words in the selection. Remember to find the base word first. Then add the meaning of the base word and the meaning of the suffix to come up with the meaning of the word.

Study and Research Skills Reading Techniques

4. This is the kind of article you might find in a magazine. You would probably want to read it just for entertainment or general interest. So you can read somewhat quickly.

CATHY RIGBY

Irwin Stambler

Cathy Rigby was born in Long Beach, California, on December 12, 1952. She was small from birth, and for several years she fought a succession^g of ills that threatened her life. But her constitution^cg proved stronger than it seemed, and after her fifth year she remained healthy and became increasingly active.

In the early sixties Cathy's father took her to a trampoline^c class. The first time she got onto the springy canvas surface, she tested it out with a few jumps. Before the session was over, she had performed several back flips. In succeeding classes she demonstrated so much acrobatic ability that her teacher suggested she should enroll in SCATS—the Southern California Acrobatic Team—coached by Bud Marquette, a U.S. gymnastics champion of the thirties.

■ If your purpose for reading was to find out what SCATS meant, you would probably skim until you saw it. Then you would read carefully only the sentence it is in.

Cathy did join SCATS in 1964 and quickly gained the attention of the entire staff. "She adapted so easily. She learned so readily. First she could do only a few cartwheels. But in a few weeks she was doing things that girls who had been working out for years had trouble doing."

Not only did Cathy demonstrate talent for acrobatics, she also showed great determination. She was willing to give up almost all other activities so that she could concentrate —hour after hour, week after week—on strengthening her muscles and developing her technique.^c She went over each routine countless times, smoothing over the rough spots and making even the most complex series of somersaults, flips, handstands, and cartwheels practically automatic.

■ The suffix -ation can mean "state of." And determine means "to have a firm purpose."

Cathy's constant training and intense desire brought early success. She won trophies and medals. She traveled to many parts of the U.S. and to several foreign countries with the SCATS—giving better and better performances and

showing a coolness under pressure so vital to success in major competition.

At the trials for selecting the American team for the 1968 Olympics in Mexico City, Cathy, only fifteen and barely four feet ten inches tall, faced opponents who had four to five years more experience. However, her performance at the trials was a major one. She won many marks of 9 or better, in some cases getting almost perfect scores of 9.8 or 9.9 from the tough-minded judges. Cathy also captivated[cg] the crowd. She won waves of applause for some of her difficult maneuvers,[c] and a standing round of applause when each routine was ended.

With Cathy and Linda Metheney as team members, most observers agreed that the U.S. had its best women's gymnastic team in history. Television viewers throughout the U.S. anxiously watched the proceedings in Mexico City as Cathy, Linda, and their teammates went up against the best gymnasts in the world.

The U.S. team gained no medals, but its performance was first-rate. When the competition was over, Linda Metheney had made it into the finals in the balance beam and Cathy had finished sixteenth overall. This was an outstanding accomplishment against the acknowledged superstars of the Russian, Czechoslovakian, Hungarian, and German teams.

During 1969 Cathy placed high in many meets both at home and abroad. More important, she added moves to her floor exercises, side horse vaulting, and uneven bars. This brought her scores in those classes more in line with her best event, the balance beam. The prime goal was the 1972 Olympics, but an important step on the way was the 1970 World Games held in Ljubljana, Yugoslavia. The World Games were attended by the same stars who generally made the Olympic teams. A good score in Yugoslavia was almost as important as an Olympic victory.

When the last gymnasts finished their performances and all the marks were in, Cathy had taken second prize and a silver medal. It was the first ever won by a woman from the U.S. in world championship competition.

Cathy continued to give excellent performances all over the world. Though the experts rated her number one in the U.S., Cathy had to fight to hold the honor, particularly against the challenge of Linda Metheney. In the Olympic semi-finals in early 1972, Cathy beat Linda and won the meet.

In the finals in May, Cathy began with a beautiful performance on the side horse. On the second day she was extending her lead with a flawless workout on the parallel bars. But she accidentally caught one toe beneath the high bar. She lost her hold and fell straight to the floor. Cathy escaped with only a toe fracture, but it seemed that the injury and the scoring loss might cost her the chance to make the team. The judges gave her an average of 8.3, far below the score she would have earned otherwise, and she dropped to second place.

Cathy showed her great courage and iron will by trying even harder the next day. In the floor exercises she executed a good series of flips, giant splits, one-arm handstands, and somersaults, and finished with a bow. But the crowd groaned when she moved off the mat—she was obviously limping. X-rays showed that Cathy had damaged her ankle ligaments.[9] She had to miss the fourth day.

Cathy's performance to that point had been so good, and her presence was so important to U.S. hopes, the Olympic committee elected her to the team anyway. She responded gratefully by going back into training barely a week after the accident. But the injury probably shook her confidence.

At Munich the U.S. team did reasonably well, but it was not to be a medal year. The Russian team included not only the long-established stars, but also a new and mighty performer, Olga Korbut. By the time the competition was over, Olga ranked equally with Cathy in the hearts of sports fans. Together they carried women's gymnastics to new heights of popularity in the U.S. and in countries where the sport had long been accepted as a major one.

After the 1972 Munich games Cathy retired from amateur[9] competition. But she continued to work for progress in her field by performing in gymnastics exhibitions and by instructing some of the eager young performers who wanted to follow in her footsteps.

■ In which of these words is the -er a suffix? How do you know?

Check the Skills

Understanding the Selection

1. Did Cathy Rigby develop her athletic ability by sitting around waiting for it to happen or did she work at it?

2. What did Cathy accomplish for herself and for American women's gymnastics?

Vocabulary Development Skills Word Structure

3. a. What does *determination* mean? The note in the margin on page 7 can help you decide.

    b. Is *-er* a suffix in the word *eager*? in the word *performer*? How do you know?

Study and Research Skills Reading Techniques

4. Suppose you were going to write a report on Cathy Rigby for your English class. Would you read this selection differently? How? Why?

Use the Skills

Understanding the Selection

1. The following selection describes an experiment to teach a chimpanzee to "talk." The experiment was planned and directed by Beatrice and Allen Gardner. As you read, decide how the Gardners' interests and abilities helped them accomplish their goal.

Vocabulary Development Skills Word Structure

2. Use what you know about suffixes to figure out some words. Notes in the margin will help. Refer to the glossary or a dictionary if you need to.

Study and Research Skills Reading Techniques

3. This selection discusses a scientific experiment. You will probably choose to read slowly to be certain you understand the information being presented.

"HURRY, PLEASE," SAID THE CHIMPANZEES

Aline Amon

Washoe was thirsty. When she saw a friend opening a soda bottle, she became impatient.

Hurry, please, she begged.

Booee wanted to play. He asked his friend, Bruno, to tickle him.

Children often ask for food and games, but Washoe, Booee, and Bruno are not children. They are chimpanzees who have learned to "speak" in the language of deaf persons. They have been taught the hand signs of the American Sign Language, or ASL.[c]

■ You will want to read this section slowly since it provides important information for understanding the rest of the selection.

In ASL the position of your fingers and the way you move your hands tell other people what you mean. You show words and ideas instead of saying them.

No one has ever been able to teach an ape to speak more than a word or two. Scientists discovered that these animals' throats cannot make all the sounds humans' can. But with a sign language instead of a spoken one, apes learn very quickly.

It started in 1966. Two scientists, Doctors Beatrice and Allen Gardner, first tried to teach American Sign Language to Washoe, a one-year-old baby chimp.

Washoe lived in her own house trailer in the backyard of the Gardners' home in Reno, Nevada. Students at the university there helped train the little ape.

These students were Washoe's foster[g] parents, teachers, and playmates. They also had to be acrobats. They chased the ape as she climbed and ran and somersaulted. They had to run even faster than the chimp to get in front of her. Then Washoe could see the signs the students were making with their hands as they "talked" to her.

All day long the students showed Washoe signs. They named the clothes she put on and the food she ate. Over and over they made the signs for *toothbrush, bath, funny, dog, tree*—whatever words matched the things Washoe was seeing or doing.

Washoe learned some signs by copying her teachers. She learned more when the students held her hands in the right position for a sign. They showed her a sign many times over until she understood.

After a while Washoe began to put two and then three signs together in short sentences. She asked for food and fun. She also apologized when she had been naughty, signing *Sorry, sorry, hug me good.*

By 1970 Washoe had become very big and strong. She could easily hurt a person without meaning to do harm. When her teachers had finished their own studies and left the university, the Gardners were without trained chimpanzee workers. They had to send Washoe away.

One student, Doctor Roger Fouts, was going on to the Institute for Primate[g] Studies at the University of Oklahoma, where there were many chimpanzees. So Doctor Fouts took Washoe with him.

When Washoe first saw other chimpanzees, she did not like them at all. She thought she was human, and called the other apes *bugs.* They could not even use sign language!

■ You know what *mother* means. Here *-ly* means "appropriate to" or "like."

Later Washoe grew to like the company of her own species.[cg] She even became quite motherly and protected a new little male chimp, Kiko. Bruno, who was a bully, and Booee, his constant companion, treated Kiko very roughly. But when Washoe arrived, she stopped the bullying. She would not let anyone hurt little Kiko.

Doctor Fouts has been teaching about a dozen chimpanzees in Oklahoma. The most exciting news is that the chimps are using ASL among themselves. Animals of one species are "talking" together in a language taught them by another species, humans!

Some of the chimpanzees that have not been trained in ASL are now making signs and seem to understand them.

Doctor Fouts thinks that they are copying Washoe and the other apes who have had ASL lessons. Now the chimps are learning from each other, not from people.

Washoe is old enough now to have babies. The scientists are curious: Will she teach signs to her own infant? Then a human language would become an ape language, passed down from one generation to the next.

Even Tarzan might be <u>jealous</u> of the people who are *really* "talking" with animals.

■ The suffix *-ous* can't help you figure out the meaning of this word.

A chimpanzee's hands signing the word *clean.*

Check the Skills

Understanding the Selection

1. What did the Gardners accomplish with their experiment? Do you think the results are important? Why do you think so?

Vocabulary Development Skills Word Structure

2. a. What does *motherly* mean?

   b. Why doesn't the suffix *-ous* help you figure out the word *jealous?*

Study and Research Skills Reading Techniques

3. Did you read this selection quickly or slowly? Why did you choose the reading rate you did?

Use the Skills

Understanding the Selection

Harold dislikes organized activities of any kind and thinks of himself as a born "lone wolf." But his teachers keep trying to get him "involved." Mr. Asbury, his history teacher, wants him to run for class president. Miss Tate, his art teacher, wants him to join the art club and make some posters for school events. Mrs. Jennings, his English teacher, wants him to work on the class newspaper. But Harold continues to avoid group activities.

1. Find out how some special knowledge Harold has forces him to accomplish something.

2. See if you think Harold really is a lone wolf.

Vocabulary Development Skills Word Structure

3. Remember to try the suffix strategy if you find a word you don't know.

Study and Research Skills Reading Techniques

4. This story is fictional and should be fun to read. You don't have to remember everything you read.

THE CAKE ICING CAPER

Shirley Lee

Even Mom and Dad had given up on trying to talk me into doing things I really didn't want to, and contented themselves with letting me go along at my own pace.

■ After you have read one or two paragraphs, you will probably be able to tell that you can read this selection rather quickly.

I'm no great athlete. I play games for the fun of it. And parties never did turn me on. So I hadn't planned to go to the class banquet.⁹

Now, don't get me wrong. I *do* love to eat. That was one reason I enjoyed visiting Uncle Earl and Aunt Belle last summer and helping out in their bakery. I learned to fry doughnuts, to mix up cake batter in the big electric mixer, and to ice and decorate cakes. But I never told anyone.

■ The final e of the base word was dropped before the suffixes -er and -ry were added. One of the r's was dropped, too.

There were two or three guys I hung around with at lunchtime. Since they didn't jump into school activities either, it was surprising that we even got around to mentioning the banquet. But Jim Thompson had a twin sister, Jody, who was gung-ho for school events.

"It's too bad about the banquet cakes," he muttered.

"How's that?" I asked.

"They can't get anybody to decorate them this year."

"Why not?"

"Because the cafeteria lady who did their decorating moved to another town. Mrs. Muffet, who's in charge, says we'll just have to make do with plain cakes this year."

"Really? I thought nearly anyone who cooked for a living could decorate cakes."

Jim gave me a funny look. "What makes you think so?" he asked. "My mom does lots of baking, but she can't do fancy things like cake decorating."

"Huh," I said, "Maybe it runs in my family or something."

"What are you talking about?" said Pete Fenton, who had been listening all this time.

"Why, cake decorating, of course," I answered. "I learned how at my uncle's bakery last summer. It's not hard."

"You what?" Jim stared at me. "Well, why don't you tell them?"

It was my turn to stare. "You know how I feel about volunteering. No, thanks."

I did my best to forget the whole thing. But the next day was the day before the banquet. It seemed we'd be the first class since the school opened to have cakes without the usual stuff all over them. So who cared? Just about everybody, and especially Jody Thompson, who wanted color photos to put in the class scrapbook.

I tried to concentrate on my history book. But I kept hearing Jody talking to her friend Samantha.

"I just don't know what we're going to do," Jody moaned. "The cakes are being baked today, but there's nobody to decorate them. I might try to do it myself."

Samantha was shocked. "But you don't know the first thing about it. You'll probably make a big mess out of it."

I sneaked a look at Jody. I shuddered to think of the way those cakes might turn out. I'd have to drop by after school and see the worst, but I'd be careful nobody saw me.

I opened the kitchen door and peeked inside. Jody was there, talking to Samantha. On the <u>stainless</u> steel table before her stood two enormous bowls of blue frosting. Spread out all around were metal icing tubes and canvas bags. On the table behind her were four large cakes.

■ Remember that -less can mean "free from."

Jody was trying to stuff huge gobs of icing into one of the bags. "If I can teach myself to use these things," she was saying, "then I can make some sort of design."

"Oh, no!" I groaned. It had taken me a couple of weeks to get that far along even with Uncle Earl's expert instructions.

I heard a step behind me, turned, and bumped into Jim. All he said was "Well?"

But he meant "Well, why don't you break down and help her?"

Then, before I knew it, I was in the middle of things. Coloring frostings, filling bags, putting on curlicue⁹ borders, drawing on the class emblem,⁹ and writing on the name and the motto. I did all four cakes in a little more than an hour.

"It was wonderful of you to help us, Harold," Jody was saying earnestly. "Think how proud you'll be at the banquet tomorrow when we tell the class what you did."

"But I won't be there," I started to say, and then I stopped. "Well, that will be great," I told her with a grin.

It felt nice to be the center of attention. I wasn't at all sure I wanted to stay a lone wolf. I mean, joining the Writers' Club might be an inspiration to me. And drawing a poster or two certainly wouldn't be all that difficult. And what was it that Mr. Asbury had said? Well, maybe the class *could* have a worse president than me!

Check the Skills

Understanding the Selection

1. What did Harold accomplish because of his special knowledge of cake decorating?

2. Do you think Harold really is a lone wolf? Why do you think as you do? Why do you think Harold never wanted to join any groups?

Vocabulary Development Skills Word Structure

3. What is the base word in *bakery*? What does *stainless* mean?

Study and Research Skills Reading Techniques

4. Did you read this selection more quickly than you did the first two selections? Why?

Use the Skills

Understanding the Selection

Benjamin Banneker was born in Maryland in 1731. His mother was a free black woman and his father was a slave. Although young Benjamin went to school for a short time, most of his education came from books borrowed from a neighbor. Still he became a great scientist.

1. Read the selection to find out what Benjamin Banneker's interests were.

2. Discover what he accomplished in his lifetime as a result of his special interests and abilities.

Vocabulary Development Skills Word Structure

3. Use what you have learned to help you figure out the meanings of words containing suffixes. Look up suffixes in a dictionary if you need to.

Study and Research Skills Reading Techniques

4. As you begin reading, think about the type of material the selection is. Adjust your reading rate.

BENJAMIN BANNEKER

Charles E. Anderson

In 1791, a black man named Benjamin Banneker served as <u>assistant</u> to the surveyor,^g Andrew Ellicott. President Washington had selected a French engineer to design the new capital city. But he was so uncooperative^c that he had to be dismissed. He took his partly completed plan with him when he left. So Andrew Ellicott was asked to prepare a new map of the city. At this point, Banneker is said to have reproduced the French engineer's plan for the city of Washington entirely from memory.

■ What is the base word?

This <u>remarkable</u> feat^{cg} was not unusual for Benjamin Banneker. He had been working similar wonders for most of his life. As a young man in Maryland, he constructed the first all-wooden clock made in America. He used only a pocketknife as a tool and a small pocket watch as a model. The clock struck the hours of six and twelve and kept accurate time for more than twenty years.

■ The suffix is -able.

A student of astronomy, Banneker accurately predicted the solar eclipse^g in 1789. Shortly thereafter he published an almanac containing tide^g tables, dates of future eclipses, <u>medicinal</u> products and formulas, and essays on many different subjects. He was the first black man to publish such a scientific book in the United States. And for ten years he published a new edition of his almanac each year.

■ Here's the suffix -al.

By the time Banneker was forty, he was known as a "self-made wizard." Scholars and curiosity seekers came from all over to see him solve any mathematical problem put to him.

■ Check your reading rate. Is it appropriate for the type of material you are reading?

But Banneker was more interested in the evils of slavery. They deeply grieved him, and he worked to abolish them. Early in 1791, he learned that Thomas Jefferson, the Secretary of State under President Washington, had doubts about the capabilities of black people. Jefferson had recommended

Banneker to Andrew Ellicott, and Banneker probably considered the famous patriot⁹ to be his friend. But this did not keep him from speaking his mind frankly.

In a now-famous letter, which he sent along with a copy of his almanac, Banneker pointed out to Jefferson that his own accomplishments proved that a black person could succeed. He asked Jefferson to help eliminate ". . . false ideas and opinions, which so generally prevail⁹ with respect to us. . . ." He also scolded Jefferson for continuing to own slaves after having written in the Declaration of Independence "that all men are created equal."

Banneker might have gestured like this to Jefferson, indicating that the lives of slaves were bound the way their wrists were.

Jefferson was so impressed by Banneker's letter that he sent Banneker a personal apology. And he also helped spread the name of Benjamin Banneker around the country and the world.

Banneker was widely known as a charming host. He was often seen escorting visitors around his farm. And he was often observed at night, wrapped in a cloak, peering into the sky and studying the stars until dawn.

Shortly before he died, in 1806, Banneker sold his farm in order to devote all of his time to scientific pursuits and to publishing a pamphlet aimed at the abolition of slavery and the promotion of peace among all races.

Check the Skills

Understanding the Selection

1. Benjamin Banneker was interested in astronomy. What is astronomy? Did you have to use a dictionary or were you able to figure it out yourself? What else was Benjamin Banneker interested in?

2. What were some of the things Benjamin Banneker accomplished in his lifetime? Do you think he ever would have written his almanac if he had been only slightly interested in science? Why do you think as you do?

Vocabulary Development Skills Word Structure

3. How could knowing suffixes help you figure out the meaning of the words *assistant, remarkable,* and *medicinal?*

Study and Research Skills Reading Techniques

4. What reading rate did you use for this selection? Why?

Use the Skills

There are some things on this earth that even scientists with their knowledge and the use of modern techniques can't explain. This selection is about one of these mysteries. As you read, you will find out about a group of people whose accomplishment was a very unusual one.

Remember to use what you have learned to help you figure out the meanings of words containing suffixes. You can use the glossary or a dictionary if you need to. Think about your reading rate and adjust it to suit the material.

This time you'll be on your own. There are no marginal notes.

GIANTS ON THE EARTH

Helen Achczynski

Can you imagine seeing an eagle with a wingspread of 624 feet? Or a bear 80 feet long from the tip of his snout to the end of his tail? Or a man 214 feet tall wearing a horned headdress? Such giants *do* exist, but, luckily for us, they are not alive. Found in the midwestern United States, these huge creatures are made of dirt and sod and are called *effigy mounds*.ᶜ An effigy is a sculptedᵍ image, and these images of animals and people are formed out of earth. Thousands of effigies, representing birds, panthers, bears, turtles, deer, beaver, and moose were once spread over 20,000 square miles in Iowa, Illinois, Minnesota, and the southern half of Wisconsin. Only a few remain today.

Fortunately, a handful of surveyorsᵍ and amateurᵍ archaeologistsᵍ recognized the importance of these uniqueᵍ earthworks and became alarmed at their disappearance. By the middle of the nineteenth century, they began to map and measure the still existing mounds. As they charted them, they began to ask questions. Who built these effigies? When were they built? How? Why? The question of *who* was finally answered when skulls similar to those of historic Indians were found in the prehistoricᵍ mounds. Archaeologists carefully studied these skulls, as well as the location of the mounds and the artifactsᵍ found in and around them. They concluded that the builders of the huge monuments were indeed ancestors of present-day Indians, possibly the Menominee and Winnebago tribes. But almost nothing is known about these ancient people except that they built their incredible mounds.

When did these people live, and when did they build their amazing mounds?

The answer did not come until 1951, when Dr. Willard Libby devised the Carbon 14 dating technique.ᶜ This system is based on the regular rate of radio-carbon decay. Since every living organism contains carbon, scientists can use the Carbon 14 dating method to determine just when in the past an organism stopped living. By testing charcoal found in the mounds, researchers discovered that the majority of effigies had been built between A.D. 500 and A.D. 1100, long before Columbus reached the shores of America.

Although laboratory techniques told researchers *when* the mounds were built, long days of field work with shovels and picks were required to learn *how* they were constructed. Archaeologists carefully studied cross sections of the mounds. They concluded that the "Effigy Indians" had no hard and fast rules for sculpting their earthen figures. In some mounds the sod[9] cover had been removed to create a complete outline of the effigy before the ground was heaped up to form its

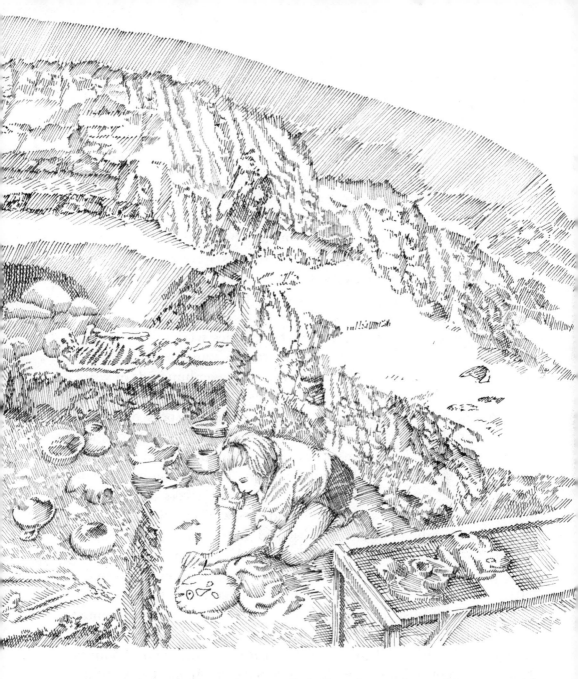

body. In others the earth was piled directly on the prairie grass with little prior preparation. Sometimes complicated layers of yellow, white, and red sand had been spread on the floor of the mound before the effigy was formed over it.

Because there are so few clues to explain why these giant earthen figures were built, many wild guesses have been made about the effigies. Fortifications, said the frontier soldier. Clan symbols, said a scholar. Game drives to capture buffalo or deer, said another. Foundations for dwelling places. Guardians of cornfields. A record of ruling families. A sign from the god Manitou that there is much game in the spirit world.

One writer called effigies "picture writing upon the earth." Like our written word, the mounds may have had several functions—to worship the Creator, to record the passage of time, to honor the memory of the dead, and to mark boundaries, springs, and trails.

An isolated[c] effigy was rare. Usually a number of figures appeared together, either grouped in a cluster or stretched out in a long procession. Accompanying the many animal figures were rod-shaped and conical earthworks. Sometimes a deeply worn trail would pass between a pair of identical mounds, and often the effigy complexes seemed to be laid out in a series of giant circles.

Many archaeologists today believe the effigies were primarily constructed as burial mounds, and that the reason some mounds contain no remains is that the bones have decomposed[g] over hundreds of years. They think that, though the Effigy Indians were probably wanderers most of the time, they returned to certain sacred spots once each year—when the ground had thawed enough for digging—to conduct burial services and religious rites. This would explain why the mounds are usually found in groups. Then, as the game in a certain region became scarce, the Indians followed the rivers and lakes to better hunting grounds, and new mound sites were established.

Perhaps if early pioneers had listened more carefully to Native Americans in Wisconsin they might have discovered more clues to solve the mystery of the effigies. In 1848, an aged Winnebago told a settler that he had heard from the lips of his father that, in the past, various tribes of Wisconsin Indians had gathered together at appointed meeting places, bringing with them heavy loads of earth from their campgrounds. When all the tribes had gathered, they would empty their burdens of soil onto one huge pile to form an animal, and then would conduct religious services. Other such stories circulated through the frontier but were never thoroughly investigated.

Today, although most of the effigies have been destroyed, a small sampling remains. Protected by state or county parks or carefully preserved by private landowners, the effigies still stretch across the Midwest, waiting for someone to reveal their secrets.

Check the Skills

Understanding the Selection

1. What was the accomplishment of the "Effigy Indians"? Do you think this was an easy thing for them to do? Why do you think as you do?

2. What special interests do you think led these people to build the effigies? Why do you think as you do?

Vocabulary Development Skills Word Structure

3. The words listed below are from the selection. In the first column, the underlined letters in each word form a suffix. Use your knowledge of suffixes to decide what each of those words means. Refer to the glossary or a dictionary if necessary. However, the suffix strategy will not help you figure out the words in the second column. Why not?

locat<u>ion</u>	region
survey<u>or</u>	ancestor
earth<u>en</u>	monument
research<u>er</u>	incredible

Study and Research Skills Reading Techniques

4. Did you read this selection quickly or slowly? Or did you read at different rates at different points in the selection? How did you decide at what rate to read?

Apply What You Learned in Unit 1

The Theme

Accomplishments

1.   We sometimes think that an accomplishment must always be an important deed that receives public recognition. But an accomplishment is actually a very personal thing. To a baby, a first step is a great accomplishment because it takes all the special skill and ability the baby has at that time.

•   Can you think of any other kinds of accomplishments that do not receive public recognition but that do give the individual a great deal of personal satisfaction? Do you think that because a person has an interest or an ability, he or she will automatically accomplish great things and receive public recognition? Why do you think as you do?

The Skills

Vocabulary Development Skills Word Structure

2.   In this unit you learned about suffixes. You will use your skill with suffixes in all your reading. The more you use your skill the easier it will become to figure out the meanings of words containing suffixes.

3.   Remember that most suffixes can be looked up in a dictionary. When you know the meaning of the base word and the meaning of the suffix, you will be able to figure out the meaning of the word containing the suffix.

Study and Research Skills Reading Techniques

4.   You learned that good readers adjust their reading rate according to their purpose for reading and to the type of material being read. You will save yourself a lot of time with your reading if you practice this skill. You won't read important materials too quickly and then have to go back and reread them because you missed important facts. And you won't spend too much time reading every word of something you are reading just for fun. The next time you begin reading something, ask yourself what your purpose is for reading and what type of material it is. Adjust your reading rate accordingly.

Compassion

Overview and Purposes for Reading

The Theme

Compassion

1.   Compassion means feeling so deeply for someone else's suffering or hardship that you are moved to help them. In what ways do people express compassion?

The Skills

Vocabulary Development Skills Word Meaning

2.   What are homonyms?
3.   When you come across a word that you know has two or more meanings, how can you decide which meaning is the right one?

Comprehension Skills Implied Meaning

4.   How can you predict the outcome of a story or section of a story?

Learn About the Skills

Vocabulary Development Skills Word Meaning

The English language has a few tricky surprises that can sometimes make reading confusing. One of these is words that sound alike or are spelled alike, or both, but have different meanings. Words like this are called **homonyms.** The underlined words in the following sentences are homonyms.

Take the <u>pail</u> of water to the house.

Bob looked <u>pale</u> after his long illness.

Two of the <u>pales</u> in the picket fence are loose.

The word *pail* in the first sentence sounds just like *pale* in the second and third sentences. But *pail* and *pale* are spelled differently and all three words have quite different meanings. Here's another example.

Judy yelled, *"Duck!"* as the ball went whizzing by.

The people fed crackers to the *duck* that swam nearby.

Homonyms can be tricky because they do have different meanings. When you meet homonyms in your reading, you have to be able to tell which meaning is intended.

The best way to do this is to use the other words in the sentence as clues. Every sentence expresses a thought or message. Choose the meaning of the homonym that fits with that message. For instance, read the two sentences at the top of the next page. They contain the homonyms *principal* and *principle.*

The school *principal* is speaking at the assembly.

The professor spoke about the *principle* of loyalty.

The clues in the first sentence tell you that *principal* is a person connected with the school. The message in the second sentence tells you that *principle* is not a person but an idea.

Homonyms can be confusing. They will not trick you if you use the clues in the sentence to help you figure out the correct meaning. Remember to think about the sense or message of the sentence.

The selections in this unit contain some homonyms. Use the sentence clues to figure out the appropriate meanings.

Comprehension Skills Implied Meaning

Good readers are active readers. One way you can help yourself be a more active reader is to learn to think along with the author of a story and figure out what is likely to happen next. **Predicting outcomes** in this way can make your reading more exciting and enjoyable, even if an author sometimes surprises you by doing something unexpected.

You can often forecast what might happen next by using your experience and by looking for clues provided by the author. To use your experience, think about what is happening in the story in terms of what you already know about life. For instance, you might ask yourself what would probably happen next in real life. This will help you to "think along" with the story.

Also, learn to look for the clues in the story regarding what is going to happen. For instance, you would figure out that something bad was going to happen next if you read the sentence below.

But that was the last happy time they had for a long while.

With this statement, the author is giving you a clue that unhappy things are about to occur.

Reading becomes more exciting when you become involved in it. One way to get involved is to predict or anticipate what is going to happen in a story. Use your experience and the clues that authors provide as you try to predict outcomes in the selections in this unit.

Selection 1

Use the Skills

Understanding the Selection

Aside from being blind, Emily Gregory is just like most other twelve-year-olds. She goes to school. She has friends. She gets angry. And she takes piano lessons.

1. See if you think Emily's piano teacher has compassion for her.

Vocabulary Development Skills Word Meaning

2. Use context clues to help yourself choose the appropriate meanings of the homonyms for the words *row* and *hide*.

Comprehension Skills Implied Meaning

3. Try to predict the music teacher's reaction to a trick Emily planned to play on him.

THE YOUNG UNICORNS

Madeleine L'Engle

Emily relaxed again and burst into a pleased, expectant[9] laugh.

"What?" Rob asked. "What's funny?"

"Nothing. At least not yet. If you come along to my lesson you'll see."

"Anything for a laugh," Dave said. "Give me your key, Emily."

On the corner of Riverside Drive stood a large old stone mansion. Dave opened the heavy blue door that led into a hall with a marble floor and wide marble stairs. At the back of the hall, double doors were open into a great living room with two grand pianos in it. By one of the pianos stood a small old man with a shaggy mane of yellowing hair.

If he had been larger he would have looked startlingly like an aging lion. He let out a roar. "So, Miss Emily Gregory!"

"So, Mr. Theotocopoulos!" She threw each syllable of his name back at him with angry precision.[9]

"Three times in a <u>row</u> you come to me late."

■ The message of this sentence tells you the meaning here is "a line or series" and not "to move a boat by using oars" or "a noisy argument."

Emily flung her head up, unbuttoning her coat and letting it fall on the floor behind her. "How late am I?"

The old man pulled out a gold watch. Temper matched temper. "Remember, Miss, that I come personally and promptly to you, instead of making you come to my studio—"

"So I'll come to your studio—"

"In my declining[9] years I must still work like a hog. One minute too late is too many of my valuable time—"

"I couldn't help it, orchestra rehearsal—"

"No alibis! And kindly pick up your coat and hang it up—"

"I'm going to!"

"—like a civilized human being instead of a spoiled rat."

Emily reached furiously for her coat. "I'm not spoiled!"

"Emily! Be courteous or be quiet!" The old man sounded as though he himself were no more than Emily's age. "I am fit to be fried."

Emily grabbed the coat and rushed towards the hall, bumping headlong into the doorjamb. She let out a furious yell, echoed by her music-master.

"If you knock yourself out you think that will make me sorry for you? Hang up your coat and come sit down at the piano. And do not move without thinking where you are going."

"Do I always have to think!" Emily shouted.

Rob, who had started automatically to help Emily, turned back to the room. He sat down on a small gold velvet sofa.

"Mr. Theo," Dave said, holding himself in control, "there is a difference between mollycoddling^{cg} her and—"

"Sit down!" Mr. Theo bellowed. "You are talking about a twelve-year-old girl, and I am talking about an artist. I will not let her do anything that will hurt her music. Now sit still and listen—if you have ears to hear."

Shrugging, Dave stalked over to his favorite black leather chair by the marble fireplace.

Out in the hall by the coatrack, Emily managed to get her coat to stay on its hook. Then, walking carefully but with the assurance^{cg} of familiarity, she came back and sat down at one of the pianos. "Then why don't you let me give a concert if you think I'm a musician?"

Mr. Theotocopoulos took her hands in his. "Why could you not come straight home from school? Cannot that so-called orchestra get along without you? And your hands are too cold to be of any use for music at all." He began to massage her fingers. "You are too young for a concert. You would be not only a child prodigy,^g you would be a blind child prodigy, and people would say, 'Isn't she marvelous, poor little thing?' and nobody would have heard you play at all. Is that what you want?"

"No," she said.

He rubbed her hands for a moment more in silence, then asked, "What is bothering you?"

"Nothing. I don't want to talk about it."

"Something at school?"

"No."

"But there is something. Yes. Bigger than something at school. I can feel it in your hands. All right. Play, and we will see what you tell me."

"I won't tell you anything."

"You think you can <u>hide</u> yourself from me when you play, hah?"

■ This can be "keep out of sight" or "the skin of an animal." Only the first meaning makes sense here.

"We'll see." Emily sounded grim, then gave an unexpected giggle. "Shall I start with the G minor fugue?"ᵍ

Mr. Theo looked at her suspiciously. "If you think your fingers are limber enough."

Emily began to play. After less than a minute Mr. Theo roared, his yellowed mane seeming to rise in rage from his forehead, "And what in the name of all I treasure is *that?*"

She stopped, turning her face towards his voice with an expression of wounded surprise. "<u>You told me last week that I was to learn that fugue backwards and forwards. That's backwards.</u>"

■ From what you've learned about Mr. Theo, chances are you expect him to be very angry at Emily's trick. But watch for an unexpected reaction that you probably could not predict.

Mr. Theotocopoulos's roars of rage turned into roars of laughter and he grabbed Emily in a huge hug of delight. "See?" he asked, more to an imaginary audience than to Rob and Dave.

"See what I mean? All right, child, let us hear. Play it backwards all the way through."

Whenever Emily was pleased with herself and her world she had a deep chuckle that gave somewhat the effect of a kitten's purr. Pleasure in her accomplishment, and it was indeed an accomplishment, made her purr now. She reached for a moment for a cumbersomeᵍ sheet of Brailleᵍ music manuscript, concentrated on it with a furious scowl, then grinned again and turned back to the piano. "I really rather like it this way. I wonder Bach never thought of it."

Dave turned to ask Rob, "Your family know where you are?"

"They knew I was going to wait after school for Emily. If anybody wants me they'll guess I'm here and come downstairs and get me."

"Quiet!" roared Mr. Theotocopoulos.

"The trouble with you," Emily said to her teacher without a fraction's hesitation in her playing, "is that you can't concentrate." She raised her hands from the keyboard. "It's rather splendid backwards, isn't it? Shall I do it forwards now?"

Check the Skills

Understanding the Selection

1. Does Mr. Theo have compassion for Emily? Why do you think as you do?

Vocabulary Development Skills Word Meaning

2. What is the meaning of *row* on page 37? of *hide* on page 40? How did context clues help you decide which homonym was the correct one?

Comprehension Skills Implied Meaning

3. Did you predict correctly the outcome of Emily's trick? What clues led you to predict as you did?

Use the Skills

Understanding the Selection

Tara never liked birds of any kind. But now, because of the winter storm, the birds in her yard need her help.

1. Find out how Tara shows compassion for the birds.

Vocabulary Development Skills Word Meaning

2. Think about the sense of the sentence and decide which meaning of *fast* is the appropriate one for this selection.

Comprehension Skills Implied Meaning

3. Try to predict how Tara will react to the birds' predicament.

TARA AND THE BIRDS

Margaret Higham

It had been raining all afternoon. Tara Chen stood by the kitchen window and traced a raindrop as it slid down the outside of the glass. She followed it with her finger till it stopped at the ledge, then looked up for another. That was when she saw the bird. It stood on the clothesline, flapping its wings but not flying. Something was wrong with its feet.

Tara didn't like birds. They squawked in her window and peered at her with beady eyes. Just thinking of their sharp beaks and their dry, scratching claws gave her goose pimples.

The rain turned to ice and struck the glass with clattering⁹ pellets.ᶜ Through the frosty pane Tara could see other birds clinging to the line. Beyond, where the clothesline joined the garage, more birds were bathing in the gutter under the roof.

The moment they climbed out, dripping wet, onto the line, their feet froze <u>fast</u> to the cord.

■ Does this mean "quick," "tight," or "to go without food"?

One bird after another stuck to the clothesline, like a row of wooden puppets. By now, the first bird had stopped fluttering. Its soggy feathers were slowly turning to ice.

Tara watched in horror. She didn't like the thought of touching birds, but she couldn't just stand by the window and let them freeze. She hesitated, then pulled on her jacket and ran outside to the clothesline stoop.⁹ She yanked the line toward her, knocking its icy coating into the pulley.⁹ The first brown bird trembled as it looked at her.

■ This should help you predict whether or not Tara will try to help the birds.

"Why, you're more scared than I am. Don't be afraid. I'm going to help you."

Tara cupped one hand over the bird's icy claws. With her other hand, she made a warm cocoon⁹ over its body, holding the small, shivering creature until her fingers ached. Finally, she tried to loosen the frozen claws that were wound tightly around the line. The bird struggled feebly.⁹

One foot came loose. Then the other. The wings under Tara's hand moved a little.

"You can do it, little bird. Come on! Flap your wings." She pushed gently against the backs of its thighs where yellow wing feathers joined the dark body.

"Fly away, little bird!"

The bird fluttered, then flew to a tall spruce tree. Tara rubbed her hands together, warmed them with her breath, and started to work thawing out the feet of the second bird in line. Then she went on to the third. Soon all birds were nestled^c safely in the spruce tree. Tara knew if any more landed in the gutter, they would skate, not swim. By now even the bristles of grass were like icicles.

Tara tried to warm her frozen hands in the sleeves of her jacket and called out, "Fly away, little birds. And if you come back tomorrow, there'll be food for you."

Check the Skills

Understanding the Selection

1. What did Tara do that showed compassion for the birds? Do you think her feelings about the birds changed after she helped them? Why do you think as you do?

Vocabulary Development Skills Word Meaning

2. Why was it obvious from the sense of the sentence on page 43 that *fast* meant "tight"?

Comprehension Skills Implied Meaning

3. What clues helped you predict that Tara would help the birds?

Selection 3

Use the Skills

Understanding the Selection

In this story Boss, a woman sheep herder, takes care of an orphan boy with no name. He had been living with some migrant workers in exchange for his wages. But he ran away when his only friend was killed in a corn picking machine. He is tired and hungry when Boss finds him.

1. Read the selection to find out how Boss shows her compassion toward the boy.

2. Try to imagine what it would be like to live as Boss does.

Vocabulary Development Skills Word Meaning

3. If you think about the sense of the sentence, you will have no trouble knowing which meaning *lean* has in this selection.

Comprehension Skills Implied Meaning

4. Try to predict whether Boss will want the boy to stay and whether he will want to stay.

THE LONER

Ester Wier

The woman bent over the sleeping boy. Traces of tears were on his face, streaks through the dust and dirt. His thin body was curled against the cold, and the straight brown hair hung ragged against his neck. "What a miserable little critter," she said softly. "I won't let a sheep get into such a wretched condition." Carefully she placed an arm underneath and slowly raised him so that he lay against her. He stirred and then lay quietly in her arms.

She carried him up the hill and across the hundred yards to the sheep wagon. Smoke curled from the stovepipe atop the sheep wagon, drifting south with the wind. The woman mounted the steps to the door, pulling it open carefully so as not to disturb the boy. Once in, she shut it behind her and looked about. The benches on either side of the long narrow room were hard and bare, so she carried the boy to the end where her bed was built crosswise into the wagon. The room was warm. The boy sighed as he turned over and adjusted himself to the softness.

The woman took off her heavy coat and old felt hat, and went to the kerosene stove. Taking a kettle, she poured water into it from a bucket, salted it, and set it on the flame to boil. She poured cornmeal into the boiling water. When the mush was ready she put it into a bowl and punctured^{cg} a can of milk. She looked at the sugar and hesitated. She didn't hold with spoiling children with sweets. She left the bowl on the stove to keep warm and went back to the bed where the boy lay.

"Come," she said, rousing^{cg} him. "Here's some food." She went back to the stove and picked up the bowl.

The boy sat up and backed into a corner of the bed. He looked around the strange room and then up at the woman. "Who're you?" he asked.

"Eat," she said. "I'll talk while you fill your stomach."

She wanted to wash his hands and face before he ate but she knew at the moment his need was more for nourishment than for cleanliness.

"Eat!" she said again. The boy stared at her, then dropped his eyes to the bowl. Picking up the spoon, he began to eat, swallowing hungrily.

"Take it slow," she said. "There's more if you want it." She sat on the bench and started to lean forward. "My dog found you a while ago, and I carried you here and put you to bed. I figured you must be hungry so I fixed you something to eat. And I wanted you to know where you were so that when you woke up in the morning you wouldn't be scared to find yourself here."

The boy listened. "Who're you?" he asked again.

"You can call me Boss, I guess. It's been years since anyone called me anything else. I've got a flock of sheep outside and this is my wagon."

The boy finished the mush. The woman refilled the bowl for him.

"Now, suppose you tell me what to call you," she said.

The boy looked at her silently for a long time. "Boy," he said. "That's what folks call me, unless they're mad at me."

■ There are two homonyms for *lean*: 1. not fat, 2. to bend or slant. Which fits here?

The woman knew she had been right about his being a stray. He was underfed, uncared for, and didn't even have a name. Right now he looked like a lonely animal fighting for its life in a world where nobody cared about it. It made her mad all over.

■ These last two paragraphs should help you predict what Boss will do with the boy.

"All right," she said. "I'll call you Boy for now." There would be time enough to find out where he belonged and decide what to do with him later.

Check the Skills

Understanding the Selection

1. What did Boss do that showed her compassion for the boy? What might have happened to him if Boss had not come along? Why do you think as you do?

2. What do you think it would be like to live as Boss does? Do you think you would be able to live like that? Why or why not?

Vocabulary Development Skills Word Meaning

3. What helped you decide that on page 48 the word *lean* means "to bend" instead of "not fat"?

Comprehension Skills Implied Meaning

4. Do you think Boss will want Boy to stay? Do you think Boy will want to stay?

   You might enjoy reading the book this selection was taken from. Its title is also *The Loner*. It was published in 1963 by David McKay Company.

Use the Skills

Understanding the Selection

1. The next selection is about sheep herding, too. Find out how Alice Yazzie helps Grandfather Tsosie and shows compassion for the lamb. The time of the poem is January. *Yas nilt'ees* means January in the Navajo language.

2. Decide for yourself how Grandfather feels about Alice.

Vocabulary Development Skills Word Meaning

3. Use the message of the sentence to figure out which homonym of the word *ground* is in this selection.

Comprehension Skills Implied Meaning

4. Use the clues in the poem to help you predict whether Grandfather will let Alice keep the lamb inside.

JANUARY
YAS NILT'EES

Ramona Maher

The snow slowed the world,
the Navajo world.
"Go see if the sheep are fine,"
Grandfather Tsosie tells Alice Yazzie.
"The hay is frozen
and so is the ground," says Alice, returning.
"The horses look like they blame me
for causing this cold."

■ Does *ground* mean "crushed into bits" or "the solid surface of the earth"?

Her nose red, her chin buried in sheepskin,
she carries the smallest lamb
into the hogan.^{cg}
"Just for the night," says Alice Yazzie
holding the lamb.
"He's all new and starry.
He's too new to be cold."
Grandfather grunts.
He doesn't say no.

Alice heats milk in a bottle
over burning piñon.[cg]
Grandfather watches.
The new lamb sucks.
The piñon burns low.
The lamb goes to sleep.
His nose is a black star.

■ These sen-
tences should
help you predict
whether or not
Grandfather will
let Alice keep
the lamb inside.

"It *is* cold out there," Alice tells Grandfather
as she goes to bed.
Grandfather nods.
He wears a red flannel shirt
Alice gave him for Christmas.
He looks at the low fire.
He looks at the lamb.
Grandfather says
to Alice Yazzie,
to Alice Ben Yazzie,
"It was almost this cold
the night you were born."

Check the Skills

Understanding the Selection

1. How does Alice Yazzie help Grandfather Tsosie? How do you know she has compassion for the lamb?

2. How do you think Grandfather feels about Alice? What makes you think as you do?

Vocabulary Development Skills Word Meaning

3. How did you know that in the poem *ground* means "the surface of the earth"?

Comprehension Skills Implied Meaning

4. Do you think Grandfather will let Alice keep the lamb inside? What makes you think as you do?

Selection 5

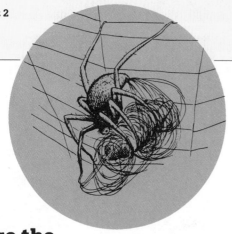

Use the Skills

The next selection is taken from a book so popular and well written that it is considered to be a classic. It is *Charlotte's Web* by E. B. White. As you read, think about the compassion the characters really have for each other, even though it may not seem that way on the surface.

There are four homonyms for the word *last.* They are *a.* coming after all others; *b.* to endure, go on; *c.* a model of the human foot, used in shoemaking; *d.* a British unit of measurement. As you read the story, decide which one is appropriate here.

In the last paragraph of this excerpt, you will find that the author tells you directly what the outcome will be.

Remember, there are no marginal notes this time.

CHARLOTTE'S WEB

E. B. White

At last^c Wilbur saw the creature that had spoken to him in such a kindly way. Stretched across the upper part of the doorway was a big spiderweb, and hanging from the top of the web, head down, was a large grey spider. She was about the size of a gumdrop. She had eight legs, and she was waving one of them at Wilbur in friendly greeting. "See me now?" she asked.

"Oh, yes indeed," said Wilbur. "Yes indeed! How are you? Good morning! Salutations!^g Very pleased to meet you. What is your name, please? May I have your name?"

"My name," said the spider, "is Charlotte."

"Charlotte what?" asked Wilbur, eagerly.

"Charlotte A. Cavatica. But just call me Charlotte."

"I think you're beautiful," said Wilbur.

"Well, I *am* pretty," replied Charlotte. "There's no denying that. Almost all spiders are rather nice-looking. I'm not as flashy as some, but I'll do. I wish I could see you, Wilbur, as clearly as you can see me."

"Why can't you?" asked the pig. "I'm right here."

"Yes, but I'm near-sighted,"^g replied Charlotte. "I've always been dreadfully near-sighted. It's good in some ways, not so good in others. Watch me wrap up this fly."

A fly that had been crawling along Wilbur's trough^g had flown up and blundered^c into the lower part of Charlotte's web and was tangled in the sticky threads. The fly was beating its wings furiously, trying to break loose and free itself.

"First," said Charlotte, "I dive at him." She plunged headfirst toward the fly. As she dropped, a tiny silken thread unwound from her rear end.

"Next, I wrap him up." She grabbed the fly, threw a few jets of silk around it, and rolled it over and over, wrapping it so that it couldn't move. Wilbur watched in horror. He could hardly believe what he was seeing, and although he detested^{cg} flies, he was sorry for this one.

"There!" said Charlotte. "Now I knock him out, so he'll be more comfortable." She bit the fly. "He can't feel a thing now," she remarked. "He'll make a perfect breakfast for me."

"You mean you *eat* flies?" gasped Wilbur.

"Certainly. Flies, bugs, grasshoppers, choice beetles, moths, butterflies, tasty cockroaches, gnats, midges, daddy longlegs, centipedes, mosquitoes, crickets—anything that is careless enough to get caught in my web. I have to live, don't I?"

"Why, yes, of course," said Wilbur. "Do they taste good?"

"Delicious. Of course, I don't really eat them. I drink them—drink their blood. I love blood," said Charlotte, and her pleasant, thin voice grew even thinner and more pleasant.

"Don't say that!" groaned Wilbur. "Please don't say things like that!"

"Why not? It's true, and I have to say what is true. I am not entirely happy about my diet of flies and bugs, but it's the way I'm made. A spider has to pick up a living somehow or other, and I happen to be a trapper. I just naturally build a web and trap flies and other insects. My mother was a trapper before me. Her mother was a trapper before her. All our family have been trappers. Way back for thousands and thousands of years we spiders have been laying for flies and bugs."

"It's a miserable inheritance,"⁹ said Wilbur, gloomily. He was sad because his new friend was so bloodthirsty.ᶜ

"Yes, it is," agreed Charlotte. "But I can't help it. I don't know how the first spider in the early days of the world happened to think up this fancy idea of spinning a web, but she did, and it was clever of her, too. And since then, all of us spiders have had to work the same trick. It's not a bad pitch, on the whole."

"It's cruel," replied Wilbur, who did not intend to be argued out of his position.

"Well, *you* can't talk" said Charlotte. "*You* have your meals brought to you in a pail. Nobody feeds me. I have to get my own living. I live by my wits. I have to be sharp and clever, lestᶜᵍ I go hungry. I have to think things out, catch what I can, take what comes. And it just so happens, my friend, that what comes is flies and insects and bugs. And *further*more," said Charlotte, shaking one of her legs, "do you realize that if I didn't catch bugs and eat them, bugs would increase and multiply and get so numerous that they'd destroy the earth, wipe out everything?"

"Really?" said Wilbur. "I wouldn't want *that* to happen. Perhaps your web is a good thing after all."

The goose had been listening to this conversation and chuckling to herself. "There are a lot of things Wilbur doesn't know about life," she thought. "He's really a very innocent little pig. He doesn't even know what's going to happen to him around Christmastime; he has no idea that Mr. Zuckerman and Lurvy are plotting to kill him." And the goose raised herself a bit and poked her eggs a little further under her so that they would receive the full heat from her warm body and soft feathers.

Charlotte stood quietly over the fly, preparing to eat it. Wilbur lay down and closed his eyes. He was tired from his wakeful night and from the excitement of meeting someone for the first time. A breeze brought him the smell of clover—the sweet-smelling world beyond his fence. "Well," he thought, "I've got a new friend, all right. But what a gamble^g friendship is! Charlotte is fierce, brutal, scheming, bloodthirsty—everything I don't like. How can I learn to like her, even though she is pretty and, of course, clever?"

Wilbur was merely suffering the doubts and fears that often go with finding a new friend. In good time he was to discover that he was mistaken about Charlotte. Underneath her rather bold and cruel exterior,^{cg} she had a kind heart, and she was to prove loyal and true to the very end.

Check the Skills

Understanding the Selection

1. How do Wilbur and Charlotte reveal compassion for each other?

Vocabulary Development Skills Word Meaning

2. Which meaning of *last* is intended on page 55?

Comprehension Skills Implied Meaning

3. What will the outcome of the friendship be? How do you know?

Apply What You Learned in Unit 2

The Theme

Compassion

1. There are many different ways that people show their compassion. Boss took an orphaned child in and gave him food and shelter. Mr. Theo helped Emily develop a talent. Alice and Tara were kind to animals. Even Charlotte and Wilbur began to develop a compassionate friendship.

• Does helping others benefit the one doing the helping as well as the person being helped? How?

The Skills

Vocabulary Development Skills Word Meaning

2.   In this unit you learned about homonyms. You found out that homonyms are different words that are spelled in the same way or pronounced in the same way or both.

3.   The message of the sentence is usually the best clue to use in determining which homonym is the correct one. If you trust your own common sense, you should have little trouble with homonyms in your reading.

Comprehension Skills Implied Meaning

4.   You can probably increase your enjoyment of reading stories by learning to predict outcomes. To do this, use your own experience and clues the author gives. How does predicting outcomes get you more involved in your reading and make it more interesting for you?

Unit **3**

Other Times, Other Places

Overview and Purposes for Reading

The Theme

Other Times, Other Places

1. How do people from different times or places live? In what ways are their lives like yours? In what ways are they different?

The Skills

Vocabulary Development Skills Context Clues

2. When you come across a word you don't know, how can you try to figure out its meaning?
3. What are synonym and inference context clues? How can they help you decide what a word means?

Study and Research Skills Study Techniques

4. How can you complete your school assignments in the least time with the least effort?

Vocabulary Development Skills Context Clues

It is not always possible to know what all the words in a selection mean before you begin to read. Sometimes you need to figure out the meaning of a word while you are reading. The words and sentences around the unknown word can help you. The hints you find in these other words and sentences are called **context clues.** There are several types of context clues.

One type is a word or phrase that has nearly the same meaning as the unknown word. These are called **synonyms.** For instance, do you know the meaning of *lenient?* Perhaps not. The following sentences contain both the word *lenient* and a synonym context clue for it.

> The judge was lenient. He always gave mild sentences to criminals.

To use a context clue like this one, follow the steps below.

Using Synonym Context Clues

1. Locate the word you don't know.
2. Read the other words and sentences around that word.
3. See if there is a word or phrase that seems to give a clue to the unknown word.

Try it with *lenient* in the sentence above. Read past the word and go to the end of the next sentence. Look for a context clue that seems to give a hint to *lenient.* The word *mild* hints at what a lenient judge does. *Mild* is a synonym for *lenient.* Now you know enough about what *lenient* means to keep on reading. You don't need to ask somebody or to look it up in the dictionary.

Another way to use context clues is to "read between the lines." Figuring out hints like this by reasoning and common sense is called inferring. For instance, you may not know the meaning of *stoop,* but the following sentence contains an inference about its meaning.

The door to the playhouse was so small that the man had to stoop to get in.

Using Inference Context Clues

1. Locate the word you don't know.
2. Read the other words and sentences around that word.
3. Use what you already know about the topic to make a good guess about the word's meaning.

See how this works with *stoop* in the sentence above. The rest of the sentence tells you that a man is going into a playhouse that has a small door and that he has to stoop to get in. Think about your own life. Did you ever try to walk into a small place? How did you make yourself fit? Yes, you bent over to make yourself shorter. This clue to the word *stoop* is enough to allow you to keep on reading.

You can be a better reader if you learn to figure out hard words by using context clues to make a careful guess. In these two examples, the clues are synonyms and inferences. You can practice using both these types of context clues as you read the selections in this unit.

Study and Research Skills Study Techniques

Studying is hard work. However, you can make it easier and at the same time you can be more efficient. The secret? Having a study plan.

A study plan will help you know exactly what you need to do and when to do it. If you organize yourself with a study plan, you will be more successful.

Making a Study Plan

1. Know exactly what the teacher wants you to find out or do.
2. Determine what you need to read or write or do to complete the assignment.
3. Decide where you can get the necessary information. Will you need to use the textbook, the library, an encyclopedia, or some other source?
4. Figure out how much time you need to do the job.
5. Be sure you know when the assignment must be done.

Vary your study plan according to the type of assignment. If you only have to read a single chapter in the textbook and it will take less than an hour, your study plan will be simple. However, you will have to give your plan more thought if you have to read many sources from the library, interview people, and take notes for a paper due in two weeks.

To help yourself study better, follow the directions listed above before beginning each new assignment. When you have made your study plan, schedule enough time to complete it successfully and STICK TO YOUR SCHEDULE! You'll find some ideas about how to use this skill as you read this unit.

Use the Skills

Understanding the Selection

1. Read the selection to find out why the right clothing is so important for the place where these Eskimos live.

2. As you read, think about the type of clothing you would wear to go out in the cold. Compare your clothing to the Eskimos'.

Vocabulary Development Skills Context Clues

3. If you come across a word you don't know that has the small letter *c* after it, look for synonym or inference context clues. Notes in the margin will give you some help.

4. Review the steps on pages 61 and 62 if you need to.

Study and Research Skills Study Techniques

5. As you read, imagine that you have been asked by your teacher to do a three-page paper on Eskimos that will be due in two weeks. You are to include information on clothing, homes, food, transportation, and daily routine. Think about how you would organize to complete the imaginary assignment. Decide whether the following article would be all you would need to complete the assignment or if you would have to go to other sources.

ESKIMOS

Mary Bringle

In a land where a ripped pair of trousers could cause a person to freeze to death, carefully made clothing is truly essential.^{cg} Although Eskimo costumes are often handsome, the Arctic people must first think of practicality. Eskimos have found that the fur of the animal skins must be worn on the outside for the best protection against the low temperatures and freezing winds. Only the undershirts, made of birdskins, are worn with the feathers against the body. The overclothing must be loose and not overlap very much. A tightly fitting jacket might make the wearer perspire, and the wet hide could become frozen stiff when taken off. In the Arctic, durable^c clothing, made to last, is a matter of life or death.

■ If you know what it feels like to be out in the cold when you aren't dressed warmly enough, you should be able to infer that *essential* means "necessary."

The basic Eskimo costume is quite similar all over the polar^g world. Sealskin boots, called *kamiks,*^c are worn with skin stockings by both men and women. A layer of dried grass, which is changed daily, is sandwiched between the two soles to provide added warmth for the feet. The Eskimo male's kamiks come up to his knees. A fox tail may be sewn around the place where boots and trousers meet to keep the cold air from seeping^c in. The woman's kamiks go all the way up the leg, where they are joined by short fox-fur shorts. The men wear longer bearskin trousers with the gleaming white fur on the outside. Both men and women wear fox-fur jackets with hoods over their birdskin shirts, and mittens made from the skins of seal or caribou. In summer, a lighter-weight seal coat replaces the heavy fox. Children dress in the same costumes. Babies ride in pouches called *amauts*^c on their mothers' backs and take their warmth from the mother's body heat.

Many Eskimo garments^c are trimmed with fox tails or the long hairs from bear manes. They can be very beautiful, depending upon the artistry of the women who designed

■ The meaning of *garments* will be clear when you find the synonym "clothes" at the end of the next sentence.

the clothes. Eskimo women cut skins without using patterns. From long practice they know just where to clip without bothering to measure. Using a curved knife with a handle in the middle of the blade, called an *ulo*ᶜ or *ulu,* the Eskimo woman cuts the hides. Then she sews them together with a thread made of narwhalᵍ sinew.ᵍ

All clothing is dried each night on hanging frameworks, suspended over a blubberᵍ lamp. But other special precautions must be taken, as well, to guard against frostbite. In the tunnel leading to every Eskimo igloo,ᶜᵍ there is a little tool which is made of bone or wood and shaped like a small sword. This device,ᶜ called a *tilugtut,*ᶜ is used for beating snow crystals from the clothing. By the time an Eskimo has crawled through the tunnel to the house's entrance, his or her clothing is free of any excess moisture and will not grow heavy or damp inside. The tilugtut is particularly important for visitors—without it their clothing would freeze as soon as they departed if there is not enough time for their clothing to dry.

Soon, however, modern dwellings and heating devices will allow the polar people the same freedom in dressing that their more modernized^c neighbors to the south have enjoyed for years. Fashions from Europe and America are already much in demand, especially for Eskimo teen-agers.

■ If your report must include information about transportation, you would have to go to another source.

Check the Skills

Understanding the Selection

1. Why is the right clothing so important to the Eskimos you just read about? How does the place where they live affect the kind of clothing they need?

2. If you were going out into the cold, what clothes would you put on? How would your clothes be like those of the Eskimos? How would they be different?

Vocabulary Development Skills Context Clues

3. As you read the first paragraph, were you able to find the meaning for *durable*? Find the synonym for *durable* in this sentence:

    > In the Arctic, durable clothing, made to last, is a matter of life or death.

4. Were you able to figure out the meaning of *seeping* as it appeared in this sentence from the selection? Or did you have to use a dictionary?

    > A fox tail may be sewn around the place where boots and trousers meet to keep the cold air from seeping in.

Study and Research Skills Study Techniques

5. Was there enough information on transportation in the selection for your imaginary paper?

Use the Skills

Understanding the Selection

This story takes place in the early 1900s in Mississippi. It describes what living conditions were like for some black people after slavery had been abolished. Although the story is fiction, it is based on fact. Some freed slaves stayed to work on the plantations because they felt there was no place else to go.

1. Decide for yourself whether Cap'n Bryant is fair to the people who work on the land.

2. Look for sentences that let you know that this story takes place in an earlier time.

Vocabulary Development Skills Context Clues

3. Use your skill with synonym and inference context clues to help figure out several words you may not know.

Study and Research Skills Study Techniques

4. Suppose you are going to write a report about the way these people lived. Decide whether this selection would give you enough information.

SETTLIN'-UP TIME

Julius Lester

On Saturday afternoon there was scarcely anyone on the Bryant plantation. Monday to Friday they worked in the fields from the time the sun was a half-circle of orange over the eastern edge of the world until it was a half-circle of red over the western edge. On Saturday, though, they were allowed to stop working while the sun still glared^c from the top of the sky. They laid their hoes across their shoulders and with much laughing and talking went to their shacks, washed, put on clean clothes, and started for Bryantown, a mile and a half of dusty road to the south. Many walked, but those who could squeezed onto already crowded mule wagons. By the time the wagons got to town, sometimes there were people hanging from the sides, their feet dragging in the dust. It was Saturday, and only those too old or too sick stayed behind.

Bryantown was two small frame houses across from the railroad tracks at the end of the plantation. The train went by twice a day, but no one had ever known it to stop.

Although everyone called it Bryantown, it didn't appear on any maps or government records. It wasn't really a town, and even if it had been, that word would not have been an accurate^cg description. In reality it was a small country of some four hundred acres of rich Mississippi delta^g land with five hundred blacks, including children and infants, ruled by Cap'n Bryant. He owned the land and the shacks the people lived in, sold them the food they ate, the clothes they wore on their backs, the cottonseed they put in the ground, and the tools they farmed with. And although slavery had been declared illegal^cg sixty years before, the blacks within Cap'n Bryant's four hundred acres lived no differently than their parents and grandparents had. Some of them still lived and remembered the day Cap'n Bryant's father had told them they were free.

On Saturday afternoon Cap'n Bryant could be found in the second of the two frame shacks. This was the store, or commissary,[c] as it was called. It was well stocked with brightly colored bolts[g] of cloth for dresses and shirts, fatback and grits, and patent[g] medicines. All afternoon Cap'n Bryant stood behind the counter, taking items from the shelves and noting the price in ink beside the person's name in his ledger[g] book.

■ Look in the first part of the sentence to find *store,* the synonym for *commissary.*

The people stood at the counter and watched while Cap'n Bryant added another figure to the long line of figures already under their names. They wondered if at settlin' up time "de ducks"[c] were going to keep them in debt for another year.

"Well, de ducks got me again this year," one would say jokingly to another on that cold November day when they lined up outside the commissary to settle[c] their accounts. "Cap'n Bryant look in that big book of his and he say he deduck for the medicine I had to have for my chillun. And he deduck for the cottonseed and the new plow and the new shoes and clothes and the food and the rent. And he put all de ducks together and he say, 'Well, Sam, you owed me two hundred dollars from last year, and the cotton you and your family raised this year brought in nine hundred dollars. But y'all spent 'leven hundred dollars for rent and the cottonseed and that new plow and all the rest. So that mean you end up owing me four hundred dollars. Thought you was gon' get out of debt this year. Well, you work hard, and I believe you might make it out of debt next settlin'-up time.'"

Check the Skills

Understanding the Selection

1. Is Cap'n Bryant fair to the black people? Why do you think as you do?

2. What clues let you know that this story takes place at an earlier time?

Vocabulary Development Skills Context Clues

3. a. Were you able to find the synonym for *noting* as it appears in the following sentence? Look at the long phrase following the word.

   > All afternoon Cap'n Bryant stood behind the counter, taking items from the shelves and noting the price in ink beside the person's name in his ledger book.

   b. Were you able to make a good guess about the meaning of *bolts* in the following sentence? Or did you have to use the glossary?

   > It was well stocked with brightly colored bolts of cloth for dresses and shirts, fatback and grits, and patent medicines.

Study and Research Skills Study Techniques

4. Do you think you would have to check other sources for more information about the way these people lived? Where would you check? How long do you think it would take you to locate the information, take notes, and then write the report?

Selection 3

Use the Skills

Understanding the Selection

Tien Pao lives with his mother and father and little sister in China during World War II. But he becomes separated from his family when their sampan home in which he is sleeping floats down river into Japanese territory. Now he is trying to find a way to get himself and his pet pig, Glory-of-the-Republic, safely back home.

1. Think about what it was like to live in Japanese-occupied China during World War II.

2. Find out why Tien Pao is afraid.

Vocabulary Development Skills Context Clues

3. Use what you have learned about synonyms and "reading between the lines" to figure out the meanings for some words you don't know.

Study and Research Skills Study Techniques

4. As you read, think about the steps you would follow to write a report on farming in China. Review the steps for making a study plan if you don't remember them.

THE HOUSE OF SIXTY FATHERS

Meindert DeJong

In the late afternoon Tien Pao suddenly could go no farther. He broke into a cold sweat, his legs trembled under him, he was nauseated with hunger. He had reached the top of a round, grassy hill. There were a few sheltering bushes, and he crawled behind them. He had to eat, had to rest. He dug his hand into the rice bowl and gulped a choking, big mouthful. Glory-of-the-Republic began tearing at the grass. Tien Pao dug his hand into the bowl again, stuffed his mouth full. Again his hand went to the bowl. He pulled it back. There was only a good handful of rice left in the bottom of the bowl. He mustn't touch it, mustn't eat it—he mustn't keep looking at it! It had to be saved for one more meal.

He heard voices. He peered° through the bushes and saw a group of boys and girls coming up the hill with baskets on their backs and grass knives in their hands. They came slowly and weakly—like old people. They even looked like old people! The skin was drawn like old paper over their cheekbones. The children stopped halfway up the hill and cut grass with their hooked knives. They stuffed whole handfuls into their mouths before they put as much as a blade of grass into their baskets. Then one little boy began to eat mud!

Tien Pao looked on, horrified. The mud-eating boy was the smallest of the lot. He kept away from the others, as if he were ashamed. He dragged himself around behind his bloated,° huge stomach. His sticks of legs looked silly under that big stomach. And now the little boy scooped up a handful of dirt again and brought it to his mouth. His sister saw it and scolded him in a tired old way. The little fellow hung his head. He slowly opened his hand and let the mud dribble^c out of it. He looked at his empty, dirty hand and began to cry.

Tien Pao looked on—sickened. His glance went from the skeleton boy with the bloated stomach to the sturdy little pig beside him. Suddenly he was desperately^{cg} afraid. Glory-of-the-Republic was food! He was in danger from these starving people.

■ You should be able to figure out the meaning for *steal* from the rest of the sentence.

Tien Pao started to steal^c away so as not to be noticed, but ten paces beyond the little boy he broke into a hard run. He had to run even though these starved, weak children could not possibly catch him and Glory-of-the-Republic. He and the pig raced down the hill and up and over the next one.

Glory-of-the-Republic could not stand the pace, nor did he like it. He began dragging on the end of the rope, and he tried to grab mouthfuls of grass in passing. Tien Pao would not let him. He did not dare stop for anything now. For now he remembered other things. All this rainy day he had

■ These sentences tell you what you would see in the farmland of China. Could you write a report from this information?

not seen one little black goat. Always before the little black goats had capered^{cg} in the mountains. He had not seen a single ox in a field, a pig in a yard, nor a water buffalo in a single rice paddy below the mountains. There hadn't even been one lean dog on any mountain path, or around the mud huts among the rice paddies. It could only mean that the Japanese had taken everything from the people, and the hungry people had eaten the dogs.

But if the Japanese had taken everything, he wasn't safe in these hills with a pig! The thought stopped Tien Pao in his tracks. He wasn't safe in daylight! He'd merely been lucky so far this dark rainy day. But the Japanese had but to get one glimpse of him with a pig, and they'd know he wasn't from this wasted land. Here were no pigs! Tien Pao stared desperately around him from the tall rock on which he was standing. He did not know what to do. He wanted to rush away from this horrible country, but it would be dangerous to take another step in daylight—sooner or later he and his pig would be seen.

■ You will find a synonym for *rooted*. But you will have to look farther than the same sentence.

Glory-of-the-Republic rooted^c about while Tien Pao stood hesitating. The little pig snorted and dug. Leaves rustled at Tien Pao's feet, pebbles rattled. He became so noisy, it finally aroused Tien Pao's attention. He looked down. Right at his feet Glory-of-the-Republic had shoved himself under a rock ledge. He'd almost disappeared, only his curly excited tail still showed. Under the ledge was a little cave. The little pig had found a cave! Suddenly Tien Pao knew what to do—hide in little caves by day, and travel by night!

He dropped to hands and knees beside the rooting pig, helped him dig out the collected leaves and debris until the cave was big enough. After a long look all around to see that no one had observed them, Tien Pao squirmed into the opening with Glory-of-the-Republic. It was a narrow little hole, but Tien Pao reached out and scraped all the leaves back into the entrance. When the cave's opening was completely closed with leaves, Tien Pao and his pig stretched out behind them to wait for the coming of night.

Check the Skills

Understanding the Selection

1. What were living conditions like in Japanese-occupied China during World War II?

2. Why was Tien Pao afraid? Do you think he was right to be afraid? Why do you think as you do?

Vocabulary Development Skills Context Clues

3. Were you able to find the meaning for *steal* as it appears on page 74? What is the synonym for *rooted* on page 74?

Study and Research Skills Study Techniques

4. Would you have to check other sources to write a report about farming in China for your social studies class? How would you make a study plan to write a four-page report?

Use the Skills

Understanding the Selection

1. The next selection is taken from a textbook that you might have in a social studies class. Read to find out what life is like for many people in India.

2. Learn about the problems that keep India a poor country.

Vocabulary Development Skills Context Clues

3. Figure out the words you don't know by using what you have learned about context clues.

Study and Research Skills Study Techniques

4. Think about how you would make a study plan if you were assigned to read this chapter as homework.

INDIA

T. A. Raman

India is part of the underdeveloped world. The countries of the world generally may be divided into two groups. In one group are countries where most of the people earn enough money to buy the things they need for a comfortable way of life. These are known as developed countries. This group includes the United States, Canada, Australia, Japan, and many of the nations of Europe. In the second group are the underdeveloped countries, where most of the people have a low standard^{cg} of living. India is one of these countries.

The underdeveloped countries are divided into two smaller groups. Countries in which industrialization^{cg} is well under way are considered partly developed. The others, called developing countries, still have little industry.

■ You should be able to figure out what *industrialization* means from the following sentence in which another form of the word appears.

Industry is developing in India. In India, as in many other underdeveloped countries, the Industrial Revolution is just beginning. About seven out of ten people in India are farmers. Most of these people are very poor. They do not use modern farming methods, and they lack power-driven machines to help them plant, cultivate,^{cg} and harvest their crops. Also, their farms are very small. As a result, these farmers produce barely enough food to feed their families.

■ What do you infer is the meaning of this word?

Compared to a developed country such as Japan, India has only a small number of factories. One reason is the lack of money to start new industries. Also, in many parts of the country there is no electric power for running machinery. Most of India's people lack the skills needed to work in modern factories. In addition, India does not have enough good roads and railroads for transporting products easily and inexpensively. Companies that have built factories here often have difficulty selling their goods because most of India's people are too poor to buy them.

Since most people in India cannot afford to buy manufac-tured^c goods, they make by hand many of the things they need. For example, many people in rural areas spin thread and weave cloth. Household articles such as dishes and furniture are usually made by village craftsmen.

Most people in India sell their handmade goods and other products in outdoor markets. There are few large depart-ment stores and supermarkets. In India, only about ten out of every one hundred workers earn a living by working in stores, or in service jobs such as repairing automobiles or selling insurance.

Like other underdeveloped countries, India must import^{cg} most of the manufactured goods that it uses. For example, much expensive machinery is purchased from the United States and other industrialized countries. To earn money to pay for imported goods, India exports^{cg} raw materials such as iron ore and farm products such as tea. However, it does not earn enough money from exports to buy all the man-ufactured goods that its people and its industries need.

India's progress has been slow. One of the reasons India has remained an underdeveloped country is that most of the people there cannot read or write. Without these skills, it is difficult for them to gain the information they need to be better farmers, to work in modern factories, or to live more productive^c and satisfying lives.

India's progress has been slow for several other reasons. Many people do not have enough food to eat, or they suffer from illness. Therefore, they do not have the energy or the enthusiasm^{cg} needed to improve their way of life. Often people are not willing to try new ideas because they cannot afford to take risks. For example, farmers are often unwill-ing to experiment with modern farming methods. They are afraid that if the experiment failed, they would be left without food and would also lose the small amount of money they had saved. They feel more secure^{cg} using the methods their parents and grandparents used.

To make progress, India must break the "vicious circle" of underdevelopment. Many of India's problems are closely related to each other. For example, if farmers in India owned larger farms and used modern machinery and fertilizers, they would be able to produce more crops. As a result, they could earn a better living and buy more manufactured goods. This, in turn, would encourage the growth of industry, which would provide jobs for millions of unemployed Indians. However, most farmers are too poor to buy the things they need in order to produce more crops. Thus they continue to live in poverty and industry fails to grow. Such a situation is called a "vicious circle."

■ How much time would you allow to read this chapter?

Check the Skills

Understanding the Selection

1. Are most people in India rich or poor? How do these people get something to eat? Where do they get household articles such as dishes and furniture?

2. What are some of the problems that keep India a poor country?

Vocabulary Development Skills Context Clues

3. What is the meaning of *industrialization* on page 77? How did you figure out the meaning of *cultivate* on page 77?

Study and Research Skills Study Techniques

4. How much time do you think it would take you to study this material?

Use the Skills

This story is about a Sioux girl's first journey away from her village. You will find out how she feels about the experience. You'll also learn something about the way the Sioux tribe lived in another time.

As you read, think about how you would make a study plan for writing a five-page report on Sioux customs. Pretend the report is due in two weeks. And remember to use what you have learned about context clues to figure out the words you don't know.

BUFFALO WOMAN

Dorothy M. Johnson

Whirlwind's mother, Many Bones, put her hands on her little girl's shoulders. She looked into her face and said, "You can go, and your father will take care of you. You will be a good girl and do exactly what you're told."

Then she turned and slipped out through the lodge doorway. She walked away with great dignity to spread the news that little Whirlwind was going to the trading post.

The horseback journey of eight days was miserably uncomfortable. The sun never came out from behind clouds. It rained most of the time, and although the grownups built a lean-to each night to keep the rain off, they were wet as they rode. They rode fast all day, careful to keep the fire in their small iron pot from being extinguished.[cg] Sometimes it was hard to find dry firewood, and they ate pemmican[g] or half-cooked fresh meat.

The men grumbled, the woman murmured sometimes, but Whirlwind was as happy as a meadowlark in the spring. She rode her own pony and led a packhorse. She gathered firewood and carried water and helped Begins Early dress out an antelope that one of the men brought down with an arrow.

As they neared the big river, they could see the buildings of the Frenchmen's trading post, surrounded by a stout palisade[c] of heavy posts standing on end. The whole party felt better. The sun came out from behind a cloud. One of the men, in sudden good humor, remarked, "It is a good thing we brought two women along. The traders will know we come in peace."

Whirlwind hardly heard the compliment of being called a woman. She was staring at the palisade and the log buildings inside. She had never seen permanent buildings before in her life. Her people had none; they moved camp very often.

How, she wondered, do they keep their camp clean if they never move it? She found out soon that they didn't keep it clean. It was dirty and smelled bad. The white men simply didn't know how to live, she concluded.

The whole party rode back and forth in front of the closed gate. They yelled greetings, so the wary[cg] traders could look them over, see they were not dressed for war, and see they had packhorses and pony drags piled high with furs and robes to trade.

The gate opened, and two men came out, carrying guns but making the sign for peace. The visitors made the same sign. Then there were loud greetings, and they were allowed to come partway inside. The Sioux and the traders alike shouted *"How, kola!"*—Greetings, friend.

That was how Whirlwind saw white men for the first time. She remembered that her grandmother had described them as dirty, with hair all over their faces. Whirlwind agreed completely. Sioux men did not have much hair on their faces, and they pulled the hairs out, one by one, because they wanted to look nice.

Check the Skills

Understanding the Selection

1. How does Whirlwind feel about her trip? How do you know?

2. What did you learn about the way the Sioux tribe lived in an earlier time?

Vocabulary Development Skills Context Clues

3. What is your best guess at what *palisade* means in the following sentence?

    As they neared the big river, they could see the buildings of the Frenchmen's trading post, surrounded by a stout palisade of heavy posts standing on end.

Study and Research Skills Study Techniques

4. Did you find enough information in this story to write a five-page report on Sioux customs? How would you make a study plan for that assignment?

Apply What You Learned in Unit 3

The Theme

Other Times, Other Places

1. People's ways of living in other times and other places may seem very different from your own. However, there may be some ways in which their lives are like yours. Just as you would take care of your cat or dog, Tien Pao was concerned about his pet pig and didn't want anything to happen to it. Whirlwind was excited about making the journey with her father, just as you probably are when you go on a trip with your family.

• What other ways can you think of that the characters from the stories are like you even though they may live in different times and places? What kinds of things do you think people all over the world have in common?

The Skills

Vocabulary Development Skills Context Clues

2. In this unit you learned that you can sometimes use context clues to help figure out the meaning of an unfamiliar word. You might find a synonym in the same sentence or in a nearby sentence. Or you might find an inference context clue.

3. Synonym context clues are found in a word or phrase that means almost the same thing as the unknown word. With inference context clues, you use reasoning and what you read "between the lines" to help figure out the unknown word. This skill will be of value to you in many situations—not only in your reading but also when people are talking and someone says a word you don't know. Practice this skill and you will find you are able to figure out the meaning of many more words than you probably thought you could. If there aren't enough context clues, you can always check a dictionary.

Study and Research Skills Study Techniques

4. Knowing how to make a study plan is a valuable skill to have, not only for your school work but also for other things you may choose to do outside of school. Once you know how to make a study plan, you can use the skill for any situation in which you want to learn something and accomplish a specific goal. What situations can you think of in which some kind of study plan would be valuable?

Unit 4

Rescues and Escapes

Overview and Purposes for Reading

The Theme

Rescues and Escapes

1. In threatening situations, what do people do to escape or to rescue someone else?

The Skills

Vocabulary Development Skills Dictionary

2. Should you look up in a dictionary every unknown word you come across in your reading? Why or why not?

3. How can you find a word in a glossary or dictionary?

4. What kinds of information about a word does a glossary or dictionary include?

Literary Appreciation Skills Figurative Language

5. How does figurative language differ from literal language?

Vocabulary Development Skills Dictionary

Imagine that you are reading a book and you meet the word *vestibule.* If you don't know the word, what should you do? First, of course, you should try to figure it out for yourself, using context clues. If this doesn't work, however, you should use the dictionary.

You know that the words in dictionaries are listed in alphabetical order. To find the word *vestibule,* then, you must first open the dictionary to the *v*'s. The letter *v* is toward the end of the alphabet, so you should open the dictionary toward the back. Then use the **guide words.** These tell the first and last entry words to appear on a page or sometimes on a spread of two pages that face each other. The guide words are in large dark type at the top of the page in most dictionaries. Look at this sample.

vessel   1.   2.   3.

veto

ves sel (ves′əl) *n.* 1 a ship or large boat. 2 a container; something hollow that can hold a substance. [< OF *vais-sel* container < LL *vascellum* < *vās* vessel]   4.

ves ti bule (ves′tə būl) *n.* 1 a passage or hall between the outer door and the interior parts of a house or building. 2 *Railroads.* an enclosed space at the end of a passenger car, serving as a sheltered entrance to the car from another car or from outside the train. [< L *vestibul(um)* forecourt, entrance]

Dictionary entries generally include several parts that give different kinds of information about the word. The labels on the sample above match the descriptions on the next page.

1. **Pronunciation.** The pronunciation is given in a code, with each symbol standing for a type of sound. Each dictionary uses a different kind of code. The complete key to the code is at the beginning of the dictionary. A shorter key is usually found somewhere on each spread of two facing pages. You do not need to memorize this code. On page 464 you will find the pronunciation key used in the glossary of this book. Take a moment now to look at it.

2. **Part of speech.** This tells whether the word is used as a noun, a verb, or another part of speech. The dictionary will also tell you if one definition of a word is a different part of speech than another definition is. In the sample entry for *vestibule* the abbreviation *n.* following the pronunciation tells that *vestibule* is used as a noun.

3. **Definition.** Most words have more than one meaning. The dictionary usually separates different definitions with numbers. In the sample entry, you can see that *vestibule* has two definitions. The most common and general meaning is listed first. A label often tells you if a definition has a special use. In *vestibule,* the second meaning is limited to railroads.

4. **Etymology.** This part of an entry tells where the word came from—its history. This part, too, often uses special symbols. The key to the code is at the beginning of the dictionary. The entry for *vestibule* indicates that the word came from a Latin word that meant "forecourt or entrance." Not all dictionaries include etymologies, but the larger ones usually do.

As you read this unit, you'll get some practice in understanding how and when to use a dictionary. You'll do this mainly by referring to the glossary at the back of this book as though it were a dictionary.

Literary Appreciation Skills Figurative Language

As you read, you need to be able to decide when words and phrases have their usual meanings and when they signal exaggerations or figurative language.

When an author describes something as being much more than it really is or could be, that's **exaggeration.** The phrase *as big as basketballs* is an exaggeration in the first sentence below. In the second sentence the phrase is used in its **literal sense,** which means with its usual or more common meaning.

1. The hailstones falling around Paul Bunyan were as big as basketballs.
2. The balls used in the game of soccer are about as big as basketballs.

In much the same way, **figurative language** suggests comparisons that are not realistic or possible. The following sentences are examples of figurative language.

1. The cat's eyes sparkled like diamonds.
2. The wind sighed and whispered in the trees.
3. He had a heart of stone.

You know that the cat's eyes could not really sparkle like diamonds, that wind can't sigh and whisper as a person does, and that no one really has a heart made of stone. But you can enjoy such uses of language.

Figurative language adds interest and fun to what you read. There are times, however, when you really need to decide whether something you read is figurative language or not. Use context clues and common sense to tell the difference between literal and figurative use of language as you read this unit.

Use the Skills

Understanding the Selection

The small European country of Hungary has been under Communist control for many years. In the early 1950s restrictions imposed on Hungarians by their government were so tight that people were rarely allowed to enter or leave the country. However, many tried to escape to freedom. These facts form the background for the following fictional selection. In it, twelve-year-old Latsi Kerék is attempting to escape to join his family in Sweden. He is going to try to cross the border at night. That day a horse drawing a cart had bolted and run toward the border fence, setting off several land mines that tore a gaping hole in the fence. Latsi hopes to escape through this hole.

1.　Find out what happens to Latsi. Think about how he feels.

Vocabulary Development Skills Dictionary

2.　Use your dictionary skills if you find a word whose meaning you cannot determine from context. Remember that a word that is in the glossary is indicated by the small letter ᵍ after it.

Literary Appreciation Skills Figurative Language

3.　Be alert to the author's use of figurative language.

UNDER THE BARBED WIRE

László Hámori

Slowly and with infinite^g care, he crept forward, following the tracks. Every time he raised his head, he could see that he was coming closer and closer to the barbed-wire^c barrier.^{g} The moon shone down through the trees, but as yet he couldn't make out the hole, which was the aftermath^g of the explosion. Suddenly there was no more grassland. Beneath his hands he could feel the earth, and he began to realize that he had reached the mine field itself. There, all the bushes and trees had been removed, and they had even plowed up the grass. Nothing was left that might shield the escapees.^{c} "This is the most dangerous point," he said to himself, making slow progress with even greater precaution.^{cg} The only thing that mattered now was to keep within the bounds of the wheel tracks and to keep pressed as closely to the ground as possible.

■ This phrase hints that *precaution* means something like "carefulness." So you probably don't need to use the glossary.

He had managed to go forward about thirty yards on the newly plowed ground when a dazzling searchlight was turned on in the watchtower. The flood of light splintered the darkness. For a moment, Latsi believed they had turned it on because they had discovered his presence. His first impulse^c was to get up and run as fast as possible. With any luck he might reach the place where the explosion had ruined the fence and escape over onto Austrian soil. And if he were to run terribly fast, perhaps they wouldn't be able to shoot him. He tensed his muscles, but at the last minute he curbed his feelings of panic.^{c} With his arms at his sides and his legs pressed tightly together, he stretched out flat on the ground. In that position, it would be more difficult for any bullets to hit him. The searchlight had made a quarter turn when it reached the spot where a motionless figure lay on the ground. Latsi's heart was pounding so hard that he felt his chest would burst; his throat was dry. For a second

■ Since light can't flood or splinter, you know this is figurative rather than literal.

■ It sounds as if the search-light is acting like a person. This is another type of figurative language.

the strong light lingered, and then it continued on its path indifferently.⁹ But the second seemed an eternity⁹ to Latsi.

By this time the light had made a half-circle turn, and Latsi, who had cautiously peeked upward, could see every thorny barb in the fence. Just as suddenly as the lights had been turned on, they were turned out again, and only a reddish glow, fast fading, remained at the point where the blinding light had originated. Everything was dark and quiet once more, and Latsi began to creep ahead again. Because of the tension his joints were stiff, but a few yards farther on, it got a little easier, and he made fairly good progress. The passage of time began to disturb him. No doubt it was quite late. He had no watch, but he had the feeling that the night was just about at an end. To be sure, the skies were still dark, but the stars had begun to fade. Dawn was advancing, and with it the dangers increased.

Lifting his head with utmost caution, Latsi took a good look around. The tracks of the wheels, which had been his guide, ended abruptly,ᶜ and he was forced to feel his way with his hands and inch his body along. A rash⁹ movement, a false touch, and a new mine could explode!

■ You'll probably have to use the glossary for rash.

About four yards farther on, he could see a dark spot on the ground. It was where the mine had burst the previousᶜ morning, blasting a hole. What if there was another mine on this side or the other side of the hole?

He didn't have time to worry about that. Although he was well aware of his peril,ᶜ he began to crawl ahead on all fours. He couldn't help himself, even though he knew that the watchtower was very close at hand! He reached the hole and his hands were touching the edge when the searchlight came on again. Like a flaming sword the beamᶜ split the darkness. Under other, more peaceful circumstances this would have been a beautiful sight, but Latsi had no time to enjoy the dramaticᶜᵍ wonder. Headfirst, he threw himself into the hole. It was deep enough so that he could curl up and not be seen in the deadly beam of light. As it had before, it returned halfway before it went out again. Darkness once more covered the field, but Latsi had no desire to leave his safe retreat⁹ in the hole.

Shivering, he tried to persuade himself to crawl out of the hole and go ahead, but he couldn't do it. While his will battled his fear, he began, involuntarily,⁹ to mumble to himself the football cheer: *"Hoop, hoop, hurrá! Hoop, hoop, hurrá!"*

And it helped. Once more he began to inch along. No longer did his teeth chatter so terribly, and he even dared to raise his head and look around. No more than ten yards away was the open gate to freedom. The explosion had blasted a couple of fence posts almost to pieces, and twisted barbed wire hung over the remnants.⁹ As rapidly as possible, he made his way toward the opening: there were five, now three yards, now one yard to go—and over there was freedom, life, and Sweden. Cautious⁹ though he was, he scratched his hand badly on some barbed wire that lay on the ground. Blood dripped from the gash onto Hungarian soil as Latsi said farewell to his homeland, the beautiful land of Hungary.

Check the Skills

Understanding the Selection

1. What happened to Latsi? How did he feel as he was trying to escape? afterward?

Vocabulary Development Skills Dictionary

2. What are the guide words on the glossary page where you found *rash*? Why is *rash* on that page instead of the one before?

Literary Appreciation Skills Figurative Language

3. How do you know the sentence below is figurative language?

   Like a flaming sword the beam split the darkness.

Use the Skills

Understanding the Selection

Several different people contributed to the invention of television. The all-important picture tube was largely the work of two young men who, unknown to each other, were working on the same idea thousands of miles apart. When the time came to patent the invention, one had proof of when he had started and the other did not. The latter was rescued in a dramatic fashion by his high school teacher.

1.   Read to discover how this rescue came about.

Vocabulary Development Skills Dictionary

2.   Use your dictionary skills when you need to. Although the article is about a technical subject, there are only a few difficult words in it. You may be able to unlock their meanings through context clues. If not, use the glossary.

Literary Appreciation Skills Figurative Language

3.   See if you agree that the author has used mainly literal language rather than figurative.

TV ON A BLACKBOARD

Tom Dowling

One of the strangest cases ever to come before the United States Patent⁹ Office concerned the invention of the television tube. And a high school teacher was the deciding figureᶜ in the case.

Justin Tolman knew a great deal about science. He recognized talents and helped to develop them in his students. He taught in Rigby, Idaho, in the 1920's. If he had not been teaching there in 1922, Philo Farnsworth might never have been recognized as an inventor of TV.

Philo was a real bug on science, and about the only person who would listen to his ideas was Tolman. Perhaps this was because the teacher was the only one around who understood most of what Philo was talking about. All others looked upon the boy as some kind of a nut who had fantasticᶜ ideas.

This boy had said it was possible to make a picture jump invisibly through the air and be seen on some kind of screen many miles away. As if that wasn't bad enough, he claimed it would be seen the very second it was happening!

But he couldn't really do it. He said he could if he had the materials—but the materials cost a great deal of money, and he had no money.

So, naturally, they all laughed at Philo Farnsworth in those days. Not so today, however. Today his name is in the history books.

But where do Justin Tolman and the U.S. Patent Office come into the picture? Well, it all started at the school blackboard, where Tolman watched Philo, then sixteen years old, make complicated diagrams⁹ of his invention. The teacher fired question after question at Philo, and the answers came right back. There wasn't the slightest doubt in his mind that, if he could get the necessary equipment, he could build a tube which would pull pictures out of the air.

Tolman believed in the boy. His explanations seemed correct in every detail. The building of such a machine, however, would be expensive.

■ You may need to check the glossary. Context clues are not very strong here for the meaning of this word.

So Philo's dream lay dormant⁹ until years later when he was called before a wealthy group of people in San Francisco and asked to describe the idea he had about a magic tube.

Once they heard him speak of his ideas, they became excited by his enthusiasm and provided him with his own laboratory᪣ in which to work. If he could actually produce the invention he claimed, they would reap꜀⁹ great returns on their investment.

It was the chance Philo Farnsworth had been waiting for ever since the days he had drawn blackboard diagrams for Justin Tolman. He had not seen his teacher since. But the day was to come when he would remember him and hope that he was still alive and that his memory and intellect⁹ were as strong as ever!

It all came about when Farnsworth and his backers filed

for patent[cg] rights with the Patent Office. The authorities there were bewildered.[c] They were receiving patent requests from another man at the same time! And each man was claiming invention of the same <u>contraption</u>![c] The other man was Vladimir Zworykin; he was sponsored by a different group of backers.

This left the Patent Office faced with the very serious problem of determining which of the two men should get both the patent rights and the fortune which undoubtedly awaited.

After considerable deliberation,[g] it was announced that the proof was up to the inventor. Each man would have to give evidence to prove when his invention was made, when he first wrote down the idea. Zworykin produced proof by showing dated sketches. These were dated prior to Farnsworth's laboratory work. Farnsworth had no proof that he'd worked out the whole thing many times on a school blackboard when he was only sixteen years old.

■ Your sense of the sentence and the word *invention* are clues that this means "something invented." So you don't need to use the glossary.

Philo Farnsworth is shown at the far left of the photograph. He is operating his first portable television transmitter unit.

Things looked bleak^c for him until he remembered Justin Tolman. He realized his old teacher was the only man in the world who had understood those diagrams. But even if he could be found, would he remember them today?

Not wanting Farnsworth to have any contact with Tolman before he could appear before the hearing board, the Patent Office itself located the teacher and brought him to the meeting. There he was asked about Philo Farnsworth's claims regarding blackboard diagrams. Did he remember them?

To Farnsworth's relief, Tolman stated that he not only remembered them but, with painstaking^c detail, he used a blackboard to prove it.

The first television camera, photographed in 1929 in Farnsworth's laboratory.

Because of the teacher's outstanding memory and because he had had faith in a sixteen-year-old boy with a dream when everyone else thought him eccentric,[9] Farnsworth's case was won, and his patents granted.

Both inventors involved in this decision have gone on to great things since that historic hearing by the United States Patent Office. Vladimir Zworykin, a great scientist, is Honorary Vice President of Radio Corporation of America (RCA) and winner of many awards, including the National Medal of Science, which is this country's greatest scientific award. Philo Farnsworth's inventions are too numerous to mention here. But neither man could ever forget a tension-packed day, a teacher, and a blackboard.

■ This is not exaggeration, as the rest of the paragraph makes clear.

Check the Skills

Understanding the Selection

1. How did Farnsworth's former teacher rescue him?

Vocabulary Development Skills Dictionary

2. How did you figure out the meaning of *diagram* and *reap*?

Literary Appreciation Skills Figurative Language

3. How did the last paragraph of the selection make clear that its first sentence was literal language rather than figurative?

Use the Skills

Understanding the Selection

1. The next story is fun to read. Watch for the worm's clever escape plan. How does it compare to Latsi Kerék's escape in "Under the Barbed Wire"?

Vocabulary Development Skills Dictionary

2. Only a few words in this selection are in the glossary. See if you can figure out their meanings from context. Check the glossary if you need to.

Literary Appreciation Skills Figurative Language

3. Watch for a different use of figurative language early in the story.

THE BLACKBIRD AND THE WORM

Stephen Krensky

A blackbird awoke one morning on a breezy day. Yawning lazily, he watched the clouds drift by, noting their different shapes. The largest was especially striking.⁹ It reminded him of a bear prowling^cg the countryside for his breakfast.

Such thoughts brought his own hunger to mind. Spreading his wings, the blackbird took flight. He searched the ground for something to eat. Before long, he captured an unsuspecting^cg worm.

"Good morning," said the blackbird. "How kind of you to join me for breakfast."

The worm glanced around for a last look at the flowers, the trees, and the sky.

"Ah," said the blackbird, following the worm's gaze. "I see you've noticed the bear."

"The what?"

"The bear," repeated the blackbird. "The big cloud that looks like a bear."

The worm laughed.

"What's so funny?" asked the blackbird.

"Are you serious?" asked the worm. "About the bear, I mean."

"Yes, why?"

The worm laughed again. "It's ridiculous, that's why."

"Oh, really," said the blackbird smugly.^cg "How would you know? After all, I have been in the clouds."

"True enough," said the worm.

"So . . ." said the blackbird.

"So what?"

"So *what*?" raged^c the blackbird. "How can you say that? With my experience, I should be the better judge."

■ Notice how both the bird and the worm talk in a modern, human fashion. This is another way to use language figuratively.

The worm shook her head. "Maybe that's your problem," she explained. "You're too close to see the clouds properly."

"Hummph!" snorted the blackbird. "I don't believe it."

"I'll show you how shortsighted you are. Look at the little cloud approaching the big one."

The blackbird looked. "You mean approaching the bear," he said.

"It's not a bear," said the worm patiently. "Anyway, what do you think the little cloud is?"

The blackbird thought it over.

"The bear is bending down," he decided. "Pawing in a stream. He is trying to catch a fish. The little cloud is a fish."

The worm sighed.

"What's the matter now?" asked the blackbird angrily.

"If you put me down, I'll explain. It's too uncomfortable this way."

The blackbird released the worm. "Now hurry up and explain."

The worm stretched happily. "All right," she said. "The big cloud is a cave, not a bear. And the little cloud is a fox, not a fish. The fox is fleeing some dogs. Notice that little dip?"

"The bear's open mouth," said the blackbird.

"Not exactly," said the worm. "It's the mouth of a cave. Too small for the dogs, but big enough for the fox to enter."

■ See if you can determine the meaning of *obvious* from context. Check the glossary if you can't.

"How can you be so sure?" the blackbird asked.

"It's obvious."^{cg}

For the first time, the blackbird doubted himself. "A cave . . ." he mused,^{cg} staring at the two clouds. "And a fox?"

■ Can you get an idea what this means from context clues? Or do you need to use the glossary?

"Precisely."^g

The blackbird frowned. He still thought the bear was decidedly pawing a fish. Turning his head one way, and then another, he tried to imagine them as a cave and a fox. It was no use.

"I was right," he said finally. "Look now. The bear is scooping the fish from the water. He will eat it for breakfast. Just as I will eat you." The blackbird looked to the ground in triumph.[g]

The worm was gone.

And when the blackbird glanced back at the clouds, the fox was entering the cave in safety.

Check the Skills

Understanding the Selection

1. How did the worm's escape plan differ from Latsi Kerék's in "Under the Barbed Wire"? Which was based on courage and which on wits?

Vocabulary Development Skills Dictionary

2. Were the word meanings you got from context close to the glossary definitions? If an unfamiliar word was not in the glossary, where would you look for it?

Literary Appreciation Skills Figurative Language

3. Why is having animals talk like people considered figurative language rather than literal language?

Use the Skills

Understanding the Selection

1. As you read the funny little poem on the next page, think why it fits with the theme Rescues and Escapes.

Vocabulary Development Skills Dictionary

2. Don't interrupt your reading of the poem to use the glossary or dictionary. Decide why you won't find the last word in the poem included in a dictionary.

Literary Appreciation Skills Figurative Language

3. Most poems use figurative language. See if this one does, too.

THE PANTHER

Ogden Nash

The panther is like a leopard,
Except it hasn't been peppered.
Should you behold a panther crouch,
Prepare to say Ouch.
Better yet, if called by a panther,
Don't anther.

■ Is this literal or figurative language?

■ What "real word" is meant here?

Check the Skills

Understanding the Selection

1. What does the poem have to do with Rescues and Escapes?

Vocabulary Development Skills Dictionary

2. Why won't you find *anther* in a dictionary? Why do you suppose the poet made up a new word?

Literary Appreciation Skills Figurative Language

3. How do you know that the second line of the poem is figurative language?

Use the Skills

This exciting story is about a double escape and rescue. Decide if you think this story could really happen. Use your dictionary skills if you need them. You know enough now not to be confused by figurative language. So relax and enjoy the story.

TWO WERE LEFT

Hugh B. Cave

On the third night of hunger Noni thought of the dog. Nothing of flesh and blood lived upon the floating ice island except those two.

In the breakup of the iceberg, Noni had lost his sled, his food, his fur, even his knife. He had saved only Nimuk, his devoted[g] husky.[g] And now the two marooned[c] on the ice eyed each other warily[cg] —each keeping his distance.

Noni's love for Nimuk was real, very real—as real as the hunger and cold nights and the gnawing pain of his injured leg in its homemade brace.[c] But the men of his village killed their dogs when food was scarce, didn't they? And without thinking twice about it.

And Nimuk, he told himself, when hungry enough, would seek food. One of us will soon be eating the other, Noni thought. So . . .

He could not kill the dog with his bare hands. Nimuk was powerful and much fresher than he. A weapon, then, was essential.[cg]

Removing his mittens, he unstrapped the brace from his leg. When he had hurt his leg a few weeks before, he had fashioned the brace from bits of harness and two thin strips of iron.

Kneeling now, he wedged one of the iron strips into a crack in the ice and began to rub the other against it with firm, slow strokes.

Nimuk watched him intently, and it seemed to Noni that the dog's eyes glowed more brightly as night waned.[g]

He worked on, trying not to remember why. The slab of iron had an edge now. It had begun to take shape. Daylight found his task completed.

Noni pulled the finished knife from the ice and thumbed its edge. The sun's glare, reflected from it, stabbed at his eyes and momentarily blinded him.

Noni steeled himself.

"Here, Nimuk!" he called softly.

The dog watched him suspiciously.

"Come here," Noni called.

Nimuk came closer. Noni read fear in the animal's gaze. He read hunger and suffering in the dog's labored[g] breathing and awkward, dragging crouch. His heart wept. He hated himself and fought against it.

Closer Nimuk came, wary⁹ of his intentions. Now Noni felt a thickening in this throat. He saw the dog's eyes and they were wells of suffering.

Now! Now was the time to strike!

A great sob shook Noni's kneeling body. He cursed the knife. He swayed blindly; flung the weapon far from him. With empty hands outstretched he stumbled toward the dog, and fell.

The dog growled ominously⁹ as he warily circled the boy's body. And Noni was sick with fear.

In flinging away his knife he had left himself defenseless.ᶜ⁹ He was too weak to crawl after it now. He was at Nimuk's mercy, and Nimuk was hungry.

The dog circled him and was creeping up from behind. Noni shut his eyes, praying that the attack might be swift. He felt the dog's feet against his leg, the hot rush of Nimuk's breath against his neck. A scream gathered in the boy's throat.

Then he felt the dog's hot tongue caressing his face.

Noni's eyes opened, staring incredulously. Crying softly, he thrust out an arm and drew the dog's head down against his own. . . .

The plane came out of the south an hour later. Its pilot looked down and saw the large, floating floe. And he saw something flashing.

It was the sun gleaming on something shiny which moved. His curiosity aroused, the pilot banked his ship and descended, circling the floe. Now he saw a dark, still shape that appeared to be human. Or were there two shapes?

He set his ship down in a water lane and investigated. There were two shapes, boy and dog. The boy was unconscious but alive. The dog whined feebly but was too weak to move.

The gleaming object which had trapped the pilot's attention was a crudely fashioned knife stuck into the ice a little distance away and quivering in the wind.

Check the Skills

Understanding the Selection

1. How do you think Noni and his dog happened to be on the ice floe? What was the biggest problem facing them?

2. Do you think the events in this story could really happen? Why do you think as you do?

3. How does the rescue in "Two Were Left" differ from the rescue in "TV on a Blackboard"?

Vocabulary Development Skills Dictionary

4. Did you use the glossary to help yourself understand the story? If you didn't need to use the glossary, how did context clues help you figure out the meaning of the words *warily, essential,* and *defenseless?*

Literary Appreciation Skills Figurative Language

5. Which of the following sentences from the story is an example of literal language and which is figurative language? How do you know?

   He saw the dog's eyes and they were wells of suffering.
   It was the sun gleaming on something shiny which moved.

Apply What You Learned in Unit 4

The Theme

Rescues and Escapes

1. You read in this unit several very different accounts of what people do to escape or to rescue someone. How did reading about rescues and escapes add to your understanding of what helps people survive and succeed?

•   Which of the five selections in this unit represented rescues? Which ones represented escapes? How are rescues and escapes alike?

•   Which characters in this unit succeeded through using their heads? Which ones succeeded through courage and endurance? In which selections were there elements of luck?

•   Do you think difficult situations sometimes uncover strengths people didn't know they had? Can you think of any examples in your own experience or that you've read or heard about?

The Skills

Vocabulary Development Skills Dictionary

2. Why shouldn't you use a dictionary first for every unknown word you meet in your reading?

3. What steps should you follow to find a word in a dictionary?

4. What four kinds of information does a dictionary usually include?

• Glossaries are different from dictionaries. Glossaries include only words in the book they are part of. And they give only the definitions used in that book. You might want to compare the entries for one or two words in the glossary in this book with entries for each of them in a dictionary. How are the entries in the glossary and the dictionary alike? How are they different?

Literary Appreciation Skills Figurative Language

5. You found out that figurative language makes comparisons or exaggerations that are not realistic or even possible. Remember to make sure as you read that you are not being confused by accepting something as literal language when it was meant to be figurative.

Apply the
Vocabulary Development Skills
You Have Learned

Apply the Skills As You Do Your Schoolwork

The vocabulary development skills you have learned in this section will be helpful to you in all subjects in school. For instance, the following short selection was taken from a social studies textbook. It tells about the widening technology gap between certain countries. Read the selection to find out what a technology gap is and why it is a problem.

Each of the vocabulary development skills you have learned will help you figure out some words in the selection. The questions at the bottom of this page will show you how. First read the questions. Then read the selection, keeping the questions in mind. Finally, after you have finished reading the selection, answer the questions.

1. **Suffixes.** The word *industrialize* in the first paragraph of the selection includes two suffixes. What are they? What is the base word? How does this help you to know the meaning of the word?

2. **Homonyms.** In the first paragraph you will come across the word *sale*. What is its homonym? What is the meaning of each word? How does the context help you to know which word is used here?

3. **Synonym and inference context clues.** What inference context clues in the first paragraph helped you figure out the meaning of *surplus*? What synonym context clues helped you figure out the meaning of *commodities*?

4. **Parts of a dictionary entry.** What steps would you follow to find the meaning of *technology* in a dictionary?

A Technology Gap Developed

As the First Industrial Revolution went on, more goods were produced than could be used by the people who made them. The more industrialized countries then began to look for customers to buy their surplus goods. Naturally they tried to sell their surplus goods to pre-industrial countries. But the people in those countries had little money or cash to complete the sale. However, they did have commodities—crops or natural resources—that the industrial nations wanted. These were such things as tea, coffee, cotton, gold, copper, rubber, and oil.

Trade made the industrializing countries grow richer. And as they grew richer, they continued to improve their technology. But the pre-industrial countries that sold resources to industrial countries did not grow richer. Their people continued to live in nonmodern ways. What is called the technology gap between the industrial and pre-industrial countries has grown wider and wider.

Thoughtful people today are concerned about the technology gap. The gap is growing larger all the time. Industrialized nations are getting richer. And they are using up more and more of the energy resources of the world.

Meanwhile, the pre-industrial nations are falling farther and farther behind. A famous British social scientist, Barbara Ward, has said that our Earth is now "a lopsided world." For every advance in technology that pre-industrial nations make, the highly industrialized nations made a hundred more.

In Barbara Ward's words, the pre-industrial nations "move at the speed of a bicycle. Their wealthy neighbors move at the speed of a moon rocket."

Apply the Skills As You Deal with the World

You will also use your vocabulary development skills when you read material outside of school. The following editorial commentary is from a newspaper. It tells how one question asked in two ways can give very different answers. Read the commentary to find out how and why this can happen. Again, read the following questions first so you see how these vocabulary development skills will help you here. Then keep the questions in mind as you read the selection. Afterward, answer them.

1. **Suffixes.** You will come across the word *motorist* in the second paragraph. What is the base word? the suffix? How does this help you understand the word as it appears in the newspaper?

2. **Homonyms.** You will also see the word *poll* in this paragraph. Its homonym is *pole.* Suppose you forgot the spelling clue. How does the context help you decide that the meaning here is "a public survey"?

3. **Synonym and inference context clues.** In the third paragraph, what synonym context clue helps you know the meaning of *subdued*? What inference context clues helped you figure out the meaning of *sedate* in the fifth paragraph?

4. **Parts of a dictionary entry.** To figure out the meaning of *coveted* in the fourth paragraph, you may have to check the dictionary. Use the skills you have learned in this book.

One question asked in two ways can bring opposite answers

Sydney J. Harris

What a lot of people fail to learn, even as they grow older, is that the way you ask a question can determine the kind of answer you get. The professional pollsters are keenly aware of this and can get different answers by asking the same question in somewhat different ways.

Some years ago, two large auto companies made expensive polls at the same time. They were trying to find out what kind of car the American motorist might buy in future models.

One company's pollster asked the direct question, "What kind of car would you like to have?" The majority of auto owners replied that they wanted a car not too big, that was also economical, functional, and subdued in looks. In other words, they wanted a plain-looking, little car.

The other company's pollster was far more sensitive to the self-deception most of us practice. He asked: "What kind of car do you think your neighbor would like to have?" And there the majority replied that their neighbors coveted large, gimmicky models that looked more like boats or airplanes.

The first auto maker nearly went broke putting out sedate little cars long before the public was ready for them. The second, however, enjoyed a banner year with its gaudy, rear-finned models. In fact, the first company was forced to retool to meet the competition.

It is much harder to devise fair and "unweighted" questions than it is to find the answers. Indeed, the most significant advances in science have come not from finding answers, but from beginning to ask the right questions in the right way. The simplest question of all, that no one asked until Newton, was "Why do apples fall down instead of up?"

Section 2　Comprehension Skills

Unit 5

Determination

Overview and Purposes for Reading

The Theme

Determination

1.   What part does determination play in success?

The Skills

Comprehension Skills Literal Meaning

2.   Why is it necessary to figure out cause-effect relationships as you read?

3.   What are some ways to do this?

Study and Research Skills Reference Sources

4.   How can you find the information you want in an encyclopedia?

Comprehension Skills Literal Meaning

Pretend you are reading a chapter about the tropics in your social studies textbook. When you get done, the teacher asks, "Why are there so many floods in the tropics?" The teacher is checking to see if you understand what causes the floods. You think about what you read, trying to remember a statement that began, "The floods are caused by . . ." or "The cause of these floods is. . . ." But there was no direct statement like that. How then can you figure out what the cause was?

One way is to watch for special signal words that sometimes tell you that the cause or the effect is being described. Follow the steps below.

Understanding Cause-Effect Relationships

1. Look for signal words like *because* and *since*. Read what comes after the signal word. This is where you will find the cause stated. The effect will be stated elsewhere in the sentence or in another sentence nearby.
2. Also look for a signal word like *so*. Following that word you will find the effect stated.

Try the Skill. Read this sentence:

> There are many floods in the tropics *because* the amount of rain is very great.

The signal word is *because*. The words following *because* tell why there are floods in the tropics.

Look at a slightly different example:

Because it rains so much in the tropics, there are many floods.

This time the word because comes at the very beginning of the sentence. However, the cause is still described in the words following that signal word.

Let's see how it works with a different signal word.

Since it rains a lot in the tropics, there are many floods.

The signal word in this sentence is since. It acts just like the word because in the previous example. Since also signals that the cause is about to be stated. The same thing is true when since appears in the middle of the sentence:

There are many floods in the tropics, since it rains so much.

The word so can also act as a signal word for cause and effect relationships.

It rains a lot in the tropics, so there are many floods.

In this sentence, the signal word so tells you that an effect is about to be stated. The cause: raining a lot. The effect: many floods.

Understanding cause-effect relationships is an important skill. Watch for words that signal such relationships as you read the selections in this unit.

Study and Research Skills Reference Sources

Where can you find factual information about many different subjects? An encyclopedia, of course!

An **encyclopedia** is usually a set of books. Each separate book is called a volume. Each volume contains many articles, or entries. The entries in an encyclopedia are listed in alphabetical order. Usually the cover of each volume tells which letters of the alphabet that volume contains.

Most encyclopedias, like most dictionaries, include guide words at the top or bottom of each page or spread of facing pages. The guide words tell the first and last entry words, so you can tell quickly if what you're looking for will be found on those pages.

Before you begin to use the encyclopedia, you should think of a key word that might be the entry word. You might have to try out several ideas before you find the entry with the information you want. And you should remember that people are always listed with their last names first.

Remember the steps listed below.

Using an Encyclopedia
1. Think of a key word that might be the entry word.
2. Choose the volume containing the letter of the alphabet your key word begins with.
3. Use guide words to find the right page.

As you read the selections in this unit, you may come across a topic that you want to find out more about. If so, try using the steps above to look up the subject in an encyclopedia.

Selection 1

Use the Skills

Understanding the Selection

In this exciting story there is no time for argument or fear. With death hovering minutes away, a determined and courageous attempt is made to save a baby in a doomed house.

1.   As you read this story, think about the characters and how they react in the face of fear and death. Watch for the determination shown by each character, too.

2.   Find out who you think the main hero of the story is. Why does the hero respond as he does at the beginning of the story and at the end of the story?

Comprehension Skills Literal Meaning

3.   As you read, try out your skill in recognizing cause-effect relationships. Look for signal words like *because, since,* and *so.* Notes in the margin will help you.

Study and Research Skills Reference Sources

4.   The man in this story says something about physics. If that interested you, how could you use an encyclopedia to find out more about it?

TIGHT SPOT

Robb White

"Because if you open that door it's going to blow up this house and all the houses on this block. And the people."

"My baby's in that room," the man said. "And I'm getting him out!"

"That way you'll kill him," George, the man from the gas company, said. "You people hold this man. Or he'll blow up the whole block. Now, where's the gas meter?"

"Under the truck," somebody said, pointing.

The big truck had slammed through the fence and come to a crumpled halt—on top of the meter and cutoff valve.

Looking in the window of the room, George saw a baby crawling around on the floor. He also saw the broken gas pipe to the stove.

The man, with two men trying to hold him, yelled, "Get him out through the window."

"I can't, since letting any air into that room will make the house blow up," George told him. "He can breathe down near the floor."

"You're killing him!" the father cried.

"I can't give you a physics lesson now. So, please, just believe me. The only way to save the baby is to get the gas turned off."

George knew what was happening, but he didn't want to tell them. Gas from the broken pipe was flowing into the room, filling it from the ceiling down. As soon as the gas came low enough to touch the burning pilot[9] light of the water heater, there wasn't going to be anything where this house was except a hole.

If I've got 20 minutes, I'm lucky, he thought. He yelled at the people, "All of you clear out. Get clear out across the road. All the way."

Two men began to lead the father across the lawn.

■ The word *because* is followed by the cause: opening the door. The rest of the sentence tells you that the effect of opening the door would be to blow up several houses.

■ Following the word *since* is the cause: letting air into the room. The effect of that would be to make the house blow up, as the rest of the sentence states.

■ If you wanted to find out if George was right about what could happen and why, you could look up the key word *gas* in the G volume of an encyclopedia.

The house was on a low, concrete-block foundation[9] with a small air vent,[9] the size of one concrete block, covered with rusty screen wire. George knocked that away with the biggest wrench he had. He began hammering at the edge of the small hole. He knew that what he was doing was useless, but he kept hammering.

Something kept tugging at his pants leg. He tried to kick it away as he hammered, but it kept on. When he looked down, there was this skinny little kid. "I can get through that hole, mister."

"No you can't, so beat it!" George moved to the window and saw the baby in the room now lying on the floor sucking his thumb.

Maybe, he thought, *I've still got 10, 15 minutes.*

Across the street the father was standing, crying. "Your baby's still OK," George yelled.

As he started to swing the wrench again he saw, inside the hole, under the house, a face staring out. "I told you I could," the skinny little kid said.

"Come out of there!" George yelled at the kid. He knew now that there would be two children, and him, going to be killed.

"I know where the pipe is," the kid under the house said. "How do you turn it off?"

"You can't! So come on out, kid, *Please.*"

The kid said, "What would you do under here, mister?"

"I'd cut it, but please come on out now."

"What with?" the kid asked stubbornly.

"With a pipe cutter, but it's too big, too heavy for you. Come on out of there," George said. But the kid just shook his head. George reached in and tried to grab him, but the kid scuttled[c] out of his reach. "You better hand it to me," he said.

George got the pipe cutter and showed it to the kid. "If I give you this, will you come out when I tell you?" The kid's hand snaked out of the hole, grabbed the cutter, and disappeared.

George got his flashlight and saw the kid scrambling under the house, kicking up a cloud of old dust. When he reached the pipe running under the floor, George said, "Just put it around the pipe and turn that shiny knob until it's tight and—"

"I *know* how to do it," the kid said. And he did.

George shone the light on him and watched him cutting. He wondered if, when he had been a skinny little kid like this, he would have had the guts this kid did. He didn't think so.

Ten minutes? Five? How many?

George got a rag and a pipe stopper, wrapped the stopper in the rag, and threw it in to him. "When you hear gas coming out of the pipe, put the rag over your nose."

"OK," the kid said.

"Then when it comes apart, shove the stopper in the pipe and ram⁹ it in with the cutter."

"The pipe's so *thick!*" the kid said, almost crying.

George thought, *If he stays under there the house will take him and the baby and me. If he comes out now it'll only be the baby—and me.*

■ Here is the word *so* signaling an effect. The cause is the fact that there is not much time left.

Unless he gets it cut. "There's not much time left, so if you want to come out, come on."

The kid didn't say anything.

Then the pipe came apart and with one smooth movement the kid had the stopper in and was ramming it tight.

The kid was looking out at him, his face bug-eyed and scared. "Is that OK?"

"That's just exactly OK," George said, then turned to yell at the father to come get his baby.

When he looked back into the hole, the kid's face was right there. "I can't get out," the kid said and began to cry.

"We'll get you out," George said, putting his hand through the hole and touching the kid's cheek. "That was a great job you did. Really great."

The kid was really crying now.

"But I can't get out," the kid sobbed.

"Then how'd you get in?" George asked him.

"I had to then," the kid said. "He isn't much fun to play with yet, but he's my brother."

Check the Skills

Understanding the Selection

1. How did George react in the face of fear and death? How about the skinny kid? the father? How were each of them determined to succeed? How do you think you might react in a similar situation?

2. Who do you think is the main hero of the story? How does he feel at the end of the story? Why do you suppose he feels that way?

Comprehension Skills Literal Meaning

3. a. Why couldn't George let any air into the room? Remember that the key words *because, since,* or *so* can help you find the answer to a cause-effect question. Check the notes in the margin if you need more help.

   b. What is the cause stated in the following sentence from the story? What is the effect? Refer to the marginal notes for help if you need to.

      "There's not much time left, so if you want to come out, come on."

Study and Research Skills Reference Sources

4. Suppose you wanted to find out if letting air into a room with leaking gas really would cause an explosion. What key words might be the entry words in an encyclopedia? If you decided to try the entry word *gas,* would you find it on a page with the guide words *gather* and *geometry*? Why or why not?

Selection 2

Use the Skills

Understanding the Selection

This selection is an autobiographical sketch. The author is a girl who loves to play soccer and baseball. She had the courage and the determination to help break down the barrier that stood in the way of allowing her to play all-star soccer.

1. Read this selection to find out what that barrier was and how it was broken.

2. Ask yourself what kind of determination Amy must have had to follow through her wish to play on the soccer team.

Comprehension Skills Literal Meaning

3. Be on the lookout for cause-effect relationships as you read. The notes in the margin will give you some hints. Remember that the words *because*, *since*, and *so* often signal a stated cause-effect relationship.

Study and Research Skills Reference Sources

4. As you read this story, you may find topics you'd like to know more about. Think about how an encyclopedia could help you.

THE BALLPLAYER

Amy Love

Amy Love plays soccer⁹ and baseball. In 1977 she was ruled off her county's all-star soccer team <u>because</u> she was female. Her parents thought the problem was important, <u>so</u> they took the issue to court.

The court ruled that such sex discrimination⁹ was illegalᶜ and ordered the soccer league⁹ to open its teams to girls.

In this article, Amy talks about her playing.

■ Here the word *because* is followed by the statement of a cause: she was female. The effect was that she was not allowed to play on the all-star soccer team.

■ In the next sentence, a cause begins the sentence, then the word *so* is followed by the statement of the effect.

After the court ruled that they couldn't keep girls out, some of the other mothers wouldn't talk to my mom. They said my parents were terrible for making trouble. Some said we ruined soccer in Danville because the all-stars had to play with a girl. But we didn't ruin soccer in Danville, we built it up! I got to play for the all-stars, and thirteen other girls who wanted to play soccer but didn't bring a lawsuit⁹ got to play, too. And next year there will be new leagues for girls; over two hundred girls already signed up!

A few coaches tried to talk me into playing in the all-girl league. But I'm not a beginner; I'm on the all-stars in my league.

In the spring, I play my other favorite position—third base. Baseball is like soccer. Absolute fun. I love to be on teams. I even think about team plays when I'm sitting in school.

I like to play Little League. And Little League doesn't care that I'm the only girl on the team!

The best thing about baseball is that you get to hit the ball. You can make lots of hits. My batting average is over .400, and last spring I almost hit a home run!

Pitching is fun, too. The pitcher is the most active position on the team. I like pitching best; you get to throw more. I throw curve balls. I pitch, and I play catcher and third base. In most games I play third. I've got to watch out for runners trying to steal from first or second, got to keep my eye on those runners, and cover third. Baseball is the *best* game. No, soccer is. No, *both!*

To be good at any game, you've got to be interested. It takes practice. You're not born with it. People play very well only after they have practiced more than others. Practice makes perfect. The practice really helps a lot—in soccer and in baseball.

At Little League we practice hitting, running bases, fielding, throwing, and sliding. I practice throwing and catching with my dad. Dad got me into baseball. We love to play catch together.

I want to become a pro.⁹ I plan to be like the Babe— Babe Ruth. No, like the Babe and <u>Pelé</u> together. I'll do <u>baseball</u> in the spring and <u>soccer</u> in the fall—just like I do now.

I'd like to play for the Atlanta Braves. Then I could live in Atlanta; that's where we lived before. Maybe I'll coach the Braves after I retire.

I'm not sure where I want to play soccer yet. The pro soccer teams are so new. I guess I'll just go with the team that wants me the most.

■ Most encyclopedias include entries for *baseball* and for *soccer*. In those articles you might also find something about Babe Ruth, who was a very famous baseball player, and Pelé, considered by many the finest soccer player of all time.

Check the Skills

Understanding the Selection

1. What barrier prevented Amy from playing all-star soccer? How did Amy and her parents change the situation?

2. How was the determination of Amy and her parents important to their success? What kind of person do you think Amy is? Why do you think as you do?

Comprehension Skills Literal Meaning

3. Read the following sentence from the selection and tell what is the cause and what is the effect. Explain your answer.

> "Some said we ruined soccer in Danville because the all-stars had to play with a girl."

Study and Research Skills Reference Sources

4. If you wanted to look up Babe Ruth in an encyclopedia, would you check the **B** volume or the **R** volume? Why?

Selection 3

Use the Skills

Understanding the Selection

1. Read this short science article to find out what being extinct means. Also discover how the dodo bird became extinct.

2. As you read, think about the determination that people today must have in order to try to prevent other animals from becoming extinct.

Comprehension Skills Literal Meaning

3. Use your knowledge of the words that signal cause-effect relationships to find several such relationships.

Study and Research Skills Reference Sources

4. Decide how you might use an encyclopedia to find out more about dodos and dinosaurs.

DODOS AND DINOSAURS ARE EXTINCT

Julian May

Once, on a faraway island in the Indian Ocean, there lived a strange bird. It could not fly <u>because</u> its wings were too small to lift its heavy body. The first people who saw it called the bird *dodo,*ᶜ a word meaning "silly."

As years went by, the island settlers brought dogs and pigs. Since these animals ate the eggs and young of the dodos, the birds began to disappear. Finally, only 200 years after people had first seen the dodo, the last of the birds died.

When all the animals of one kind disappear, that kind of animal is said to be extinct.ᶜᵍ The dodo became extinct about the year 1681.

People have caused some animals to become extinct, as happened with the dodo. But we cannot be blamed for all extinct animals. Fossils,ᶜ or traces in the rocks, show us that living things have been on earth for more than a billion years. And almost all of the creatures we know from fossils are extinct. Human beings did not cause this; we have only been on earth for about two million years. The real secret of <u>extinction</u> lies in the way that animals adapt.ᵍ <u>Dinosaurs</u> are a good example. <u>Since</u> they could not adapt to changes in the world around them, they became extinct.

The study of extinction and why it happens is important to us today. People still destroy animals and plants through carelessness.

Many beautiful and interesting birds, mammals, reptiles, and other living things will disappear forever unless we help them to survive.

■ The signal word *because* tells you that a statement of a cause follows.

■ *Extinction* is probably not an entry word in an encyclopedia, but *dinosaur* probably is.

■ Another cause-effect relationship is stated here. The word *since* is the clue.

We must save the other living things of Earth. We need them if we are to survive ourselves. Without plants and animals, human beings would become as extinct as the dodos and dinosaurs!

brontosaurus

pterodactyl

Rodriquez
solitaire

dodo

guagga

passenger
pigeon

Check the
Skills

Understanding the Selection

1. If a certain kind of animal is said to be extinct, what does
    that mean? How did the dodo bird become extinct?

2. Why do you think it will take determination to prevent other
    animals from becoming extinct?

Comprehension Skills Literal Meaning

3. Why did dinosaurs become extinct?

Study and Research Skills Reference Sources

4. If you wanted to look up *dodo* in an encyclopedia, would you
    find it on a page with the guide words *Dodge, Grace H.* and
    dogwood? Or would it be on a page with the guide words
    Dearborn and *decathlon*? Explain your choice.

Use the Skills

Understanding the Selection

In this selection you will learn some of the tricks used by magicians, and you will learn how to do a magic trick.

1. As you read, think about how well prepared someone must be in order to do a magic trick.

2. Decide whether confidence and determination are necessary to successfully complete a magic trick.

Comprehension Skills Literal Meaning

3. Watch for some important cause-effect relationships in this selection. Marginal notes will give you some hints, but you shouldn't need to depend on them much by now.

Study and Research Skills Reference Sources

4. Decide how you could use an encyclopedia to find more information about magic tricks.

THE SECRETS OF ALKAZAR, MASTER MAGICIAN

Allan Zola Kronzek

When I was a young magician, nothing excited me more than going to a magic store. I longed to own the dazzling⁹ magic store items. But on my allowance I couldn't afford a single one. I complained about my lack to Alkazar, the master magician who had accepted me as a student.

"Don't be so glum," Alkazar advised me. "Magic comes from you—not from a store. There are dozens of excellent magic tricks that you can make yourself."

And to prove his point, Alkazar taught me a startling illusion⁹ that required only a coin, a napkin, a salt shaker —and the art of misdirection.ᶜ

In the entire realm of magic there is no skill more important than skill in misdirection. Misdirection is the art of making an audience see what *you* want them to see, while secretly doing something you don't want them to see. To do it skillfully, you need to be a very good actor.

■ If you're interested in finding out more about magic and illusions, where might you look in an encyclopedia?

The key to misdirection lies in learning to control people's attention, and Alkazar gave me a set of rules to follow in performing nearly any illusion of magic. It is with his permission that I pass these rules along to you.

Rule 1: The audience will look at what moves. They will also look at what makes noise. What doesn't move and doesn't make noise doesn't attract attention.

Rule 2: The audience will look where you look. If you look at your foot, they will look at your foot. When there is something you don't want the audience to see, don't look at it. If you don't want them to look at the ceiling, don't look at the ceiling; look at your foot.

Rule 3: The audience will treat as important what you treat as important. The audience will treat as unimportant what you treat as unimportant. In magic you nearly always treat something important as if it is unimportant. Likewise, you treat something unimportant as if it is important.

Of course, the reading of these rules will do you no good unless you put them into practice. The following illusion, called "Passing Through," is an ideal place to start because the misdirection is built right into the trick.

While seated at a dinner table with friends, Alkazar announces that he is going to perform a miracle.[9] He is going to cause a coin to pass *through* the table. A quarter is borrowed and placed on the table a foot or so in front of the magician. Next, some handy object—a salt shaker, for instance —is covered with a napkin and placed on top of the coin.

With all eyes upon him, Alkazar chants his magic words and orders the coin to pass through the table. Everyone is silent and watching. Dramatically, Alkazar places his empty left hand under the table to receive the coin, and with his right hand lifts the shaker to show that the quarter has vanished.[c] But much to the great wizard's[9] surprise, the coin is still there. The magic has apparently failed.

But wait. Alkazar suddenly notices that the coin is lying heads up instead of tails up. No wonder the magic didn't work. He turns the quarter over, covers it with the salt shaker, and again utters some magical words. But again the magic fails.

By this time the audience is beginning to wonder if Alkazar is really a magician. Indeed he is—and now he proves it.

Once again the coin is covered. "Atoms and molecules," chants the mystifier,[9] "by the power that is mine, I order you to make way. Oomash kabasi zid!" Without warning, Alkazar slams his right hand down upon the napkin, and—lo and behold—it is smashed flat against the table. The coin is still there, but *the salt shaker has vanished and is immediately brought up from under the table.* An impossible demonstration of one solid object passing through another has apparently taken place. As for the quarter, Alkazar returns it to its owner with a smile and says, "Sometimes the powers of magic surprise even me."

In this trick Alkazar uses misdirection and surprise to throw the audience off guard. Here's how it's done.

When you cover the salt shaker, squeeze and mold the napkin around the top and sides so the shape of the shaker is clear. Make certain that the napkin hides the entire shaker, especially at the bottom where the napkin spreads out onto the table.

■ What is the cause-effect relationship stated here?

Now, the first time you pick up the shaker and napkin to show that the coin has "disappeared," lean forward slightly to get a closer look at the coin, and at the same time bring the hand with the shaker to the edge of the table, loosen your grip, and secretly let the shaker drop into your lap. If you are using misdirection well, no one will pay the slightest attention to what you have done. You have made the audience think you are doing a coin trick, so their attention will be on the quarter. And that's where your attention should be, too. Remember Rule 2: What you look at, they will look at.

■ Here is another clearly stated cause-effect relationship.

Now, you have in your hand a napkin that, after some practicing, you have kept in the form of the salt shaker. Magicians often call such a hollow form a *shell.*[c] Place the shell over the coin and continue as described above. (Alkazar turns the coin over as an added bit of misdirection.)

The second time you peek at the coin, don't move the
shaker more than a couple of inches away from the coin,
and people will never remember that you moved it farther away the first time. When you are ready to conclude
the trick, your empty left hand picks up the shaker from
your lap and moves under the table as your right hand
slams down on the napkin. Immediately bring the shaker
up for all to see, and the illusion is perfect.

Here are five important tips about this illusion from Alkazar's Black Notebook:

1. Just as you must make the coin seem important to the trick, you must make the salt shaker seem unimportant.

2. Always handle the shell as if it really contains the shaker.

3. Learn what kinds of napkins will hold a shape. Large paper napkins are ideal. Newspaper is an excellent substitute.

4. Add or subtract from the trick whatever makes it work best for you. Many magicians, for instance, "steal" the shaker on the second peek. It's a matter of choice.

5. Don't do a trick. Do magic.

Check the Skills

Understanding the Selection

1. To do a magic trick well, in what ways must you be prepared?

2. Why do you think confidence and determination are important for a magician to have?

Comprehension Skills Literal Meaning

3. Why will the audience pay attention to the quarter instead of the salt shaker as you do the "Passing Through" trick?

Study and Research Skills Reference Sources

4. Harry Houdini was a very famous American magician who astounded people with his tricks, especially escapes, in the early part of this century. If you wanted to find out more about him, where in an encyclopedia could you look?

Selection 5

Use the Skills

Doug thought he hated ballet. But one day he went with his mother to see the ballet "The Nutcracker" because his sister was performing in it. Doug became very excited during that performance. He seemed to see things about ballet he had never noticed before.

As you read, see what a determined person Doug is. Be on the lookout for words that signal cause-effect relationships. Make sure you understand the cause and the effect in each relationship. If you get interested in the story, you might want to find more information. Watch for topics that could be entry words you might look for in an encyclopedia.

There are no marginal notes to help you this time. You are on your own!

DOUG MEETS THE
NUTCRACKER

William H. Hooks

Doug couldn't get that dumb ballet⁹ out of his head. It kept popping up in his mind at the strangest moments.

He tried several times to ask his sister Julie about her ballet classes. But the words stuck in his throat. Finally, he did ask.

"Are there any boys in your ballet class?"

"Why?" replied Julie. "I thought you hated ballet."

"Just asking. Well, are there?"

"Well, for your information, we have twenty girls and three boys in the class. And it's not fair."

"What do you mean? You don't think the boys should be there?"

"No, it's not fair that the boys are all on scholarship and the girls have to pay," explained Julie. "We girls are thinking about a girls' liberation movement to protest."

"Why do the boys go for free?"

"Because the school can't get them to come any other way. They're all like you and hate ballet. Or else they're scared people are going to call them sissies for taking classes."

Doug kept silent.

"You have to be a lot stronger to do ballet than you do to play baseball," Julie continued. "One of the guys in my class can do a shoulder lift⁹ with me and he's only your age."

"Come on, anybody could do that," replied Doug.

"You think so, huh? Well, it's hard."

"I'll bet I could do it easy as anything."

"Bet what?" chided Julie.

"Bet you my new T-shirt."

"I've got myself a T-shirt!" squealed Julie.

"Not yet. First show me what that guy does to do a shoulder lift. Then I'll show you I can too do it."

"O.K. You stand behind me. I wish we had a mirror. It's a lot easier to show with a mirror. . . ."

"There's one on the bathroom door," said Doug. "We can swing it out into the hall."

"Now stand behind me with your hands around my waist," said Julie as they stood in front of the mirror. "Then we are going to *plié* at the same time."

"What do you mean, *plié?*"

"It's just French for 'bend.' It means bend your knees. All ballet terms are in French. Now you start with a *plié* and you end up with a *plié*. Watch and I'll show you how."

"O.K.," said Doug, copying her movements. "Now what happens in between?"

"You try to lift me to your shoulder. You fail. And I have a T-shirt."

"Don't go counting your T-shirts yet. I think I ought to have three tries. You always get three tries in all the stories."

"O.K., I'll be big-hearted since it takes years of training to do this lift. Let's go. First, we *plié* together. Then as we straighten up, I'll jump and you lift me so I sit on your shoulder."

"O.K.," said Doug solemnly.

"*Plié*. Lift!" commanded Julie.

Doug pushed upward. But Julie got only as far as his chest.

"Put me down!" Julie ordered. "If you don't make it on the first lift you can't force the weight on up. Ready again?"

Doug's arms felt a little trembly. But he answered, "Ready."

"*Plié*. Lift!" Julie went higher this time. She was half onto his shoulder but slipping downward. Doug staggered.

"That was better," exclaimed Julie. "Ready for number three?"

Doug was breathing hard and his face was flushed. He nodded.

Julie landed on Doug's shoulder. Solid. The landing was firm but Doug's knees weren't. They were all rubbery and wobbly. He staggered. Julie's weight shifted backward. That threw Doug into reverse. Julie leaped neatly from his shoulder just before Doug crashed to the floor.

"I won!" yelled Julie. "The T-shirt is mine!"

"That's not fair. I did the lift," groaned Doug. "We just bet on the lift. You didn't say anything about staying up. I got you onto my shoulder, didn't I?"

Mom came in. "What's all this?"

"It's nothing, Mom. I'm O.K."

"Mom, we bet Doug couldn't do a shoulder lift. He lost."

"I did the lift. I put her on my shoulder. I did it. I slipped on the floor and fell afterward, but I did the lift."

"Falling down out of the lift means you didn't do it," argued Julie. "The T-shirt's mine. Isn't it, Mom?"

"It sounds like a tie to me," replied Mom.

Doug said, "Mom, I have a question I want to ask you."

"Sure, Doug, what is it?"

"Can I take ballet lessons?"

Check the Skills

Understanding the Selection

1. Is Doug determined? How do you know? Do you think he will pursue his interest in ballet? Why do you think so?

Comprehension Skills Literal Meaning

2. Below is a stated cause-effect relationship in two separate sentences. What is the signal word? the cause? the effect?

    "Why do the boys go for free?"
    "Because the school can't get them to come any other way."

Study and Research Skills Reference Sources

3. Suppose you wanted to find out more about ballet in an encyclopedia. What key word do you think might be an entry word? Could you find the entry on a page with the guide words *ball bearing* and *Baltic Sea*? Why or why not?

Apply What You Learned in Unit 5

The Theme

Determination

1.   In this unit you read about several people who were successful because they were determined. Can you think of other people you've known or heard about who were like this? How can you use this knowledge in your own life?

Amy in "The Ballplayer" and Doug in "Doug Meets the Nutcracker" were both determined to do things that traditionally were not expected for people of their sex. You might want to discuss with your teacher or classmates what you think of such changes in expected roles.

The Skills

Comprehension Skills Literal Meaning

2. You found many cause-effect relationships as you read this unit, and you could see why it is important to understand them. You'll come across many of these in your reading of science and history materials. Watch for them!

3. Remember that words like *because, since,* and *so* often signal cause-effect relationships.

Study and Research Skills Reference Sources

4. In this unit you've seen that your interest in a particular topic can be expanded by checking an encyclopedia. An encyclopedia is a valuable source of information. Knowing how to use an encyclopedia can be important, especially when you're doing schoolwork. Next time you do a research project in one of your classes, remember to use what you learned in this unit about finding the information you need in an encyclopedia.

Unit 6

Concern for Others

Overview and Purposes for Reading

The Theme

Concern for Others

1.   How does a concern for other human beings affect a person's life?

The Skills

Comprehension Skills Implied Meaning

2.   Why is it necessary to know what the main ideas are in what you read?

3.   What steps can you follow to figure out the main idea when it is not actually stated?

Literary Appreciation Skills Types of Literature

4.   What is the difference between fiction and nonfiction? between a biography and an autobiography?

Learn About the Skills

Comprehension Skills Implied Meaning

Read the following paragraph. Can you tell what the main idea is?

> Not a breath of air stirred over the open prairie. The clouds were like cotton. The sky had a hazy look. The horses hung their heads as they waded through the dust. The riders slouched in their saddles.

Figuring out the **main idea** in what you read is sometimes difficult because the main idea is hinted at rather than actually stated. You have to "read between the lines" to find it. It is necessary to know what the main idea is in order to really understand what you're reading. You can help yourself do this by practicing these steps:

Finding the Main Idea

1. Look for the details that are stated.
2. Think about how these details are all related or what they all have in common.
3. Think how you could label all those details. This label is the main idea.

Look again at the paragraph about the prairie. What are the details? They include the following: *not a breath of air stirred; the sky had a hazy look;* and *the riders slouched in their saddles.* How are these all related? What do they all have in common? If you put them all together, what do they lead up to? They all suggest uncomfortable weather. Therefore, all the details in the paragraph could be put under a label about how very hot and dry it was. This is the main idea of the paragraph.

Try the Skill. Use the same steps on a more difficult paragraph. What is the main idea of this one?

> More than two hundred years ago, a young man named Croisilles was returning from Paris to Le Havre, his native town. He was the son of a goldsmith. His father had sent him to Paris on business. His trip to the great city had turned out very well. The joy of bringing good news caused him to walk with more bounce than usual.

This paragraph may seem harder because not every detail points to the main idea. For instance, the mention that it happened more than two hundred years ago is not connected enough to other details to lead to the main idea. The main idea is hinted at by the details that *the young man's father had sent him to Paris on business,* that *the trip had turned out well,* that *he was bringing good news* and that *he walked with more bounce than usual.* Think about how these details can be related to each other. They all can be thought of as a group described by a label about the success of the young man's trip. So the main idea is that the trip was successful.

Remember to look for the details and figure out how they are related. Doing that will help you find the main idea of something you read. You will have a chance to use this important skill in this unit.

Literary Appreciation Skills Types of Literature

You probably already know that there are several types of literature.

Fiction is a work of imagination, not necessarily based on fact. Fiction includes stories, novels, folk tales, and fables. Poetry and plays, which are very easy forms of writing to identify, are also fiction.

Nonfiction refers to all material that is about real people, things, and events rather than imaginary ones. Nonfiction is factual. Many kinds of writing are nonfiction. Some of these are articles, essays, encyclopedia entries, biographies, and autobiographies.

A **biography** is the story of a real person's life written by someone else.

An **autobiography** is an account of some real person's life written by that person.

In a **biographical sketch** an author tells about only part of someone else's life, rather than all of it. What do you think an **autobiographical sketch** is?

It's often important for you to know if what you're reading is fiction or nonfiction. And if you're reading about someone's life, it helps to know if it's a biography or an autobiography.

This unit includes examples of several types of literature. You'll see how to really tell which is which.

Selection 1

Use the Skills

Understanding the Selection

Did you ever wonder what it's like to work "behind the scenes" at a television station? In this selection a young woman gives you some idea of her job at a New York station.

1. Read to learn of some of the work that must be done before a news program goes on the air.

2. Note how the author is concerned about others following her lead.

Comprehension Skills Implied Meaning

3. As you read, notice how details add up to main ideas. The marginal notes will help.

Literary Appreciation Skills Types of Literature

4. Since Susan Collins is a real person, you should be able to decide immediately that this is nonfiction. Watch for clues that tell you whether it is biographical or autobiographical.

BREAKING INTO TV

Susan Collins

I've been here for eight months. My first day at WCBS-TV was the day I was interviewed⁹ for the job. I had just graduated from college. Several months before, I had spoken to the news director about working here. My chances didn't look too good at that time. So I was pretty surprised when I came in for another interview and found myself right on the job, starting that day.

■ Several details here add up to the main idea that Susan Collins works for WCBS-TV.

It felt as though I were being thrown into a lion's den.ᶜ I didn't know what to do. The other two production assistants⁹ took me under their wings. They showed me what I was supposed to do with the script,⁹ and everything went fine.

In my first weeks here my job was working with the scripts for the six o'clock news. These contain all the material that will be on the program. They are very long, and there are copies for every person on the program. They have to be separated, put in the right order, and given out to the different people.

That may sound easy, but it isn't. You have to be very careful to make sure of the order. You also make changes on all the scripts as they are needed. These changes can be made until the program goes on the air.

I became the first woman staff production assistant on the local news. It was a very good chance for me. I hadn't studied journalismᶜ or communicationsᶜ in college. But by my junior year I knew that this was where I wanted to work when I graduated. That summer I took several classes at schools that specializedᶜ in TV. Those classes gave me some background. Even so, becoming a production assistant was a better job than I had expected.

■ The author is clearly writing about some of her own experiences. So you know that this is an autobiographical sketch.

As you can tell, I enjoy my work, although it's not all fun and games. The good part about it for me is feeling that what I do is important. The bad part is that there's a lot of wear and tear on my nerves.

■ The main idea is that the author has a responsible job. All the details in the paragraph can be described by this idea.

I'm responsible[c] for several tasks. One is to make sure the script is distributed.[c] Another is ordering all the photos or drawings we need.

Since news changes every day, and new things and people become important, there are always new pictures to order. We order them from a picture service. We have to be sure that they get here by 4:00 P.M. The art department needs time to put them on the slides you see on the screen. I also have to put the slides in the order in which they will appear on the program. We can't have the anchorperson[g] talking about the President while we show a picture of Queen Elizabeth.

Some days I work from 11:00 in the morning to 6:00 in the evening. Other days I do the morning news. That means being here from 6:00 A.M. until 2:00 in the afternoon. Most of the time I am here from about 4:00 in the afternoon until about 11:30 at night. That's when I do both the 6:00 and 11:00 P.M. shows. It's a hard schedule.

The end of any work day finds me pretty tired, even when things are going smoothly. When the unexpected happens, I'm in trouble. Every change means a lot of extra work. Sometimes all the slides are ready when a big story breaks. Then all the slides have to be reshuffled.

I know I'm learning skills that will be useful in whatever I do later. Being able to work under pressure makes you feel more confident. Being efficient makes you better in anything you do.

There are also creative parts to this job. One of these is picking the kind of pictures you think will look best on the screen.

I think you have to have the right kind of temperament[g] to last in this job. One thing you can't afford to do is get angry easily. If people are fighting with each other, everything will fall apart. You have to keep your cool when the going gets rough.

This is especially important for a woman. My staying together and not pulling my hair out will make it easier for the women who come after me. As the first, I have to show that I can do the job. People notice what I do. As more women come into the technical⁹ fields, men are learning that we can be trusted to hold up in tight spots.

Not only am I a woman, but I'm a black woman. That puts me in two minority⁽ groups in TV. Yet this has never bothered me. I have the feeling that you can do whatever you set your mind to.

Check the Skills

Understanding the Selection

1. What are the author's main duties as a production assistant? Why do you suppose that she writes "the end of any work day finds me pretty tired"?

2. How does Susan Collins hope to prove that women work well in the technical fields? How does she think this will make it easier for the women who come after her? Does this show that she has a concern for others?

Comprehension Skills Implied Meaning

3. The main idea in the first paragraph is that the author works at WCBS-TV. You could figure that out by deciding it is the way to describe how the following details are related.

   I've been here for eight months.

   My first day at WCBS-TV was the day I was interviewed for the job.

Literary Appreciation Skills Types of Literature

4. How did you know that Susan Collins was writing about her own life?

Use the Skills

Understanding the Selection

Feeling that you are odd or different can be uncomfortable. The following poem is about that experience.

1. See if the person in the poem feels concern for others.

Comprehension Skills Implied Meaning

2. Poems, too, have main ideas. To find the main idea, decide how the details are related, just as you do with other types of literature.

Literary Appreciation Skills Types of Literature

3. Poetry is an easy type of literature to identify because of the way words and lines are arranged on the page. Unlike most other types of writing, poems usually have a definite rhythm. Sometimes poems include rhyming words, too, like *worry* and *hurry*. Watch for other rhyming words in this poem.

GROWING: FOR LOUIS

Myra Cohn Livingston

It's tough being short.

Of course your father tells you not to worry,
But everyone else is giant, and you're just the
    way you were.
And this stupid guy says, "Hey, shorty, where'd
    you get the long pants?"
Or some smart beanpole asks how it feels to be
    so close to the ants?
And the school nurse says to tell her again how
    tall you are, when you've already told her.
Oh, my mother says there's really no hurry
And I'll grow soon enough.

But it's tough being short.

(I wonder if Napoleon got the same old stuff?)

■ Here are two words that rhyme.

■ Every line that begins with a capital letter tells a detail. All those details add up to the simple main idea that it's tough to be short.

Check the Skills

Understanding the Selection

1. Napoleon was emperor of France from 1804 to 1815. He was an extremely short man. The person in the poem wonders if Napoleon was treated as he was. Does this show a concern for others? Why do you think as you do?

Comprehension Skills Implied Meaning

2. The details in the poem add up to the main idea that it's tough to be short. This is a clear and simple main idea.

Literary Appreciation Skills Types of Literature

3. Words rhyme when they sound alike at the end, even if they are not spelled alike. Are enough and stuff rhyming words?

Selection 3

Use the Skills

Understanding the Selection

In this excerpt from a Norwegian book, we meet Mikkel and his older brother Teddy. Teddy is retarded. Teddy's parents, and especially Mikkel, want to keep Teddy with them. Teddy accidentally knocks out a boy's teeth in a handball game. The boy's friends threaten to call the police and have Teddy locked up. Mikkel decides to hide Teddy in the mountains, and the brothers are just starting out as the excerpt opens.

1. See how Mikkel's actions show his concern for Teddy.

2. Notice how Mikkel adjusts his actions to suit Teddy's abilities.

Comprehension Skills Implied Meaning

3. If you have trouble deciding what the main idea of a paragraph is, watch for details that give you a clue. Use notes in the margin for help.

4. Remember to use the steps. They are on page 149.

Literary Appreciation Skills Types of Literature

5. Since Mikkel tells this story, it often seems to be an autobiographical sketch. However, it is really part of a novel that is fiction. You would not be able to know this just from the selection here. You'd have to read the book in order to decide on your own what type of literature it is.

DON'T TAKE TEDDY

Babbis Friis-Baastad

It would be safer to take the path through the little rowan^g wood where there wouldn't be many people. But even the wood, which we know so well, seemed eerie^g today. <u>The bunches of red berries looked so angry. They hung like danger signals above us. From time to time a cluster^c would slap my face. "Stop! Go back!"</u>

No, I had to pull myself together and quit feeling I was in a horror movie. Everything was the same.

Teddy had stopped to shake down rowan berries, but they refused to fall, even though he said, "Pom-pom" to them.

"Hurry up. We have to catch the bus." But of course it didn't help to talk to him like that. Teddy can't hurry.

If he gets frightened and tries to run, it's like stepping on the gas pedal in a carnival^g car: the speed doesn't increase more than there is electricity in the motor. And there isn't much electricity in Teddy's motor. He lifts his feet high in the air, but they don't go very far.

At that moment he wasn't even stepping on the gas. He jogged and stood a little, trotted five steps, and then stopped again. Each time I had to hold back a twig or branch for him, he stopped and held it too.

"We're going in a car, Teddy! Car! Brrrr." He laughed loudly at my engine noises and tried to imitate them. Some kind of humming noise came out of his mouth, and we droned noisily through the last group of trees.

When we finally reached the main road, the bus was waiting at the stop, and everyone had boarded it except the conductor. He looked up and down the road to see if any more passengers were coming.

I nodded and waved at him, and once Teddy had caught sight of the bus, had no problem hurrying him along.

■ These details could all be labeled "scary" or "strange" or "forbidding." So that mood is probably the main idea of this paragraph.

If only we didn't see anyone we knew. Neighbors might get curious and ask where I was taking Teddy, and later on they might inform[c] the police.

Sure enough! Mrs. Gren from the store was sitting up front. Fortunately,[c] she was talking to another woman and didn't see me struggling to get Teddy in the back door.

His legs always have trouble with stairs, and the steps were very steep. "Here we go. That's right—fine." The conductor used a hold[c] for people with bad legs, and we were inside.

There was room near the back. I pushed Teddy into a seat, and he pulled himself over to the window. Good, that meant I could hide him a little with my body and the rucksack.[g] Mother, Father, and I always try to hide him when we're among strangers.

But generally Teddy manages to get himself noticed, and now he was already rocking himself on the seat. He rocked and pushed as if he were trying to pick up speed in a swing. At the same time he went on droning as he had in the wood: "Brrr—doon—doon . . ." I sank back in relief as the real motor started up and drowned Teddy's voice.

The conductor was a real friend. "One and a half. Right." That was that, and he went to the next person.

■ These all add up to the general idea that Mikkel was very relieved that the conductor did *not* pay any special attention to them.

No surprise because a half-fare passenger paid for a great big boy. No glaring as if Teddy were the man in the moon or an orangutan.[g] Not even an understanding smile and a "Say, would you like to play with the ticket?" so that people would turn to look at the sweet child, while I would reach for the ticket, because Teddy can't grasp it. Oh! I knew it all so well.

We drove past my school, and I looked with mixed feelings, as people say, at the low, pale blue building. Not that I usually long for vacation to end, but it was somehow strange to think that the other children would go back to school without me, that I might never return.

Check the
Skills

Understanding the Selection

1. Mikkel's deep concern for Teddy caused Mikkel to decide they had to run away. Do you think this was a wise decision? Why or why not?

2. In what ways did Mikkel adjust his actions to what Teddy could do?

Comprehension Skills Implied Meaning

3. a. What is the main idea of the first paragraph of the selection? Use the marginal note for help in answering.

   b. In the second paragraph from the end of the selection, how do the details help you decide what the main idea probably is? Remember to use the note in the margin.

4. Read again the steps on page 149 that you can use to find the main idea. Think how those steps were part of finding the main ideas in the paragraphs mentioned in the question above. Now keep this in mind and see if you can figure out why the main idea of the whole selection is summed up in its title "Don't Take Teddy."

Literary Appreciation Skills Types of Literature

5. Because this selection is realistic fiction, you may feel especially interested in knowing that Mikkel succeeds in hiding his brother in the mountains until the threats to have Teddy locked up are abandoned. Later, Teddy is able to receive the special education he needs and still live at home with Mikkel and their parents.

   If you'd like to read the whole book, ask a librarian or your teacher for help in finding it, if necessary. The title is *Don't Take Teddy*. It was written by Babbis Friis-Baastad and published in New York City by Scribners in 1967.

Use the Skills

Understanding the Selection

Eugenie Clark's work with sharks and other ocean creatures has made her famous around the world. The next selection tells how she first became interested in ocean life.

1. As you read, notice the warm relationship between Eugenie and her working mother.

2. Families are based on each member's concern for the rest of the family. How is this concern brought out in this selection?

Comprehension Skills Implied Meaning

3. If you have trouble figuring out the main ideas as you read, remember to look first for the way the details are related. Marginal notes show you two clear examples.

Literary Appreciation Skills Types of Literature

4. Is this fiction or nonfiction? biographical or autobiographical?

EUGENIE CLARK BEGINS HER LIFE'S WORK

Ann McGovern

"Wake up, Genie," Mama called. "We have to go downtown soon."

Eugenie Clark mumbled into her pillow. Who wants to go downtown on a Saturday? But Grandma didn't feel well and needed peace and quiet. There was no place for nine-year-old Eugenie to be except with Mama at work.

Mama worked in a big building in downtown New York City. She sold newspapers in the lobby.

Eugenie's father had died when she was a baby. So Mama had to work extra hard to earn enough money to take care of the family. Working extra hard meant working Saturday mornings, too.

The subway train pulled into their station and they got out. A sign at the top of the subway stairs said: TO THE AQUARIUM.⁹

"A good idea," Mama said. "I'll leave you at the Aquarium and I'll pick you up at lunchtime. That will be more fun for you than sitting around the newsstand."

Eugenie walked through the doors of the Aquarium and into the world of fish.

She walked among the tanks filled with strange fish. Then she came to a big, mysterious looking tank at the back. She stared at it for a long, long time. The green misty water seemed to go on and on. She leaned over the rail, her face close to the glass, and pretended that she was walking on the bottom of the sea.

■ What main idea do the details in this paragraph lead you to?

Eugenie went to the Aquarium on all the Saturdays of autumn and winter.

Eugenie read about fish, too. She read about a scientist who put a diving helmet on and walked on the bottom of the sea with the fish swimming around.

"Someday I'll walk with the fish, too," she said.

In the summertime, Mama took her to the beach. Mama had taught Eugenie to swim before she was two years old.

When Mama came out of the water, her long jet-black hair streamed down her back. Eugenie thought Mama looked like pictures she had seen of beautiful pearl divers[c] of the Orient. Mama was Japanese.

Mama was a good swimmer, and Eugenie loved to watch her swim with long, graceful strokes.

Now, in the autumn and in the winter, Eugenie watched the very best swimmers—the fish in the Aquarium. She found all the fish fascinating[g]—the smallest fish glowing like tiny jewels and the fish with fluttering fins that looked like fairy wings. But it was the biggest streamlined fish in the Aquarium that she came back to again and again.

She watched the big shark swimming, turning, swimming, turning, never resting its long, graceful[c] body. She watched it and lost track of time.

"Mysterious shark," she thought. "Someday I'll swim with sharks, too."

Miss Reilly, Eugenie's favorite teacher, took Eugenie's class on field trips. Eugenie hoped that they could come to the Aquarium. Miss Reilly had said she would like the class to see "Genie's fish."

"Genie's fish. Genie's fish." An idea began to grow.

■ Don't let the everyday talk confuse you as to whether this selection is fiction or non-fiction. The author has used her imagination to add interest.

"Just think," she said to Mama one day. "Some people have beautiful fish in their own home and watch them all the time. Mama, Christmas is coming soon." Eugenie crossed her fingers and made a wish.

After lunch, Eugenie and Mama went to a pet shop to pick out the Christmas present. They chose a large aquarium with gravel and stones. They bought plants to make it look natural. They got snails to keep it clean.

Then came the best part—picking out the fish.

Before long, the small apartment was crowded with fish of all kinds. Mama became fascinated with fish, too.

Sometimes she would bring home little white boxes with fish swimming inside. When that happened, Eugenie knew that Mama had spent her lunch hour and maybe her lunch money in the pet shop.

Eugenie joined the Queens County Aquarium Society and became its youngest member. She learned how to keep good records of her pets. She wrote down their scientific names, the date she got each fish, and what happened to them.

■ What is the main idea of this paragraph?

Her life's work had begun.

Check the Skills

Understanding the Selection

1. What are some examples of the warm relationship between the mother and daughter?

2. Is this relationship built on a concern for each other? Why do you think as you do?

Comprehension Skills Implied Meaning

3. a. Find the marginal note on page 163. Reread the paragraph next to it. Do you agree that the main idea of that paragraph is that Eugenie was completely fascinated by the aquarium and its fish? Why or why not?

   b. Reread the paragraph next to the marginal note at the top of this page. Every sentence in that paragraph gives a detail you can use to figure out the main idea. What do you think is the main idea?

Literary Appreciation Skills Types of Literature

4. This is a biographical sketch, covering Eugenie Clark's early years. What clues in the selection could help you decide this? The selection is the first part of a book entitled *Shark Lady: The Adventures of Eugenie Clark*. The author had to imagine exactly what the people might have said to each other. How did this help to make the selection seem more realistic?

Use the Skills

For many years, an unwritten law barred black players from both the major leagues and minor leagues of American baseball. About 1945, the president of the Brooklyn Dodgers, Branch Rickey, decided it was time to do something about this injustice. He asked a talented young black player, Jackie Robinson, to come to see him. As you read about this historic meeting, notice that both Rickey and Robinson were concerned about the rights of others.

If you have any trouble understanding the main ideas throughout, remember to focus on the connections among the details. Decide whether this is a biographical sketch or an autobiographical one. This time you're on your own, with no marginal notes to help you with your skills.

BREAKTHROUGH
TO THE BIG LEAGUE

Jackie Robinson and Alfred Duckett

"Do you have any idea why I want to talk to you?" Mr. Rickey asked me. "Do you really understand why you are here?"

"Well, I was told you wanted to talk to me about your new Brown Dodgers Club."

"The truth is you are not here as a candidate for the Brooklyn Brown Dodgers," Mr. Rickey said. "I've sent for you because I'm interested in you for the Brooklyn National League Club. I think you can play in the major leagues. How do you feel about it?"

There it was! The realization of a dream I'd been pushing out of my mind because I simply couldn't believe it would ever come true.

How did I feel? It was hard to say. I didn't know how to put it into words or how to marshal[g] my thoughts. I was dazzled,[g] shocked, delighted, scared to death.

"You think you can play for Montreal?"

"Yes," I said.

Montreal! The Brooklyn Dodgers' top farm club! This was the training school, the trial division to which Dodger hopefuls were taken, some of them failing, some emerging[g] as major league stars.

With dramatic[g] suddenness Mr. Rickey wheeled his swivel[g] chair to face me. He pointed a finger challengingly.[g]

"I know you are a good ballplayer," the Brooklyn boss said. "What I don't know is whether you have the guts."

"Guts," I repeated to myself wonderingly. I'd had a lot of things said about me, but no one had ever accused me of being a coward or running away from an issue—or even a fight.

What did Mr. Rickey mean? His voice was deep and rumbling as he told me.

"I'm going to tell you the truth, Jackie. I've investigated you thoroughly. They said at UCLA that in basketball you had trouble with coaches, players, and officials. I just want to tell you that my investigation convinced me that the criticisms are unjustified,⁹ that if you'd been white it would have been nothing. The thing I want to convince you of is that we can't fight our way through this, Jackie. We've got no army. There's virtually⁹ nobody on our side. No owners, no umpires, very few newspapermen. And I'm afraid that many fans will be hostile.⁹ We'll be in a tough position, Jackie. We can win only if we can convince the world that I'm doing this because you're a great ballplayer and a fine gentleman."

Mr. Rickey continued and it was almost as if he were talking to himself as well as to me. His sincerity charged the atmosphere⁹ in that office.

"So there's more than just playing," he said. "I wish it meant only hits, runs and errors—only the things they put in the box score.⁹ Because you know—yes, you would know, Jackie—that a baseball box score is a democratic⁵ thing. It doesn't tell how big you are, what church you attend, what color you are, or how you voted in the last election. It just tells what kind of baseball player you were on that particular day."

"It's the box score that really counts—that and that alone—isn't it?" I asked.

"It's all that *ought* to count! But it isn't! Maybe one of these days it *will* be all that counts. That's one of the reasons I've got you here, Jackie. If you're a good enough man, we can make this a start in the right direction. But let me tell you, it's going to take an awful lot of courage. Have you got the guts to play the game no matter what happens?"

He had left his desk and was leaning over in front of me, his face close to mine, his eyes measuring me.

"I think I can play the game, Mr. Rickey," I said. My nervousness was leaving me. I was filled with an excitement about what this man wanted to accomplish.⁹ It wasn't just making me the first in the majors. It wasn't just the buildup of one new star. We were standing at a closed door where many had knocked and none had been admitted. We were going to take hold of the knob, turn it, and walk in. But we had to walk carefully or it wouldn't work.

Mr. Rickey began to predict the kind of problems I would face. He told me I'd have to hold my temper. I must never lose sight of our goal.

What was this white man asking of me? Was he calling upon me to sell my manhood, my (inbred⁹) (militancy,⁹) for some fame and money which might come to me?

"Mr. Rickey," I demanded suspiciously, "are you looking for a Negro who is afraid to fight back?"

The (depth⁹) and passion of his voice and the classic simplicity of his reply thrilled me, shook me back into an understanding of what Branch Rickey was actually fighting for.

"I'm looking for a ballplayer, Jackie," he rumbled, "with guts enough *not* to fight back."

Check the Skills

Understanding the Selection

1. In the incident described in this selection, how did Jackie Robinson and Branch Rickey both show their concern for others?

2. Why had Rickey investigated Robinson's background? What did Rickey mean by having "guts enough *not* to fight back"?

3. Why do you think Rickey chose Robinson as the player for the difficult task of breaking baseball's color barrier?

Comprehension Skills Implied Meaning

4. The following paragraph from the selection has an important main idea. Pay careful attention to the way the details in the paragraph are related. Then decide what you think the main idea is.

   > How did I feel? It was hard to say. I didn't know how to put it into words or how to marshal my thoughts. I was dazzled, shocked, delighted, scared to death.

Literary Appreciation Skills Types of Literature

5. Is this selection a biographical sketch or an autobiographical one? Explain your answer.

Apply What You Learned in Unit 6

The Theme

Concern for Others

1. The selections in this unit all gave examples of people whose concern for other people—or lack of it—affected their lives deeply. Most of these people combined their concern for others with their own goals. For example, Jackie Robinson's dream was to play in the major leagues. His reason for having that dream was not just his concern for other black baseball players who would follow him. It was his own dream for himself, too. Do you think this kind of balance is a good thing? Why or why not?

• Do you think that a concern for others is the mark of a special person? What people can you think of who have shown interest in the welfare of other people?

• What kind of world do you think it would be if everyone thought only of themselves and their own interests and welfare?

The Skills

Comprehension Skills Implied Meaning

2. Understanding the main idea of what you read
    means knowing what it is really about. This is
    especially important when you are reading the
    kinds of nonfiction you meet in your classes at
    school. When you read textbooks or other mate-
    rials in your history, science, math, or arts classes,
    make sure you understand the main ideas.

3. Remember to watch for the details and think how
    they all are related. Then think of a label or de-
    scription that fits the main idea.

    Try these steps on your very next reading assign-
    ment in science or math. You'll find they will help.

Literary Appreciation Skills Types of Literature

4. When you're looking for information, make sure
    you're reading nonfiction, which is based on fact.

    You'll discover that an autobiography often tells
    more about a person's private thoughts and feel-
    ings than a biography does. Why do you think this
    is so?

Unit 7

Leaving Home

Overview and Purposes for Reading

The Theme

Leaving Home

1.   Everybody leaves home eventually. How does being away from home alter a person's viewpoint? What are some of the reasons for a person leaving home? What is the lure of "far away places"?

The Skills

Comprehension Skills Critical Reading

2.   What is the difference between a statement of fact and a statement of opinion?

3.   What steps can you follow to distinguish between fact and opinion?

Literary Appreciation Skills Story Elements

4.   What are the different points of view from which a story or article may be written?

Learn About the Skills

Comprehension Skills Critical Reading

Some people believe everything they read because they think that if it is printed, it must be true. This is not so. Everything you read was written by a person. And people often express their own opinions. Good readers know how to tell the difference between fact and opinion. Do you?

Look at the following statement. Is it fact or opinion?

Hockey may be the fastest sport of all.

You should be able to tell that this statement is an **opinion** because the writer uses the word *may.* Authors often label their opinions by using words such as *may, could, ought,* and *might.*

Another signal of opinion is the use of emotional words. For instance, see if you think the following statement is a fact or an opinion.

The mayor wisely ignored the whining of the people who had fought against him.

You can tell this is an opinion because of the words *wisely* and *whining.* Both are emotional words that signal opinion. Remember a **fact** is a statement of information that can be proved or checked. There would be no way to prove that the mayor's action was wise, for example.

Some statements of opinion are even more difficult to recognize, such as this one:

Cats are the best pets for children to have.

You must be particularly watchful when you read a statement like this one because it is written as if it is a fact. There are no special signal words to alert you that it is an opinion. Instead, you must use the whole statement as your signal by asking yourself, "Would everybody agree with this?'' If your experience tells you that some people think differently, then the statement is probably opinion.

You can usually tell fact from opinion, then, if you follow these steps:

Distinguishing Between Fact and Opinion

1. See if the statement contains words that label opinions, such as *may, could,* and so on.
2. See if the statement contains emotional words that cannot be proved or checked. If so, then the statement is probably opinion.
3. Ask yourself if everybody would accept the statement. If not, it is probably opinion.

Try another example to see if you can tell fact from opinion. Which of the following two statements is opinion?

1. Sacramento is the capital of California.
2. Sacramento is the greatest city in California.

The second is an opinion. The clues are the emotional word *greatest* and your knowledge that there is no way to prove what ''the greatest'' means. The information in the first sentence could be checked. What you already know about the world helps you realize that records exist about such things.

Knowing how to distinguish between fact and opinion will help you be a more careful and thoughtful reader. You will learn more about this skill as you read this unit.

Literary Appreciation Skills Story Elements

When people write stories, they decide through whose "eyes" the readers are going to "see" the story. In other words, the author chooses a **point of view.**

Recognizing what point of view a story is told from can help you understand and appreciate the stories you read. You will know different things about what is happening in a story depending upon the point of view. For instance, when the story is being told by a main character, you know what that main character knows and feels. You don't know what other people in the story know and feel because the character telling the story can't know all those things and still be believable.

When authors write from a main character's point of view, they use the words *I* and *we* frequently. *I* refers to the character telling the story, so the point of view of the story is that character's. This is called the **first person point of view.** This point of view often makes a story seem much more real.

Most stories, however, are written as though the author has complete knowledge of all the characters and of the details of many happenings, even those that occur at the same time. This is called the **omniscient point of view** because *omniscient* means "knowing or seeing everything."

Authors think carefully about whose "eyes" should be used in telling a story. When they choose one point of view over another, it is usually for a good reason. As you read the selections in this unit, notice who is telling each story. See if you can figure out why the authors chose the points of view they did.

Use the Skills

Understanding the Selection

1. For centuries the excitement of going to sea has persuaded people to leave home. Sailors who left home in the 1800s had to face the danger of sea monsters! Were the monsters real or imaginary? Find out as you read the next selection.

Comprehension Skills Critical Reading

2. You'll discover in this selection that opinion can sometimes change into fact. Watch the notes in the margin. They'll help you see how this happened with the descriptions of some sea monsters who were originally thought to be imaginary.

3. In this selection it is very important to remember that one way to distinguish between fact and opinion is to decide if everyone would accept the statement. Also remember to watch for emotional words and words that label opinions.

Literary Appreciation Skills Story Elements

4. This selection is an article rather than a fictional story. However, you should be able to identify the selection's point of view as omniscient. If you have trouble deciding why this is so, check the marginal note near the end of the selection.

THE LARGEST SEA MONSTER IN THE WORLD

Daniel Cohen

Two hundred years ago a book was published that described the kraken[c] as "incontestably[g] the largest sea monster in the world. . . ." The book said that the kraken was "round, flat, and full of arms." Another book described the sea monster as looking like "a tree pulled up by the roots." Tales were also told of the kraken grabbing ships in its arms and pulling them under the waves. Sailors were very much afraid of meeting the monster.

Have you ever heard of the kraken? Probably not.

But there are a couple of well-known sea creatures that have many arms, or tentacles.[c] They are the octopus and the squid. You <u>may</u> know what an octopus looks like. It has a round head and body with eight tentacles. The squid is a close relative of the octopus, but it is sausage-shaped and has ten tentacles. Eight are of one length, and two are longer.

■ This word labels the sentence as opinion. All other sentences in this paragraph state facts—everyone would accept them because they can be proved.

The octopus and the squid are found in most of the world's oceans. Fishermen often use them for bait, and in many countries people eat them. For a long time people believed that the creatures grew to no more than a foot or two in length, so when a French scientist suggested that the kraken might really be a giant squid or an octopus, <u>no one agreed</u>. Most scientists thought the kraken was a sailors' tall tale; only sailors and travelers were sure it was a special monster.

■ This tells you that at that point a statement about the existence of the monster was *opinion*.

People kept on sighting the kraken. Some French sailors even came close to capturing one.

In 1861, the French ship *Alecton* was off the island of Madeira when the crew sighted a kraken. They fired shots, to no effect. Finally, they wounded it with a harpoon[cg] and slipped a rope around its tail, planning to haul the monster back to port. It was too heavy. As they pulled the kraken out of the water, the tail snapped, and the huge, ugly body dropped back into the sea.

When the *Alecton* reached port, the sailors told their story. But without evidence, few people believed them.

There were also many reports of the remains of strange creatures being washed ashore. In October, 1673, after a tremendous storm off the coast of Ireland, the people of Dingle-I-Cosh found a dead monster on their shore. It was over twenty feet long and had two huge eyes and ten tentacles.

A carnival[g] owner named James Steward cut off two eight-foot sections of tentacle to exhibit[c] in his show. The rest of the carcass[c] washed back into the sea.

Steward's description of the monster sounded like carnival exaggeration, and the tentacles could have been many things. So nobody took Steward's story seriously.

Many other stories weren't taken seriously, either. Several seaside towns reported dead monsters on their beaches—monsters like the one at Dingle-I-Cosh. Sailors told of seeing creatures like the one captured and lost by the men of the *Alecton*. Reports kept coming from all over the world.

By 1870, there was too much evidence to ignore. The kraken *was* real, and it *was* a giant squid. Giant squids live deep in the ocean; they are rarely seen at the surface, and no one knows just how large they can grow.

■ Because there was more proof, the existence of the monsters began to be accepted as fact instead of opinion.

The largest squid ever recorded was found on November 2, 1878. Stephen Sperring, a fisherman from Thimble Tickle, Newfoundland, was out in his boat with two other men. They spotted a big object in the water, and thinking it was part of a wrecked ship, they rowed toward it. To their horror, they found that "the thing" was very much alive.

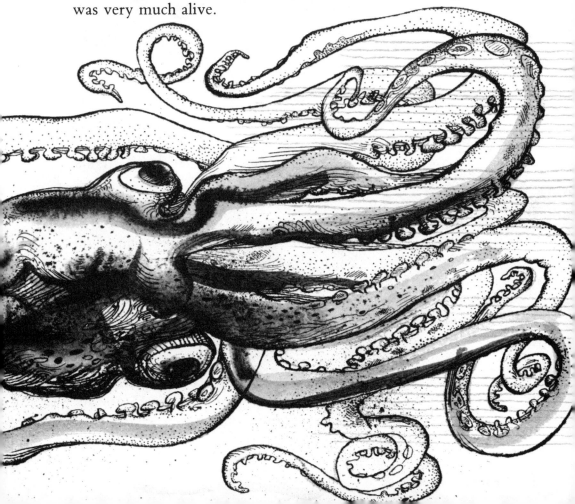

The creature had been stranded^c in the shallows,^g and it beat at the water with its tail and immense^c tentacles. The monster's eyes were particularly frightening; they looked human, but were more than a foot and a half across.

Sperring and his companions had seen many strange sights in the sea, but none compared to this giant squid. They watched the creature for a while. It was wounded and very weak, and they were able to get close enough to slip a rope around its tail. They tied the other end of the rope to a tree; when the tide went out, the giant squid was left high and dry and soon died.

The fishermen cut up the monster and used it for dog food, but before they did, they took some rough measurements. The giant squid was fifty-seven feet long from tip of tail to tip of tentacle.

The Thimble Tickle squid is the largest giant squid ever measured, but they can grow much larger. Some authorities^c think that giant squids may reach lengths well over two hundred feet—nearly as long as a football field!

■ The author seems to have complete knowledge of the subject in the article. He does not refer to himself as *I* and he is not personally involved in the action. So this selection is told from the omniscient point of view.

Try to imagine yourself as a sailor in the days of wooden ships. If you looked overboard and saw a sausage-shaped body longer than your boat, big staring eyes, and ten long tentacles, you would be sure you had seen a monster. And you would be right. The kraken turned out to be a *real* monster—a giant squid.

Check the Skills

Understanding the Selection

1. Were the sea monsters real or imaginary? How do you think those sailors who faced the monsters felt about leaving home?

Comprehension Skills Critical Reading

2. Why were the early descriptions of the sea monsters considered opinion? Why were later statements about them fact?

3. The key to answering the questions above is deciding whether or not everyone accepted the statements about the monsters. The change in most people's attitude came about when the descriptions could be proved and checked. Only then were the descriptions clearly *fact* and not the opinion of a few frightened sailors.

Literary Appreciation Skills Story Elements

4. What clues in the selection indicate that it is told from an omniscient point of view? Think about the sailors on the *Alecton* who lost the kraken they tried to haul back to port. How would this article be different if it had been written in the first person point of view by one of them?

Selection 2

Use the Skills

Understanding the Selection

In the 1930s the Nazi government of Germany began a systematic persecution of German Jews. This was to reach its full effect in the 1940s with the deaths of six million Jews in German extermination camps. It was a disaster that shocked the entire civilized world. In this excerpt from the novel *Journey to America* you will meet a Jewish family that was able to escape this holocaust. As the excerpt opens, the ship carrying several members of the family is about to reach New York.

1. Read to share in the joy of the narrator and her sisters and their mother as they find a new home in a new country after being forced to leave the old home and country that they loved.

Comprehension Skills Critical Reading

2. Even in a work of fiction, you can separate fact from opinion. Ask yourself if this could have happened exactly as it is described. Watch for words that label opinions.

Literary Appreciation Skills Story Elements

3. There is a clue word in the first sentence that tells from which point of view the story is written. Look for it.

END OF A JOURNEY

Sonia Levitin

The next day, it was said, the next day we would see land.

Night brought a change in mood,[g] a great excitement, an air of celebration.[c] People danced in the dining room and the ship's orchestra played happy tunes, while newly found friends exchanged addresses.

The next morning everyone was up early, crowding at the rails, straining to see the first glimpse of land. We stood close together, the four of us, and several times there was a false cry—land!—then disappointment and Annie's questions, "When? When?"

For nearly two hours we stood. Then, suddenly there began a murmur,[c] rising to a shout, until it spread the length and breadth of the ship. "America! America! I see it! Look!"

People shouted wildly as they pressed closer and closer to the rail to see the dim, distant outline of the Statue of Liberty. Parents held their little children high on their shoulders that they might see. I strained on tiptoe, shouting at the top of my lungs while I stared at the statue and the buildings in the distance, thinking it might be a dream, but the throbbing inside me was real, very real.

"I'll never forget this sight," Mother whispered.

Beside us an old woman wept, her head pressed against her husband's shoulder. "America! God be praised!"

On and on the shouting, the waving, the tears. The ship seemed to rock and sway with it, and then I heard the first strains of music from the ship's orchestra. If people didn't know the words, they sang the tune.

"America! America! God shed His grace on thee."

Amid the streaming crowd we made our way down the gangplank.[g] When we stood on firm ground, my legs

■ Here's the clue word that tells you the point of view.

■ This sentence is made up largely of information that can be accepted as factual. The only opinion word is *happy*.

■ The word *seemed* labels this as a statement of opinion.

still swayed from the motion of the sea. I saw a bearded young man beside me stoop down and gather up a handful of soil, and everything he felt showed in his eyes.

■ This is opinion. The narrator could not be certain that everything the man felt showed in his eyes. And it is not likely that everyone would agree.

For a few moments we stood lost in the tangle of people, all waiting for someone, all wondering where to go. We began to walk, following painted arrows. We passed through many rooms and saw many people who looked at our papers. Then, suddenly, Mother stopped short.

I can't remember what I said or did, but I heard the shriek⁹ from my sister Ruth, and I suppose my own voice mingled with hers, "Papa! Papa!" It was as if I had been hurled through space and dropped here, straight into Papa's arms.

With all the crowd milling past, Mother and Papa drew close in a long embrace.ᶜ At last Papa exclaimed, "Annie, darling, don't you know me?" For my little sister Annie hung back, clutching Mother's hand.

Now Annie came forward and said with a strange, shy look, "Are you my Papa? Are you really?"

"Oh, yes, my little Annie! I am, and I love you." Papa scooped her up into his arms, and Annie buried her face in his neck. "Yes," she sighed. "Oh, Papa!"

"Come now," Papa said, with his arm around me. "There's time for talk later. I want to hear everything. But now," he said, his voice husky, "let's go home. It's just a little apartment, and I don't have much furniture yet."

"It will be beautiful," Mother whispered.

Home, I thought, home was a feeling more than a place. I gave Papa's hand a squeeze and he smiled down at me. Yes, we were home.

Check the Skills

Understanding the Selection

1. This story of leaving home had a happy ending. Why do you think that this reunion was more joyous for all concerned than an ordinary family reunion? What are some of the ways in which the author indicates this happiness?

Comprehension Skills Critical Reading

2. a. In the second paragraph, why might the narrator's reference to "happy tunes" be considered an opinion?

   b. How do you know that the following sentence is opinion?

   It will be beautiful.

Literary Appreciation Skills Story Elements

3. How did the clue in the first sentence help you decide that this was written from the first person point of view?

Selection 3

Use the Skills

Understanding the Selection

The Navajo Indians had made their home in northern Arizona for hundreds of years when, in 1863, the U.S. government forced them to move to Fort Sumner in eastern New Mexico. U.S. soldiers, who were called "the long knives" by the Navajo, took them on a forced march that brought great hardship to these proud people. These facts form the background for Scott O'Dell's fictional novel *Sing Down the Moon*. In this excerpt, you'll meet Bright Morning, a young Navajo woman, and Tall Boy, the man she loves. Tall Boy had joined a Navajo attempt to stop the march, which failed.

1. As you read, note the powers of endurance shown by Bright Morning and her family. How would you react if you were torn away from your home and forced on such a cruel march?

Comprehension Skills Critical Reading

2. Use your skills to distinguish fact from opinion.

3. Remember to watch for words that label opinions, like *may* or *could*, and emotional words like *shamed* or *happy*.

Literary Appreciation Skills Story Elements

4. There are two clue words in the first paragraph to help you determine the point of view from which the story is written.

THE LONG TRAIL

Scott O'Dell

The sky was gray and the air smelled of bitter winds. The Long Knives drove us along the river and through the portals⁹ of the canyon.⁹ Like sheep before the shepherd, we went without a sound.

■ This comparison represents the narrator's opinion.

By noon on that day snow fell out of the gray sky. A sharp wind blew against us. The Long Knives made camp in a wooded draw and told us to do likewise. We stayed there in the draw until the snow stopped, until two days had gone. Then on the third morning we set off again.

My father asked one of the Long Knives where they were taking us. The soldier said, "Fort Sumner." He pointed southward and that was all.

■ The point of view should already be clear.

On that day we met Navajo from Blue Water Canyon, more than fifty of them. They came down from their village, driven by the Long Knives. Their clothes were ragged and all were on foot. Most of them were old men and women, but one girl about my age was carrying two young children on her back. They were heavy for her and I asked if I could help her carry one of them.

The girl's name was Little Rainbow. She was small but pretty like a flower and her children, a boy and a girl, looked like flowers too, with their round faces and big dark eyes. She gave me the girl and I made a sling and carried her on my back the rest of that day.

Toward evening we came upon another band of Navajo. There were about a hundred of them, a few on horses. They belonged to the Coyote Clan⁹ and had been on the trail for a week, prodded along by five soldiers.

We lighted fires that night and had a gathering. The Long Knives left us alone, but we could see them watching us from the trees while we chanted⁹ our songs

and our prayers. Little Rainbow came and we sat together in the grass, playing with the children. She took the girl with her when she went off to sleep, but in the morning gave her back to me.

Sometime in the night, Tall Boy slipped into our camp and lay down by the fire. We found him there in the morning, his clothes torn and his feet bare and bleeding. He ate the mush⁹ I brought to him but would not talk. He had the same <u>shamed</u> look about him that I had seen when he fled from the Long Knives, his lanceᶜ lying broken upon the ground.

■ Note the emotional word *shamed.*

The trail led south and eastward across rough country and we went slowly because of the old people. We had two wagons with good horses but they were not enough to carry all those who needed help. We made scarcely a league⁹ during the whole morning.

At noon two large bands of Navajo overtook us. They were mostly men, some of them wounded in a fight with the Long Knives. They went by us with their eyes on the ground, silent and weaponless.

That afternoon we saw many bands of Navajo. They came from all directions, from the high country and from the valleys. It was like a storm when water trickles from everywhere and flows into the river and the river flows full. This was the way the trail looked as night fell, like a dark-flowing river.

Little Rainbow did not come for her child when we camped that night and I asked my mother what I should do.

"There is nothing to do," she said.

My sister said, "You were foolish to take the child. You have enough to carry without her."

"We will find the girl tomorrow," my mother said, "or she will find us. In the meantime she knows that her child is safe."

We did not find her the next day. Tall Boy went out looking at sunrise, but soon returned, saying that a soldier had threatened him. The soldier told him to go back to his clan and not to wander around or someone would shoot him.

All day as we trudged᠌ eastward I looked for Little Rainbow. I asked people I did not know if they had seen her. Everyone shook their heads. In a way I was glad that I did not find her. I was carrying three rolled-up blankets and a jar filled with cornmeal. It was a heavy burden᠌ even without the little girl. But she was good all the time, making happy sounds as the two of us went along.

As on the day before, Navajo by the hundreds came out of the mountains and forests to join us.

The river flowed slower now and many old people began to falter.᠌ At first, the Long Knives rode back and forth, urging them on if they lay down beside the trail. But so many fell that afternoon when the cold wind blew from the north that the soldiers did not take notice anymore, except to jeer᠌ at them.

The march went on until dusk. Fires were lighted and people gathered around them. Our clan said little to each other. We were unhappy and afraid, not knowing where we were driven.

"The soldiers tell me that it is a place of running water and deep grass," my father said. "But it lies a long walk to the east."

He said this every night as we huddled around the fire. I think he believed it. He wanted us to believe it, too.

"Cast your eyes around," he said. "You will see many people sitting beside their fires. They are hungry but not starving. They are cold but they do not freeze. They are unhappy. Yet they are alive."

■ The mother's statement, as heartfelt as it may be, still represents an opinion.

"We are walking to our deaths," my mother said. "The old die now. The young die later. But we all die."

Tall Boy stared at the fire, saying nothing. He had said little since that day when he tried to throw his iron-tipped lance and had failed. The Navajo, his people, were captives of the Long Knives and there was nothing he could do to free them. Once he had been haughty,᠌ his wide shoulders held straight, his black eyes looking coldly at everyone. I wished, as I sat there beside him, that he would act haughty once more.

My sister took the little girl from my lap, where she was sleeping. "She is heavy," Lapana said.

"No wonder," my mother answered. "She eats a lot, as much as I do almost. And food is scarce. Every day there will be less until there is none."

I took the child back and wrapped her in a blanket and lay down with her in my arms.

The fire died away and I could see the stars. I wondered what the little girl's name was. She was like a flower, like a flower in a spring meadow. I gave her that name—Meadow Flower—as she lay beside me.

Check the Skills

Understanding the Selection

1. How did Bright Morning and her family show their powers of endurance after being forced to leave home? How did Tall Boy react? How would you react?

Comprehension Skills Critical Reading

2. Why is the following a statement of opinion?

    We are walking to our deaths.

3. What word in the following sentence labels it as opinion?

    He had a shamed look about him.

Literary Appreciation Skills Story Elements

4. This selection is written from the first person point of view. What clues in the story could help you figure this out?

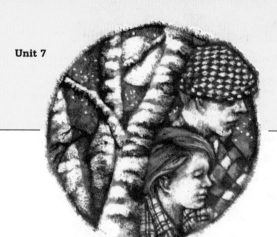

Use the Skills

Understanding the Selection

The Great Depression of the 1930s was the worst this country has ever known. By 1933—when the next selection takes place—more than 15 million men and women were unemployed. Many left home, including hundreds of thousands of teen-agers.

1. Read to hear a boy called Texas explain why he left home. He is talking to a young college teacher who was collecting material for his 1934 book *Boy and Girl Tramps of America.*

2. Imagine yourself in Texas's place. What would you have done?

Comprehension Skills Critical Reading

3. As Texas talks, look for statements of fact and statements of opinion.

4. Refer to the steps on page 174 if you need to, but you should remember them pretty well by now.

Literary Appreciation Skills Story Elements

5. You should find it very easy to identify the point of view in this selection.

BEFORE
THE BIG TROUBLE CAME

Thomas Minehan

"It wasn't so bad at home," says Texas to me in the early weeks of our wandering, "before the big trouble came." The other boys have gone to sleep. Texas and I are sitting on a log near a jungle campfire and talking of other days.

"Before the big trouble came," he goes on and his eyes are somber⁹ in the firelight. "We got along pretty good. Dad, of course, never was very well. He was in the war and he got some kind of sickness, I guess, but he couldn't get a pension.⁹ He was always sick for about a month every year, and that meant that he had to look for a new job each time he got well. If he had been husky it might have been easy to get a good job, but he was small and then sick, you know.

■ Fact or opinion?

"But we got along swell before the big trouble came, even if there were seven of us kids. I shined shoes in a barber shop. Jim carried papers. And Marie took care of Mrs. Rolph's kids. Mother always did some sewing for the neighbors. We had a Chevvie⁹ and a radio and a piano. I even started to high school mornings, the year the big trouble came.

"Dad got sick as usual but we never thought anything of it. When he comes to go back to work he can't get a job, and everybody all of a sudden-like seems to be hard up. I cut the price of shines to a nickel but it didn't help much. I even used to go around and collect shoes and shine them at the houses or take them away, shine and return them, but even then some weeks I couldn't make a dime.

"Mrs. Rolph's husband got a cut and she fired Marie. Jim had to quit the paper route because he lost all his cash customers, and the others never paid. Nobody wanted Mother to sew anything. And there we were, seven of us kids and Dad and Mother, and we couldn't make a cent like we could before the big trouble came."

Texas pushes a piece of birch into the fire. I throw in a pine knot. The embers[c] crackle and hiss. A cone of sparks and white smoke rises straight into the air. The smoke turns darker. There is a pungent[g] smell of resin[g] as the pine knot flames and burns. The night is becoming cold. We nudge closer to the fire, warming our shins. Texas stretches his hands, slender and delicate as a girl's, strong as a pianist's, toward the flame.

■ The point of view should be very clear to you by now. Is it first person or omniscient?

Were his hands, I ask myself, so slender and translucent before the big trouble came—before that monstrous depression, that economic juggernaut[g] that was to crash through his home, cast him out upon the road, and make him perhaps a bum for life?

"But the big trouble came," he continues, caressing his chin with warm palms, "and there we were. Oh, we tried hard enough, and everybody did their best. Marie made the swellest wax flowers. The kids peddled ironing cloths. Mother tried to sell some homemade bakery, and Dad did everything. We did our best, I guess, but it wasn't good enough, for the big trouble had come and nobody had any money.

"Dad gave up pipe smoking in the fall. All last winter we never had a fire except about once a day when Mother used to cook some mush or something. When the kids were cold they went to bed. I quit high school of course, but the kids kept going because it didn't cost anything and it was warm there.

■ Could this be proved or checked?

"In February I went to Fort Worth. Mother used to know a man there, and she thought maybe he could help me get a job. But he was as hard up as anybody else. I didn't want to return home and pick bread off the kids' plates so I tried to get work from a farmer for my board. Instead, I got a ride to California. Near Salinas I worked in the lettuce fields, cutting and washing lettuce. I made $32 and I sent $10 home. But that was my first and last pay check. I got chased out of California in June."

The fire flickers and ebbs.ᶜ We pull a night log into the embers and prepare to join our companions in sleep. I turn my back to the fire and face the eternal stars.

"Since then," concludes Texas and his voice sounds far away and distant as the stars blinking unconcernedly down on me, "I just been traveling."

Check the Skills

Understanding the Selection

1. Why did Texas leave home? Do you think his reasons were good ones? Why or why not?

2. What else do you think he could have done? What do you think you might have done?

Comprehension Skills Critical Reading

3. a. What clue tells you that the following sentence states an opinion?

    He was in the war and he got some kind of sickness, I guess.

   b. Is the following sentence fact or opinion? How do you know?

    The high school didn't cost anything and it was warm there.

4. Explain how watching for words that label opinions helped you answer question 3a above. How did deciding whether a statement could be proved give you the answer to 3b?

Literary Appreciation Skills Story Elements

5. What clues helped you decide that this selection is told from a first person point of view?

Use the Skills

Dawan lives in a village in Thailand, in southeastern Asia. She wants very much to go to high school, but there isn't one nearby. She gains a scholarship to a high school in a distant city. But now that the day to leave home has come, she is beginning to have second thoughts about going. As you read, note that Dawan's thoughts are a mixture of fact and opinion. Note, too, how she deals with her conflicting thoughts about leaving home.

You're on your own. There are no notes in the margins this time. Try out what you've been learning in this unit.

DAWAN IS
LEAVING HOME

Minfong Ho

Peering^c out from the leafy shelter of the path, Dawan watched the crowd of villagers gathered around her home. Naked babies scurried^{cg} between people's legs chasing chickens. A cluster of solemn young monks^g talked in low whispers among themselves. Little children peeped out from behind the curtain of their mother's sarongs.^{g}

Dawan caught glimpses of a few people who were special to her. Her teacher was standing rather awkwardly by himself. Bao was carelessly holding onto her baby brother.

Dawan stared at all this bustle for a moment, then hastily retreated into the shadows of the tree. But her mother, tying the last rope around her daughter's luggage, caught sight of her. She straightened up and hurried over to her daughter, shouting, "There you are! I was getting worried, child. Your father has already gone out to look for you. We thought you had suddenly decided not to go. It's a good thing you didn't run off. Why, look at all the people here to see you off. . . ."

By this time the villagers were swarming around, fussing and cooing over her. Dawan cringed back, muttered something about having to change her clothes, and wiggled her way through them. She clambered^c up the ladder to the hut, which she knew would be empty except for her grandmother.

In the dim light of the house, Dawan saw a pair of steady eyes gleaming in the corner. "Don't be afraid, child. Calm down," her grandmother said gently. "I have put your new clothes and shoes on the matting there. Are they all waiting for you outside?" She clucked^c softly, "Never *mind*, child, take your time."

Dawan smiled gratefully at her grandmother, and walked over to the piece of matting where her new things lay waiting. As she bent down to put her shoes on, she realized that she was still clutching her brother Kwai's discarded lotus^g bud in her hand. Tossing the bud aside, she dressed hurriedly, her nervousness increasing as she heard the sound of the heavy old bus rumbling in. Outside, the noise of the crowd grew, like palm trees rustling in the wind before a monsoon[g] storm.

"Child, you come here."

Dawan obediently crawled to the corner where her grandmother sat. She knelt down in front of the old woman, hands neatly folded and head bowed. This was the leavetaking that pained her most.

In a voice slow and heavy with age, the old woman said, "You have a long life ahead of you yet, child, and this is just the first step. If you're this timid now, how on earth are you going to face all the struggle still before you? Gather yourself together, and face the world out there with clear bold eyes. You hear me?"

Dawan nodded, but did not budge. It was the rhythm more than the meaning of the aged voice that calmed the young girl.

Her grandmother gave her a gentle shove. "Well, child, you must go now. You've packed everything you want to take with you, haven't you?"

Dawan stared at her blankly, then shook her head. "No, no, I can't go yet!" she blurted out. "Please Grandmama, I'm not ready. I haven't packed everything yet. There's the sunrise I want to take, and the bridge over the river-bend. And, oh Grandma, how can I pack Kwai, and home here, and the chickens, even the bullfrogs in the forest, and . . ." She could feel a sob rising from her throat, but could not stop it.

Already it seemed as if these precious drops of childhood were slipping through her fingers, like sun sparkles when she washed her hands in the river. Dawan glanced down at her one outstretched hand, and it looked so small, so helplessly empty. She wept then, shoulders hunched over as sob after sob was wrenched[c] from her thin frame.

The old woman reached out and cupped her granddaughter's ears with her hands, but Dawan only shook them off.

"Let me cry, Grandmama," she sobbed brokenly.

So the grandmother withdrew her hands, and waited patiently until Dawan's sobs began to subside.[c]

After a while the gentle older woman got up and went to the rain-barrel. There, she picked up a small jar and scooped some fresh rainwater into it. Walking back to where the lotus bud lay on the matting, she bent over and put it carefully in the jar.

Dawan wiped away her tears with the back of her hand, and

watched curiously. There was a solemnity about her grandmother's movements that suggested a sacred⁹ ritual,⁹ like the sprinkling of holy water over a newlywed couple.

It was not until the old woman had unhurriedly reseated herself beside Dawan that she handed the glass jar to her granddaughter.

"Hold on to this lotus carefully, child," the grandmother said. "Watch it unfold during your long bus ride to the City. It's like yourself, this lotus bud, all shut up tight, small and afraid of the outside. But with good water and strong sunlight, it'll unfold, petal by petal by petal. And you will too, Dawan, you will unfold too."

Check the Skills

Understanding the Selection

1. Why do you think Dawan suddenly felt that maybe she didn't want to leave home after all?

2. How did her grandmother help her make the important decision to go as planned?

3. Do you think Dawan might regret her decision? Why or why not?

Comprehension Skills Critical Reading

4. Which of the following sentences from the story states a fact? Which states an opinion? What clues help you decide?

> It's a good thing you didn't run off for the day.
> I have put your new clothes and shoes on the matting.

Literary Appreciation Skills Story Elements

5. This selection is an example of an omniscient point of view. Why do you suppose the author chose this point of view rather than the first person?

   This excerpt is from the novel *Sing to the Dawn*. The novel ends as Dawan leaves the village, bound for the city and high school.

Apply What You Learned in Unit 7

The Theme

Leaving Home

1.   Going away from home can be an important step toward independence, even if it's a painful one. Dawan's experience is a good example. But leaving home can be tragic if someone isn't really ready to go or is forced to go. Texas is a sad example. And we react with horror to the true stories of the Navajo in America and the Jews in Germany being driven from their homes.

Think about how these people probably changed because of leaving home.

•   Some people are so excited about traveling or seeing far away places that they leave home eagerly. This is certainly true of most explorers, from Columbus to the astronauts. Can you think of other examples?

The Skills

Comprehension Skills Critical Reading

2. Distinguishing between fact and opinion is an important reading skill. This unit has given you some practice in developing this skill. Remember to use what you have learned as you read advertisements and newspapers. Be especially careful to sort fact from opinion before you decide who to vote for or what product to buy.

3. Remember to watch for words that label opinions and for emotional words. Decide, too, whether the information can be proved and if everybody would accept or agree.

Literary Appreciation Skills Story Elements

4. Next time you read a story, determine whether it is being told from an omniscient or first person point of view. Remember that a first person point of view is limited to what the narrator knows. How will this affect what you find out about people and their activities in the story?

Unit 8

Reactions to Fear

Overview and Purposes for Reading

The Theme

Reactions to Fear

1. How do people and animals react to fear? Do the reactions vary? How?

The Skills

Comprehension Skills Interpretive Reading

2. How can you make your reading exciting?

3. How can you use your imagination to make what you read more interesting to you?

Vocabulary Development Skills Context Clues

4. When you come across a word in your reading that you don't know, how can you figure out its meaning without using a dictionary?

Learn About the Skills

Comprehension Skills Interpretive Reading

Suppose you are reading a newspaper article about dreams. It says that you remember only the dream you had just before waking up. You might react by saying to yourself, "I wonder why that is so." Or you might say, "I don't believe that. I remember all my dreams." Questioning like this can make interesting and exciting things start to happen. You might talk to people about dreams, think more about your own dreams, or read other articles about dreams. In other words, you might **get involved with what you read so that you extend it into your life.** You might add your own thoughts, feelings, and experiences to what the author says, too.

This is one of the things that makes reading exciting. Reading becomes a springboard to help you broaden your experience and understand both the world and yourself better.

Sometimes you may extend your reading very carefully and deliberately. For example, you may check an encyclopedia for more information about an interesting topic you meet in your reading.

Sometimes this kind of follow-up on something you've read is much less planned. For example, reading an article about Martin Luther King, Jr., might make you really stop and think about the nature of violence. Or reading about Marie Curie might remind you that women certainly can and do make successful scientists.

Using what you read doesn't help anyone but you. No one but you *really* knows how you've grown or changed because of what you have read.

It doesn't have to be heavy, though. Just for fun, think back to "Dawan Is Leaving Home," which you read earlier in this book. Let your imagination take you past the end of that story. What might happen to Dawan in her new school? If that wasn't one of your favorite selections, try the same kind of thinking on one you particularly liked.

This unit will help you get into the habit of extending what you read. You'll find it's an enjoyable habit to have!

Vocabulary Development Skills Context Clues

Good readers do not necessarily know in advance the meaning of all the words they meet. Good readers just don't stop or give up when they come across words they don't know. They often simply make a good guess about the meaning of the word and keep right on reading.

Of course, for this to work, you must know how to make good guesses. One way is to use what you already know about the subject to help you figure out what the unknown word probably means. Try an example. Read the following sentence.

> The flame of the candle flickered but did not go out when the wind blew the door open.

Do you know what *flicker* means? If you don't, you can use what you know about candles and flames to make a good guess. Have you ever watched the flame of a candle when there is no wind? when there *is* a wind? What is the difference in the flame? The movement of the candle flame in the wind is called *flickering.* This is the way to use what you know about the topic to make a good guess regarding the meaning of an unknown word. This saves you time and helps you read more smoothly and quickly.

The selections in the following unit contain several words you may not know. Try to guess what these words mean by using what you already know about the subject. However, don't hesitate to use the glossary or a dictionary if good guesses still don't seem to help.

Selection 1

Use the Skills

Understanding the Selection

Manolo Olivar's father, who was a great bullfighter, was killed in the bullring when Manolo was only a baby. Manolo has studied to become the kind of bullfighter his father was. Now he must decide whether this is what he really wants to do.

1. Read the selection to find out how fear affected the lives of Manolo and his father's old friend, Alfonso Castillo.

2. Find out whether Alfonso Castillo thinks that fear is sometimes a good thing.

Comprehension Skills Interpretive Reading

3. One way to extend your reading is to add to your understanding of people by reading about those you would never know otherwise. You will probably never be a bullfighter. And chances are that in "real life" you'll never meet one, either. But you can find out how it might feel to be one by reading this selection.

4. When you have finished reading, decide for yourself what Manolo's decision was about becoming a bullfighter.

Vocabulary Development Skills Context Clues

5. Try using context clues to figure out the meanings of words you don't know. Use what you already know about the subject to make a good guess. Remember that the small letter^c after a word tells you that context clues are there.

SHADOW OF A BULL

Maia Wojciechowska

"Your bull today is called 'Castalon the Second'," said the Count. "It is a fine animal."

Manolo, his eyes on the floor, knew that the Count was waiting for a reply, waiting for assurance^{cg} that he, Manolo, would try his best. But the words would not come.

■ Your own experience in talking with adults, especially adults in authority, will help you decide that *assurance* here means something like "promises."

"Would you leave us alone for a moment?" It was Castillo who had spoken. Manolo did not look up to see the Count leave. But he did look at Alfonso Castillo when he began to speak.

"The fate^c of a brave animal should never be anything but a noble^g death after a noble fight. But it is not the same with a person's fate. A person is not like a fighting bull. A person's life should not be all fighting, but also giving, loving. A person's life is many things. There are many choices: to do the right thing, or to do the wrong thing; to please yourself, or to please others; to be true to your own self, or untrue to it."

For the first time since he had awakened that morning, Manolo felt the reality^g of hearing words and seeing things. It was not that the fear had left him, it was still inside of him, but now his mind was functioning.^c He repeated to himself Castillo's last words. His mother had said almost the same thing to him when she spoke of his father.

"No one but your father really knew why it is that I am sitting here, in this wheelchair, rather than standing next to you." Alfonso Castillo's voice was no longer gruff,^c but soft. "Some ten years ago, a bullfighter who claimed I ruined his career by my criticism^{cg} of it challenged me to fight a bull. I could have laughed him off. At first I did. Then I wondered if I had rejected^{cg} the challenge out of intelligence^{cg} or out of cowardice.^{cg} I was on my way to a ranch where I was going to find out the answer when my car ran off the road. I think it was the fear I felt while driving toward the bull that caused the accident. Just thinking about coming face to face with the animal, I discovered how powerful fear can be. While writing about bullfighters, I was aware that they feared the danger of gorings,[g] of death, but I thought them to be brave because they were able to conquer the fear, able to drive it far away from their minds, to be free enough of it to do their jobs. That day, because of the accident, I did not find out if I could do that. But since that day I've encountered other fears, in all kinds of situations. And since that time I have found that you cannot confuse bravery or courage with lack of fear. Real courage, true bravery is doing things in spite of fear, knowing fear.

■ This description can help you understand how a bullfighter feels.

"But I did not mean to talk about myself. I wanted to give you advice. Adults are always doing that; it's one of their occupational hazards.[g] Don't let people push you. If you are honest with yourself, you will do the pushing. But only when it is important, important to you. I knew your father well, maybe better than any other person he ever considered his friend. If he were alive, I am sure you would not be here today. He would have understood that you are not a carbon copy of him, and you would have known it also. I do not think you want to be a bull-fighter. I do not believe you are like your father. Be what you are, and if you don't yet know what you are, wait until you do. Don't let anyone make that decision for you."

■ These comments from Alfonso Castillo help you figure out what decision Manolo will make. They are also a clue to the fact that Manolo has not really wanted to be a bull-fighter.

Castillo waited for Manolo to say something, but there was no need now. Suddenly it seemed that the burden Manolo had carried for so long, weighing him down, was gone.

"Thank you," Manolo said gratefully, "thank you, Señor Castillo, for helping me to make a decision."

Check the Skills

Understanding the Selection

1. What caused fear in Manolo? What had happened to Alfonso Castillo because of his fear?

2. Does Alfonso Castillo think that fear can be a good thing? Why do you think as you do?

Comprehension Skills Interpretive Reading

3. How do you think it would feel to be a bullfighter? Remember to think beyond what the story says. Add your own thoughts to those of the author.

4. What decision do you think Manolo made about being a bullfighter? Why do you think so?

Vocabulary Development Skills Context Clues

5. Because you do not have experience with bullfighting, you probably couldn't figure out the meaning of *gorings* in this sentence:

    They feared the danger of gorings, of death.

    Remember to use the glossary or a dictionary when context clues don't seem to help with an unknown word.

Selection 2

Use the Skills

Understanding the Selection

1.   The following article describes a real situation in the life of a hermit crab. See if you agree with the author's idea that the crab might react with fear.

2.   Find out why the hermit has to go up on the beach in spite of the danger.

Comprehension Skills Interpretive Reading

3.   As you read, try to imagine what life is like to a hermit crab.

4.   Think about other ways in which you might extend into your own life something you have read in an article like this.

Vocabulary Development Skills Context Clues

5.   Remember that using what you already know about a subject can help you figure out what some words mean.

SPRING COMES TO THE OCEAN

Jean Craighead George

The first outward sign of spring in the ocean was a lazy drift of seaweed. The sargassum weed^c left the stillness of the winter sea and moved in rafts^g and floes^g northward in the Gulf Stream.

A hermit crab at the edge of the water on Florida's Key Largo felt the warming of the water. He ran up the cool beach with just his feet sticking out of his gray and sea-worn conch shell. At a pile of seaweed he stopped.

He saw the beach. That was important! And he saw the shells splattered over it. Shells were the most necessary things in the world to this crab. He climbed onto the seaweed. His thousand-faceted compound^g eyes saw a conch shell a thousand times. In his mind's eye, however, he saw only one shell, just as our two eyes bring but one picture to our brain. He ran toward the shell, for he was about to molt^c and grow bigger and he could not stay in his old house another day. He pinched the shell. A hard foot shot out and clamped his. The hermit crab turned away. The shell was occupied by another of his kind who would fight until death to keep his home.

As he came to fallen palm fronds,^{g} he felt his outside coat loosen at his back. It would soon drop away, and he would have to shed it. At that time he must have a shell.

Most of the other hermit crabs on the beach were not in his predicament.^{cg} Some had carried empty shells in their big left claws for weeks. So had this crab. But during the night a fisherman had dropped anchor on him, and he had snapped into his shell in alarm. The anchor had rolled over beside him. But when the crab reached out to snatch his precious shell again, it was gone! Another hermit crab had snatched it and was toting^c it behind a coral fin. The hermit could not get it back.

■ Think how big an anchor would look to a crab.

There was little time to waste; he turned immediately to find another shell. By dawn he was still unsuccessful, and so he had come ashore for a last desperate search before the birds awoke.

Just as he was leaving the sea, the hermit crab took a deep draught[c] of water, filling his mouth and wetting his gills so that he could travel on land. With the sea in his body he could stay ashore for several hours. The water bubbled and circulated around his mouth as he crawled over the brown leaves.

Beyond a seed pod of the royal palm he "felt" an empty shell. His need catapulted[cg] him over the pod, and down upon the hermit holding the shell. The other crab was smaller than he. His grip on the shell was light, and he held it at a distance. As the time to change shells draws near, the hermits clutch their new homes tighter and hold them closer.

The first hermit slammed his pincer on the edge of a big conch. He pulled. The defending hermit pulled back.

They fought many minutes. Suddenly the first crab's eyes saw sea gull wings. The birds had awakened. He snapped into his shell. The second one grabbed his conch shell and ran. A gull saw him move and dropped from the sky. As the gull snatched the little runner in its hard beak, the crab let go of the shell. It tumbled and rolled into the palm fronds. The first hermit waited until the shadow of the bird was gone. Then he thrust his head out. Where his opponent[cg] had been lifted into the air lay the empty shell.

He dashed to it. He ran with it into a pile of dried seaweed. Among the twisted leaves he found a dome-shaped room.

For a moment he rested. Then he came out of his shell, halfway, feeling a strange hermit-crab fear. He now had to shift shells, the most dangerous event in the life of a hermit. First he unhooked the muscle at the spiral end of his old shell. Then he pulled himself out. He stood vulnerable,[cg] so that even a windblown grain of sand could kill him. His exposed belly was so delicate^c that a nodding grass blade could cut him in half. But he must change! He slashed his tail through the air and stuck it into the new shell. Backing carefully, he reached his tail down and around until he felt the last coil of the shell. Then he hooked onto it with a grip so strong that few could pull him out. When at last he had a firm hold, he contracted^g all his muscles and slammed himself deep into the shell. It was big and roomy. He relaxed.

■ It is easy to get interested in the remarkable information presented in this article. You could follow up by checking other sources for facts about crabs.

Check the Skills

Understanding the Selection

1. Do you think that a hermit crab might feel fear the way people do? Why or why not?

2. Why was it absolutely necessary for the hermit to go up onto the beach? What might have happened to him if he hadn't left the water?

Comprehension Skills Interpretive Reading

3. If a hermit crab could talk, how do you think he would describe his life and how he feels about it? Use your own imagination as well as what you read in the article.

4. How else could you extend this article outside of this book? The last marginal note gave you one idea. What others can you think of?

Vocabulary Development Skills Context Clues

5. Were you able to make a good guess about the word *predicament* in the following sentence from the selection? Or did you need to use the glossary?

> Most of the other hermit crabs on the beach were not in his predicament.

Use the Skills

Understanding the Selection

Jumping down seven steps may not seem like a big accomplishment to you. But to Mikael, who is younger than you are and who has asthma, it is something he wants very much to do. He hasn't been able to do it yet because he has such a hard time breathing whenever he tries. His asthma causes him to wheeze and feel that he can't catch his breath.

1. Read the selection to find out why you think Mikael tries to jump each time from a higher step, even though his asthma makes him feel afraid.

Comprehension Skills Interpretive Reading

2. As you read, think about how you might feel if you were Mikael.

Vocabulary Development Skills Context Clues

3. When you come across a word whose meaning you don't know, remember to trust your own general knowledge and make a good guess first.

THE TOP STEP

Gunilla B. Norris

Mikael jumped. His feet hit hard and his head felt jarred.ᶜ But he'd done four steps. Some days he couldn't do that at all. Five were as far as he'd ever dared.

On the fifth step he stood very still. He could see his footprints from the last time he jumped. They seemed small from where he stood. Mikael drew himself up. He wasn't going to think about how far it was. He'd jump from the fifth step, and then there'd be only two more.

Mikael swallowed and then he jumped, landing hard again. His head throbbed.ᶜᵍ But he'd done what he'd done only once before! The warm feeling spread all through him. His breath was coming faster now, and he could feel his cheeks burning with excitement.

■ You'll know what *throbbed* means here if you remember what it's like to be nervous and trying hard.

Now the sixth step, and then there'd be only that last step, the top step!

Mikael felt his toes curl in his brown school shoes—curl around the edge of the sixth step as if to hold on and as if to push off. Could he do it? Could he really do it?

Now he took two deep breaths—breaths so deep that the cool air hurt his chest. Was there a little catchᶜ in his chest? Had he heard a little peep down in it? "Never mind the peep," he scolded himself, "just jump right down."

■ Think back to when you were little and determined to do something, even though you were afraid.

Mikael closed his eyes. His whole body was tight. He couldn't do it. He just couldn't. Now his toes cramped around the edge of the step. And then somehow he let himself drop.

When he landed, he fell down and his head hit the wet sand of the courtyard.ᵍ For a while he just lay there. The enormityᵍ of it! He'd jumped despiteᵍ himself, higher than ever! Why, he'd almost jumped from the top step! It felt as if he had.

Mikael got up. But his legs felt all trembly from being excited and scared. Mikael stumbled, and just then there was Monica coming back from the candy store. She was blowing big bubbles with her new gum. He could make little bubbles that popped right away. But the bubbles Monica could blow were as big as her face and they never popped in her hair or on her nose. She could do so many things Mikael couldn't do. But he'd tell her this time!

"I jumped down the steps!" he cried excitedly.

Check the Skills

Understanding the Selection

1. Why do you think Mikael kept jumping even though he was nervous and afraid?

Comprehension Skills Interpretive Reading

2. How do you think you would feel if you were Mikael and couldn't run and jump the way others do? Does trying to answer that question help you understand Mikael a little better? Why or why not?

Vocabulary Development Skills Context Clues

3. After Mikael jumped and landed hard, his head throbbed. What do you think *throbbed* means? Were you able to make a pretty good guess? If you want to see how close you were, you can look up *throb* in the glossary.

Use the Skills

Understanding the Selection

Stacy lived in western Texas. She was angry with conditions at home, so she ran away. After she had calmed down a bit, she realized she had walked pretty far out into the desert and didn't know how to get back.

1. Find out how Stacy reacts in a frightening situation.

Comprehension Skills Interpretive Reading

2. Think about what people would have to know and do to survive for any length of time in the desert.

3. Decide for yourself what kind of creature Stacy meets.

Vocabulary Development Skills Context Clues

4. Use what you already know to guess the meanings of some of the words you don't know. Turn to the glossary or a dictionary if you have to. But always try context clues first.

SHELTER FROM THE WIND

Marion Dane Bauer

Stacy's head was light with the heat, her eyes gritty and burning, her tongue thick when she crested[c] a hill and dropped down a gully[cg] where a lone cottonwood tree rustled in the wind. Near the base of the tree, water seeped[c] out from under some rocks and disappeared into the surrounding ground without a trace.

Stacy knelt on the ground and scooped a small hollow at the base of the dampened rocks. Slowly it filled with water. She bent over to drink, feeling the sand between her teeth. Finally, her thirst still unsatisfied but no longer an agony,[g] she crawled into the shade of the cottonwood. Looking around briefly to check for snakes, she lay down with her head pillowed on her arm and was almost immediately asleep.

■ Do you think this was a good thing to do? Why or why not?

The western sky was coloring when she woke up, startled by an approaching loud roar. Hardly having time to recollect[c] where she was, she gathered herself into a ball at the base of the tree and looked through the leaves. A small plane passed over her close and then circled to pass again. That was Mr. Shannon's plane. He was probably out looking for her.

■ If you've ever been startled out of a sound sleep, you should be able to guess what *recollect* probably means here.

Mr. Shannon was a rancher. He had survived the dust bowl years in the 1930's, the dirty thirties people here called them. Now he owned one of the largest ranches in the area. But he always seemed to Stacy to be withered[c] and dry, as though he had never gotten enough water in all the years of prosperity.[g] Stacy held her knees tightly and made herself small in the shade of the tree. The plane had rumbled out of sight before she realized again how thirsty and hungry she was.

Stacy sat watching the sky turn a pale gray, then charcoal. The horizon was a black line—infinitely[cg] distant. She shivered. All of the warmth seemed to leave the air

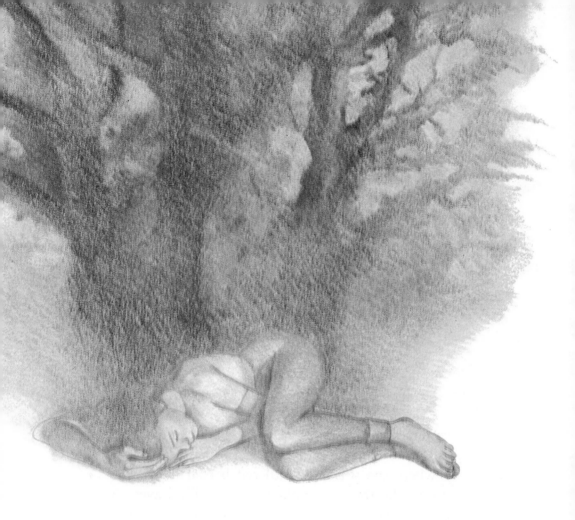

in this high panhandle[g] country the moment the sun set.
She tried again to get some water and then curled up,
pressing herself against the ground for warmth. Her
tongue filled her mouth again. She wondered how long it
took to die of thirst.

The stars were shining pinpricks in a black enamel cup.
There was no moon, and the stars gave only the illusion[g]
of light. The wind soughed.[g] The leaves of the cottonwood tree rattled and whispered constantly. There was
no other sound. She thought about her comfortable bed
at the front of their apartment. The wind sounded different from her bed. Out here the wind cried like a lonely

child, but Stacy didn't cry. She lay still and listened. She felt exposed,⁹ as though night eyes watched her and only she could not see.

Stacy awakened in the darkness to feel breath on her neck. Some shape loomed over her, sniffing. It was like a dream where you are running but are held fast to the ground and your cries of terror are soundless. Stacy closed her eyes tightly. In a moment she would wake up. Something cold and wet touched her cheek, and she screamed. She screamed and screamed, but the creature, whatever it was, had bounded away with her first cry.

■ What kinds of animals do you know that might fit the descriptions underlined?

Check the Skills

Understanding the Selection

1. How did Stacy react to her fearful situation? Why do you think she reacted as she did?

Comprehension Skills Interpretive Reading

2. Describe the desert area where Stacy fell asleep. What would you have to know and do to survive there? What should you take with you?

3. What kind of animal do you think scared Stacy? Was it likely to be a snake? Why or why not? Could it have been a coyote or a mountain lion? Why do you think as you do?

Vocabulary Development Skills Context Clues

4. The note in the margin on page 219 can help you locate the word *recollect*. In your own words, tell what you think it means.

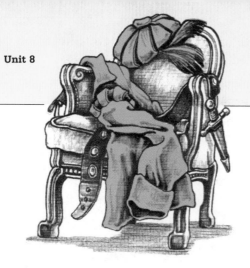

Use the Skills

The next story is about a kind of fear that you may have experienced—the fear of getting up in front of a group of people. As you read you will find out how a young actor named Robin deals with his fear.

The time of this fictional story is the 1500s. The place is a theater in England. A company of actors is putting on the new play *Romeo and Juliet* by William Shakespeare. The play and its author are real, as is the fact that Shakespeare often acted in small parts in his own plays.

As you read, compare Robin's feelings with your own in similar situations. Remember to first make a good guess about the meaning of any unknown words.

This time there are no marginal notes to help. You're on your own!

THE WONDERFUL WINTER

Marchette Chute

From somewhere came the sound of a trumpet, three sharp blasts. It was the signal for the play to begin, and Robin's heart gave an uncomfortable jump and moved into his stomach. His dinner was there already, and the two did not get along well together. He decided that he would sit down to steady his legs.

Robin tried to imagine what it was going to be like, coming out on the stage and facing all those eyes. What if he made a mistake, as he had at the first rehearsal? What if he fell and ruined the play? He could not even remember how the dance in this act began. He tried frantically° to remember, but his brain seemed to have turned to lead.

A group of actors had stationed themselves near him, waiting for their cue.⁹ There was Mr. Shakespeare, who was playing Benvolio, Mr. Burbage as Romeo, and Mr. Sly as Mercutio, along with two boys carrying torches and four hired actors with masks in their hands. They were on their way to Lord Capulet's party. And in a few minutes Robin would have to get up and go there, too. There was nothing he could do to make time stop moving.

Mr. Shakespeare gave him a friendly smile and Robin stared back at him dumbly. His hands were shaking and his feet seemed to be frozen so that he would never be able to move them again.

Mr. Shakespeare leaned forward and put his hand on Robin's shoulder. "Stand up," he said in a low voice, "and take as deep a breath as you can. Then take another one. Everyone gets stage fright° at first, and some of us get it every time the trumpets sound. I do, for one. Pay attention to your breathing and don't think about anything else."

Robin got to his feet. If even the great Mr. Shakespeare was frightened, at least it was not a kind of strange disease that had singled out Robin for special attack. He took a very deep breath, sucking in his stomach and filling his lungs, and held it for as long as he could. Then he took another, concentrating on what he was doing, and noticed that his legs were a little steadier.

His friend Sandy went by, giving him a cheerful grin. "Here we go," he said. "And another one tomorrow."

Robin passed Mr. Purdy, who was gripping the script and following each line with a long careful forefinger and then, all at once, he was on the stage. There was a sea of faces beyond, but Robin did not look at them. He concentrated on Lord Capulet, who was advancing in the splendor^g of a furred scarlet robe with a smile of welcome on his face.

"Come, musicians, play!" said Lord Capulet, and from somewhere came a lively tune, mostly strings but with a fife^g in it

somewhere. Robin found his partner, and to his great surprise his legs did exactly what they had been trained to do. He could feel them moving forward and backward, rising and falling, with no real help from him at all. Nothing seemed to go wrong, and when the music stopped, the roof had not fallen in.

The scene was over. Robin knew the rest of the story, but he was too excited to take off his costume and drop back into the everday world again, so he stood by Mr. Purdy a few minutes and watched the show.

Check the Skills

Understanding the Selection

1. What do you think stage fright is? What was Robin afraid might happen to him out on the stage?

2. What was Shakespeare's advice to Robin about handling his fear? Do you think it's good advice? Why or why not?

Comprehension Skills Interpretive Reading

3. Have you ever been in a situation similar to Robin's? Did that help you understand Robin and the whole selection?

4. Do you think Robin will experience the same feelings before the play begins the following night? What makes you think as you do?

5. How could you find out more about *Romeo and Juliet* and Shakespeare if you were really interested?

Vocabulary Development Skills Context Clues

6. What's your best guess at the meaning of *frantically* in this sentence?

> He tried frantically to remember, but his brain seemed to have turned to lead.

Apply What You Learned in Unit 8

The Theme

Reactions to Fear

1. Many situations can cause fear. Fear is often healthy because it forces us to protect ourselves. Fear can signal a really dangerous situation, as it did for the hermit crab and for Stacy in the desert. Or it can signal a situation that's just uncomfortable or possibly embarrassing, as it did for Robin before the play.

- Think of times of fear you've experienced, observed, or heard or read about in other books. Do you think people are often able to act in spite of being afraid? Do you think fear is a natural and common feeling?

The Skills

Comprehension Skills Interpretive Reading

2. In this unit you found several suggestions of ways to make reading a more exciting experience for yourself. You'll learn to develop your own ways to do this, especially when you read something that really interests you.

    You may have to make a more determined effort when you must read material that isn't about a favorite subject of yours.

    Remember that one way to do this is to think how what you read is related to your own life.

3. Use your imagination to go beyond what the book says. For example, the next time you read a history assignment, think about how it really might feel to live in the time and place described.

Vocabulary Development Skills Context Clues

4. You've seen several examples of ways to use your own experience to make a good guess about the meaning of a word you don't know. You will find this a useful skill whenever you read. Remember that it doesn't always work, though. You may still have to rely on other kinds of context clues or on a dictionary if necessary.

Apply the
Comprehension Skills
You Have Learned

Apply the Skills As You Do Your Schoolwork

The comprehension skills you have learned in this section will be very helpful when you read materials assigned in school. You will see that this is so as you read the following short selection taken from a social studies textbook. In it, you will discover that there is a certain kind of social scientist called a cultural anthropologist. Read to find out what one famous cultural anthropologist learned about two different cultures.

As you read, what you've learned about comprehension skills will be useful. See how by keeping the following questions in mind as you read. After you finish, answer the questions.

1. **Cause-effect relationships.** A cause-effect relationship is stated at the end of the second paragraph. What signal word is the clue? What is the cause? What is the effect?

2. **Main idea.** What is the main idea of the first paragraph? Remember to think of a label that covers the details.

3. **Fact and opinion.** Is the following statement from the selection fact or opinion? How do you know? Think whether it could be proved that Dr. Benedict has these ideas.

   According to Dr. Benedict, the idea of order is basic to Japanese culture, just as the idea of equality is basic to the culture of the United States.

4. **Following up and extending.** Do you agree with Dr. Benedict that equality is basic to the culture of the United States? Why do you think as you do?

Focus on the Social Scientist

Ruth Benedict was a cultural anthropologist who did much of her work "in the field." This means that instead of depending on books, Dr. Benedict observed and studied people living their everyday lives. Ruth Benedict frequently lived with the people of the cultures she studied. She lived, for example, for a time among the people of the Zuni tribe of New Mexico. Today almost every cultural anthropologist lives with the people being studied.

In her famous book *Patterns of Culture*, Ruth Benedict explained her view of culture as a series of patterns which affect every part of life. For example, Dr. Benedict found moderation to be a pattern among the Zunis. That is, the Zunis hardly ever show strong or violent emotions. Sometimes, though, strong emotion cannot be avoided. This is usually true of people in every culture when a relative dies. The Zunis are very sad when a relative dies. However, they try not to show the grief they feel because their basic behavior pattern is one of moderation.

In 1946, Ruth Benedict published a study of Japanese culture called *The Chrysanthemum and the Sword*. In this book, she states that "taking one's proper place" is an important pattern in Japanese culture. Each person has a proper place in relation to other family members and others in the community. According to Dr. Benedict, the idea of order is basic to Japanese culture, just as the idea of equality is basic to the culture of the United States.

Apply the Skills As You Deal with the World

You'll find that you will need to use these comprehension skills when you read material outside of school, too. The following article from a newspaper is an example. It tells about a missing airplane pilot. Read to find out what was strange about this. Discover how the skills work here again by thinking of the following questions as you read. Answer them afterward.

1. **Cause-effect relationships.** There is a cause-effect relationship in the last sentence of the third paragraph. What is the cause? the effect? What is the signal word?

2. **Main idea.** What is the main idea of the fourth paragraph? How do you know?

3. **Fact and opinion.** Is the following a statement of fact or opinion? How did you decide?

    It is possible that he could have become disoriented.

4. **Following up and extending.** What do you think happened to Frederich Valentich? Why do you think as you do? Where would you look to find more information on UFOs?

Missing Australian pilot feared "held by people from another planet"

MELBOURNE, Australia (UPI) —The father of a young pilot missing in a small aircraft since Saturday night said Tuesday he believes his son is alive and being "held by people from another planet."

Frederich Valentich, 20, vanished Saturday night on a flight from Melbourne to King Island, 130 miles to the south. His radio went dead at 7:12 P.M., shortly after he had reported that a mysterious object was hovering over him.

The elder Valentich said that despite an intensive air and sea search, no trace of his son or his Cessna plane had been found. "Since no sign of my son or his plane was found, I believe more strongly that he was taken by some strange people for some reason or another," he said.

Officials said weather conditions at the time Valentich disappeared were ideal, with almost unlimited visibility and a mild breeze. They said Valentich had been flying for 18 months and was compiling hours for his pilot's license. He was not an experienced flyer and never had flown to King Island in darkness before. "It is possible that he could have become disoriented," an official said. "The aircraft could have inverted and he could have seen the reflection of the Cape Otway and King Island light-houses on the clouds above him."

Veteran aviator Arthur Schutt, head of an aviation company, has discounted suggestions that young Valentich was flying upside down.

Valentich's disappearance has revived sighting of UFOs in the state of Victoria.

Bank manager Colin Morgan and his wife reported seeing a large, glowing, star-shaped object hovering in the sky for nearly an hour Saturday night near Geelong, 35 miles southwest of Melbourne.

Barbara Bishop of Queenscliff, a suburb of Melbourne, said she briefly saw "what appeared to be a Ferris wheel" in the western sky about 8:40 P.M. Saturday night, less than two hours after the plane disappeared.

Section 3　Study and Research Skills

Unit 9

Ways and Means

Overview and Purposes for Reading

The Theme

Ways and Means

1.	What procedures, or ways and means, are necessary to do certain things? Is understanding ways and means important when you want to know how to do something?

The Skills

Study and Research Skills Study Techniques

2.	Why is it necessary to know how to follow directions accurately?

3.	What steps can you take to make sure you follow directions accurately?

Vocabulary Development Skills Word Meaning

4.	What are homonyms? How can you figure out the meaning of homonyms you meet in your reading?

Learn About the Skills

Study and Research Skills Study Techniques

Knowing **how to follow written directions** is a skill that is very important, both in school and out of school. The first thing to remember is to read *all* the directions before you start doing anything. This will help you know what you'll end up with! Read the directions in the following paragraph.

> Are you hungry? Try this recipe. First, cut in half lengthwise a long loaf of unsliced French bread. Next, spread both halves with softened butter and some mayonnaise. Then, on the bottom half of the loaf, place slices of salami sausage and boiled ham. On top of the meat, put slices of cheese. Top the cheese with sliced tomatoes and onion. Next, place the top half of the loaf back on to make a long sandwich. Cut it into four pieces. Invite three friends. After you have admired your Poor Boy sandwich, start eating!

If you follow these directions, what will you make? Probably right now you couldn't just go put together the sandwich because you wouldn't remember everything you were supposed to do. You would want to have a copy of the recipe with you in the kitchen, so you could check it as you worked.

That's the second important thing to remember about following directions. You often need to reread them as you do each step.

You can help yourself learn to follow directions by remembering to do the steps listed on the next page. Read them carefully. You may want to refer to them later.

Following Directions

1. Read all the directions before you start to carry them out. Make sure you understand what the end result will be.

2. Figure out what materials you will need. Collect them and, if necessary, make them ready to use. Remember that everything you need may not be listed. You'll have to use common sense, too.

3. Decide what you should do first, second, and so on.

4. Notice any special information you must remember.

5. If there are any illustrations or diagrams, look them over carefully to find out how they can help you.

6. Reread each step before you actually do it.

Think about these steps as you review the recipe. First, you know you will end up with a Poor Boy sandwich if you follow these directions. Second, you will need bread, butter, mayonnaise, salami sausage, boiled ham, cheese, tomatoes, and onions. The directions don't say so, but common sense tells you that you'll need a knife, too. Third, figure out the proper sequence of the steps. Do you put the meat on before or after the mayonnaise? Fourth, there doesn't seem to be any special information you need to remember in this recipe, unless it's to make sure the bread you choose is not sliced in the usual way. Fifth, in this case, there is no illustration or diagram that helps explain.

You'll have a chance to try out your skill in following directions as you read this unit.

Vocabulary Development Skills Word Meaning

There are many words in English that sound alike or are spelled alike, or both, but that are really different words with different meanings. Such words are called **homonyms.** When you come across homonyms in your reading, you need to use your own common sense as well as the sense of the sentence to decide which meaning is intended.

With homonyms that are spelled differently, the spelling can be a clue—if you remember which spelling goes with which meaning! Of course you can turn to a dictionary for help if you need it. Read the sentences below.

1. There are several *deserts* in the southwestern United States.
2. John never *deserts* us when we need him.
3. The careless boy got his just *deserts* when he tripped over his untied shoelaces.
4. My favorite *desserts* are pie and pudding.

By the sense of the sentence, you could figure out that in the first sentence the word *deserts* names something—that is, it is a noun. You probably know that a desert is an area of dry and sandy land. So it is likely that you decided that was the appropriate meaning of the word in that sentence.

In the same way, you probably realized that in the second sentence *deserts* means to go away and leave alone.

You may not have known that *deserts* can also mean deserved or appropriate punishment. But the whole of the third sentence gives you clues that that is likely.

Chances are you had no trouble understanding *desserts* in the last sentence!

You'll get more practice using your skill with homonyms as you go through this unit.

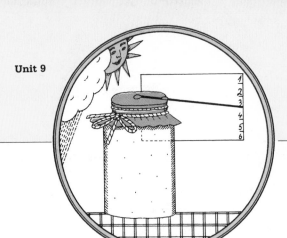

Use the Skills

Understanding the Selection

1.   How would you like to be able to forecast the weather? The following selection explains the ways and means to build a device that will help.

Study and Research Skills Study Techniques

2.   Try your skill in reading directions. Notes in the margin will help. Review the steps on page 236 if you need to.

Vocabulary Development Skills Word Meaning

3.   Decide how you could figure out the meaning of *piece* here if you forgot the spelling clue difference between the words *piece* and *peace*.

BUILD A BALLOON BAROMETER

John Waugh

It's easy to build a simple barometer that you can use to help forecast weather. You'll need a wide mouth jar, such as a peanut butter jar, a large balloon, a broom straw or pipe cleaner, and some glue, paper, and string.

■ Here is the end result and a list of materials.

Smear a little butter around the rim of the jar, and then cut the neck off the balloon so you can stretch the large part over the jar's mouth. Pull the balloon down, and tie it with the string. The rubber cover on the jar should be airtight,[g] so check to see that there are no holes in the balloon or folds at the jar rim; the butter will also help to keep it airtight.

■ More materials and the first steps. Scissors are needed, even though they aren't listed.

Now take the broom straw or pipe cleaner, and glue one end to the middle of the rubber cover so that the straw sticks out six inches or more over the edge of the jar. Put one drop of glue just at the point where the straw rests on the jar's edge.

Changes in the weather are usually accompanied by changes in the weight of the air, or air pressure,[c] which your barometer will measure. When the glue is dry, press lightly in the middle of the rubber with your finger and notice how the free end of the straw moves up and down. As the weight of the air changes, this will make the straw pointer go up and down in the same way, although much more slowly. Moist air, which you can often feel shortly before a rainstorm, is lighter than dry air; this may not seem right, because, of course, water is heavier than air. That is *liquid* water, though. When water evaporates[g] into the air, like steam rising from a teakettle, for example, it becomes lighter than the air. That is why clouds, which are made of water vapor,[c] float high above us.

■ Special information. It tells why a barometer works.

Put the barometer in a place where you can watch it, but where it won't be disturbed for at least several weeks. Behind the straw pointer, arrange a piece of paper with numbers on it to mark the rise and fall of the pointer each day. The barometer must be inside your house where the temperature stays about the same every day. (Changes in temperature can affect it, but this is not what you are trying to measure.) Check your barometer at the same time every day, and write down what number it is pointing to. Observe how the pointer moves with the weather. Quite

■ Does this mean a portion of something or a state of calmness?

■ This illustration shows how to follow the directions. Step 1—materials needed. Step 2—the cover on the jar. Step 3 —the straw in place. The finished barometer is shown on page 238.

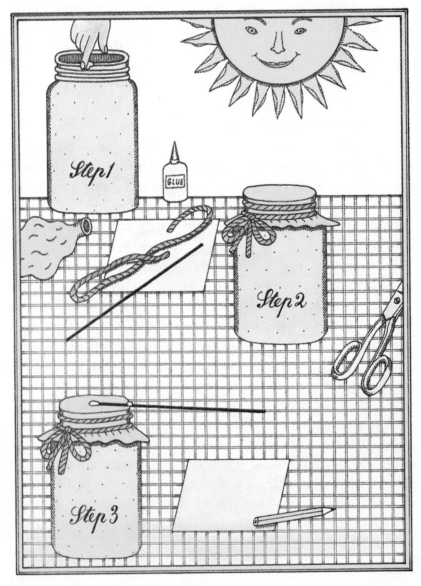

Step 1

GLUE

Step 2

Step 3

often, when the pointer begins to rise, it means that clear days are ahead; if it begins to fall, rain or heavy clouds are probably on the way.

Get a book from your school library that tells what kinds of weather different types of clouds bring. For example, a *thunderhead*,ᶜ a dark cloud that reaches high up into the air, usually means a thunderstorm. If one of these is headed your way, the barometer reading will fall very quickly!

Watch the clouds and your barometer daily; your ability to predict the weather will get better and better.

Check the Skills

Understanding the Selection

1. A barometer can be the means, or the device, to measure changes in air pressure. In what way does this help forecast the weather?

Study and Research Skills Study Techniques

2. Suppose you decided to actually make the balloon barometer described in this selection. How would you use the steps listed on page 236?

Vocabulary Development Skills Word Meaning

3. What does the word *piece* mean on page 240?

Selection 2

Use the Skills

Understanding the Selection

1.   This short selection is fun and easy. It tells how to create an optical illusion, or a sight that appears to be something it is not. Look for a description of the way it works.

Study and Research Skills Study Techniques

2.   These directions are easy to follow. What will be the end result?

3.   What materials will you need?

Vocabulary Development Skills Word Meaning

4.   Decide on the meaning of the word *nail* in this selection.

FLOATING FRANKFURTER

Martin Gardner

To see this curious optical illusion, first place the tips of your index[g] fingers together, holding them about three inches in front of your eyes as shown. Look *past* the fingers, focusing[c] your eyes on something in the distance.

■ You can figure out what materials you need.

Now separate the tips of your fingers about half an inch. You'll see a sausage-shaped finger, with a nail at each end, floating, all by itself, in the air between your fingertips!

■ Is this a metal fastener?

This is what happens. By focusing on a distant point, you prevent the separate images[g] of your finger (one image in each eye) from coming together. Your left eye's image of your left finger and your right eye's image of your right finger overlap to form the solid-looking frankfurter that seems to be floating in space.

Check the Skills

Understanding the Selection

1. In what way does this optical illusion work?

Study and Research Skills Study Techniques

2. What will be the end result of following these directions?

3. What materials do you need? Follow the directions. Did you see the "floating frankfurter"?

Vocabulary Development Skills Word Meaning

4. What kind of nail is referred to?

Use the Skills

Understanding the Selection

1. Driving requires knowledge of special ways and means. Understanding traffic signs is an important one. The following excerpt from a state driver's training manual explains the way some signs direct traffic.

Study and Research Skills Study Techniques

2. Think how your skill in following directions can help you learn to obey these traffic signs when you drive.

Vocabulary Development Skills Word Meaning

3. Context clues and common sense will help you understand the meaning of *post* in this selection.

TRAFFIC SIGNS

When you drive you are responsible for your safety and the safety of others on the roads and highways. Traffic signs help to provide for that safety. You must follow the directions given by the traffic signs.

There are different kinds of highway signs. You must obey them in the same manner as traffic laws. Following are some examples of such signs and their meanings.

The octagon,ᶜ or eight-sided, sign always means stop. When you come to it, you must make a complete stop at a marked stop line before entering the intersection.ᵍ If there is no stop

■ Special information.

line, stop before entering the crosswalk on your side of the intersection. If there is no crosswalk, stop before entering the intersection at a point from which you can best see oncoming traffic. After stopping, you must not start again until you yieldᵍ the right-of-way to pedestriansᵍ and closely approaching traffic, if the intersection is with a through highway. If it is a four-way stop, wait your turn. In either case, you must wait until it is safe to continue.

The sign in the shape of a triangle means yield. You must slow down to a speed that is reasonable for existing conditions and stop if necessary for safety. If you must stop, do so at a marked stop line or a crosswalk. After slowing or stopping you must yield the right-of-way to other vehicles in the intersection or those approaching closely on another roadway, and to pedestrians.

Horizontal⁹ rectangles are generally used for guide signs, which show location, direction, or other special information.

Vertical⁹ rectangles are generally used for regulatory signs, which tell you what you must do in a given situation.

Others shapes are reserved for special purposes. Examples are various shields for route markers and the two crossed panels used at railroad crossings.

The end of a no-passing zone. Warning! Passing still is not allowed unless it is safe to do so.

This sign means that you are to stop at the line when you come to a stop sign or signal, if the stopping place is not located at the sign.

This very important sign is posted on one way streets and other roadways that you cannot enter, including exit ramps from expressways.[9] You will see this sign only if you enter a one way route from the wrong direction.

This sign is usually used, in addition to the "Do Not Enter" sign above, on expressway ramps. It is posted on the exit ramp farther from the crossroad than the "Do Not Enter" sign, and is seen only by traffic about to enter from the wrong direction.

This sign is used at intersections where the signals may be complicated or confusing. It tells you to watch the traffic light which controls the road or lane in which you are traveling.

Sometimes the pictured "4-way" sign is mounted just below a stop sign. It means there are four stop signs at this intersection and traffic from all directions must stop. Depending upon the number of intersecting streets, "3-way" or "5-way" signs may also be used.

These signs prohibit[9] certain kinds of turns. A red circle with a red slash from upper left to lower right means NO. The picture within the circle shows what is prohibited.

This sign tells you where to drive when approaching traffic islands, medians[9] or obstructions in the center of the roadway. You must drive to the side indicated by the arrow.

  You may go only in the direction of the arrow.

  The larger sign gives you advance warning; the smaller tells what the speed limit is.

 Signs like this always inform you of the maximum speed limit.

To help make our roads and highways safe, drivers must always obey traffic signs.

■ This is the reason for following directions.

Check the Skills

Understanding the Selection

1. Signs are one means of directing traffic. What are some others?

Study and Research Skills Study Techniques

2. How can knowing how to follow directions help you learn to drive? How can it help you as you drive?

Vocabulary Development Skills Word Meaning

3. What helped you decide that *post* in the selection did not have the same meaning as it does in *post office*?

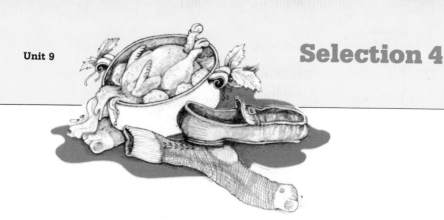

Use the Skills

Understanding the Selection

1. Most people do not agree with the old saying "the end justifies the means." This saying means that if a goal is worthwhile, it is acceptable to do anything to achieve it. See if you think the end justifies the means described in the humorous poem on the next page.

Study and Research Skills Study Techniques

2. If you follow these directions, what will be the end result?

Vocabulary Development Skills Word Meaning

3. Decide how you could know that *sew* was meant instead of *so* in the poem if you didn't see the spelling.

MY RULES

Shel Silverstein

If you want to marry me, here's what you'll
   have to do:
You must learn how to make a perfect
   chicken-dumpling stew.
And you must sew my holey socks,
And soothe⁹ my troubled mind,
And develop the knack⁹ for scratching my back,
And keep my shoes spotlessly shined.
And while I rest you must rake up the leaves,
And when it is hailing and snowing
You must shovel the walk . . . and be still when I talk,
And—hey—where are you going?

■ The end result.

■ What's the homonym for this word?

Check the Skills

Understanding the Selection

1.   Do you think the end justifies the means that are described in the poem?

Study and Research Skills Study Techniques

2.   What is the end result mentioned?

Vocabulary Development Skills Word Meaning

3.   How could you know that *sew* and not *so* was meant in the poem if you only heard it?

Use the Skills

It may surprise you to learn that your score on a test tells more than how well you know the subject. Your score also tells how well you take tests. The following selection describes some helpful ways and means of test-taking. Perhaps it will help you raise your test scores!

You'll need to remember your skill in following directions as you read. Homonyms should pose no problem in this selection. This time there are no marginal notes to help you. You're on your own!

HOW TO TAKE A TEST

Megan Lee

You *can* improve your test scores! Of course you know that to get a good grade on a test you must study well and know the subject. But you can also help yourself get better scores by learning how to take a test.

First of all, be prepared. Study the material that will be covered by the test. Organize your study time so that you can get a good night's sleep before taking the test. You'll do much better if you're rested and relaxed. Try to feel confident rather than worried. Worry and tension make it harder to think clearly.

When you get the test, read all the directions very carefully. Make sure you understand exactly what to do. Many points can be lost, for example, if you mark only one answer to multiple-choice questions when the directions tell you more than one may be correct.

After you read the directions, take a few minutes to look over the whole test. Don't read it. Just get an idea of how long it is and what sections or different types of questions it has. Figure out in a general way what is expected of you.

Be sure to schedule your time. Find out how much time you are allowed. See if some sections of the test are worth more points than others. If so, plan to spend more time working on those. Reserve some time for review after you have finished the whole test.

Begin taking the test by first answering all the questions that are easy for you. Questions that give a choice of answers should be done first. These are called objective questions. They may be true-false, multiple-choice, or matching questions. Essay questions which require you to write a paragraph or more will take longer and should be done later. If you start with the essay questions, your time for taking the test may be up before you have time to answer the objective questions!

Read each question and all its possible answers very carefully before you answer. Think about what you are doing. It is easy to lose points through carelessness.

In true-false questions, watch for words in the question that hint at the answer. Words such as *always, never, all,* and *none* tell you that to be true the statement must have no exceptions.[9] Words that indicate an exception is possible include *many, some, usually, often,* and *more.*

Pay attention to the information given in the questions. You may learn an answer to another question elsewhere on the test.

It is usually a good idea to guess, if you don't know an answer. Usually test directions will tell you if you should not guess.

If you come to a question you don't know, make a note by it. Then quickly guess at the answer and mark your guess. Your little note, perhaps a check mark or an asterisk, will show you where those guesses are after you have completed all the easy questions. It is better

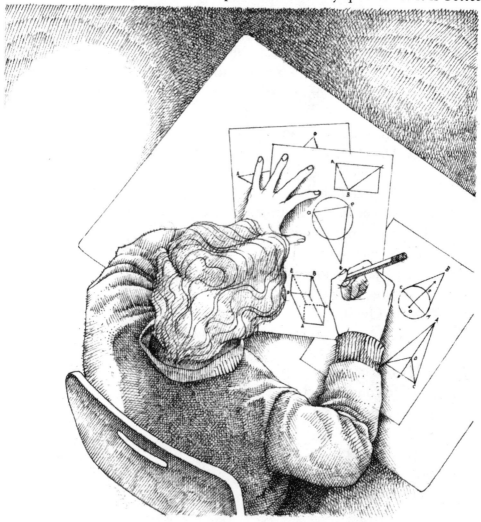

to guess than to leave the answer blank. One reason is that you can't possibly get credit for an unanswered question. With a guess, at least you have a chance. And you may not have the time to go back to the question. Also, it takes time to read a question and to think about it, even if what you think is "I don't know this one." So you might as well guess, since you have already invested time in the question.

After you have finished all the questions that were easy, review. Try to answer or guess at any you did leave blank. Check your answers if there is time.

Remember that taking tests is a skill that improves with practice. The more tests you take, the better you'll do it!

Check the Skills

Understanding the Selection

1. What are some of the ways and means of test-taking? Do you think they can help you? Why or why not?

Study and Research Skills Study Techniques

2. The selection didn't list any materials needed to take tests. What supplies do your common sense and experience tell you will be necessary?

Vocabulary Development Skills Word Meaning

3. Suppose your teacher said the following sentences to you. How would you know the difference in meaning between the homonyms *allowed* and *aloud?*

    You are *allowed* thirty minutes for this test. Do not talk *aloud* as you take it.

Apply What You Learned in Unit 9

The Theme

Ways and Means

1. Understanding ways and means is important when you want to know how to do something. In this unit you found several examples. The "Floating Frankfurter" is an interesting one. The poem is a silly example! It would be both interesting and useful to build the barometer. And the ways and means of test-taking and understanding traffic signs are really necessary to know.

•   Knowing how something works can be valuable even if it's not an activity you want to carry out yourself. For example, it will help you be a better citizen if you understand the ways and means of the government. Someday you may have your own car. You may not want to be a mechanic. You may not want to repair your car yourself. But it would still be a good idea to know generally how a car works. Why do you think this is so?

The Skills

Study and Research Skills Study Techniques

2.   This unit has shown you some different types of directions. To get good results, you need to follow directions carefully. Use what you learned about following directions in your classes in gym, science, and math. Follow the directions about test-taking in all your classes!

3.   Remember the steps on page 236. They will help you follow directions well.

Vocabulary Development Skills Word Meaning

4.   Most of the time, homonyms you meet in your reading will not trouble you. If they do, remember to use context clues, the sense of the sentence, and your own common sense.

Unit 10

Understanding Nature

Overview and Purposes for Reading

The Theme

Understanding Nature

1. How can you better understand nature? Why is it important to do? How can modern science sometimes help?

The Skills

Study and Research Skills Parts of a Book

2. How can you get information from a graph?

3. What steps can you follow to figure out graphs?

Literary Appreciation Skills Style and Intent

4. How can you "read between the lines" to better understand what the author's purpose is? Why is it sometimes important to figure out what an author is trying to say to you?

Learn About the Skills

Study and Research Skills Parts of a Book

Factual information is often presented in the form of graphs. Graphs summarize facts and their relationship to each other in a way that is usually quicker and easier to read than a long explanation written in sentences.

To read graphs efficiently, you need to do the following things.

How To Read Graphs

1. Read the title or caption to find out what information the graph will give you.

2. If there is a key to symbols or abbreviations, look at it carefully.

3. If it is the kind of graph or table that is presented in columns:

   a. Read the labels of the columns across the top or bottom of the graph. Also read the labels down the side.

   b. Find specific information by locating the spot where the bar, line, or symbol in an up-and-down column meets the one in a column going across.

Try the Skill. Suppose you wanted to find out about the home runs hit by Babe Ruth when he played in the World Series. It would be easier to get some facts from a graph like the one on the next page than from a long article about the history of the World Series. Look at the graph. Then use the steps above to answer the questions that follow the graph.

Babe Ruth's Fifteen World Series Home Runs

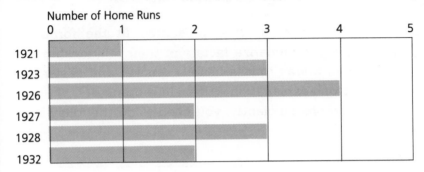

Number of Home Runs

| | 0 | 1 | 2 | 3 | 4 | 5 |

1921
1923
1926
1927
1928
1932

1. What information does the graph give you?

2. Is there a key to abbreviations or symbols?

3. a. What are the labels of the columns across the top? What do they mean? You're right if you decided the labels are 0, 1, 2, 3, 4, and 5 and that they indicate the number of home runs.

   What are the labels of the columns down the side? What do they mean? The labels 1921, 1923, 1926, 1927, 1928, and 1932 are the years in which Babe Ruth hit home runs in the World Series.

   b. In which year did Ruth hit the most world series home runs? At a glance you'll see that 4 is the highest number. Follow that bar back to the label 1926.

   How many home runs did Ruth get in 1928? This time find 1928 at the side. Follow the bar across. Then follow the line where the bar ends up to the line's label at the top. You'll see that Ruth hit 3 homers in 1928.

You'll have a chance to learn more about reading graphs as you go through this unit.

Literary Appreciation Skills Style and Intent

Authors usually have a certain purpose for writing. They may want to entertain. They may want to help you understand the world. Or they may want to persuade you to act or think in a certain way. It often helps you to better understand what you read if you try to figure out the author's purpose. Read the following paragraph. Think about the author's purpose.

> <u>A crossing guard has not been assigned to the intersection of Wood and Central Streets.</u> I estimate that twenty to thirty pupils would normally cross Central at this point. Now they must walk two blocks down Central and cross at either Green or Scott Street. Rather than do that, some cross at Wood. <u>This can be dangerous because of the heavy traffic on Central at all hours of the day.</u> There are two large schools just north of Central. They could divide the small cost of a crossing guard. The PTA should look into this matter.

By paying attention to the words and phrases used, you can figure out that this author's purpose is to persuade. The first sentence underlined gives straightforward factual information. But the author shows concern about the situation, as shown in the second sentence underlined. This writer draws a conclusion regarding what should be done, how it could be done, and who could do it. So she is trying to convince you to agree and perhaps to help accomplish that goal.

Sometimes an author's purpose is very clear and is stated. Other times you may have to "read between the lines" to figure it out.

As you read the selections in this unit, try to determine what purpose each author had for writing.

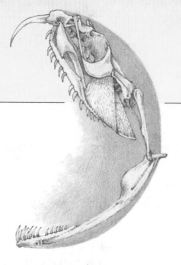

Use the Skills

Understanding the Selection

1.   Read the selection to find out how to recognize some common poisonous snakes of North America. Notice that the picture above shows the open jaws of a snake skeleton.

2.   Modern science has taught us about poisonous snakes. Look for examples of information that people of one hundred years ago probably didn't know.

Study and Research Skills Parts of a Book

3.   The graph for this selection presents two kinds of information about snakes. You'll have to read the key to find out what each color means. When a bar stops between numbers, you will have to estimate where the bar stops. Use your skill in reading graphs to figure out the information presented in the graph. Marginal notes will help you. Look back at the steps on page 259 for help if you need it.

Literary Appreciation Skills Style and Intent

4.   As you read, think about the author's purpose for writing the article. Is it to inform, to entertain, or to convince? Remember to pay close attention to the way the author presents the information.

OUR POISONOUS SNAKES

George Laycock

All who roam the outdoors should recognize poisonous snakes. North America's poisonous snakes are coral snakes and pit vipers. Pit vipers include copperheads, cottonmouth water moccasins, and rattlesnakes. All have small openings between their eyes and nostrils.[g] These are heat sensing organs that help snakes locate prey.[g]

Most poisonous snake bites do not cause death. But all are dangerous and require a doctor's care at once. The best advice is to stay alert[g] and use common sense.

In snake country, wear long trousers and high boots. Watch where you walk or sit. Don't put your hands onto rocky ledges or logs where you can't see, or step over logs without first looking on the other side.

Snakes stay out of the way of people if they can, but are likely to strike if they are touched or surprised. They do not have to be coiled to bite.

Poisonous snakes are part of the balance of nature. There is usually no reason for killing one. The following descriptions will help you recognize some of the more common venomous[c] North American snakes.

■ The author tells you, in this sentence, that his purpose for writing the article is to help you recognize poisonous snakes.

Timber Rattlesnake. Most often seen in the eastern U.S., timber rattlers live along rocky ledges, but move through the forest searching for food. They average 4 feet in length, with a 1½-foot striking distance. Their bite can be fatal[g] to humans. They eat small rodents,[g] birds, toads, and squirrels.

Prairie Rattlesnake. This greenish-yellow snake, with brownish patches on its back and a V-shaped mark above each eye, measures 2½ to 5 feet. It is found across the Great Plains to the Pacific and from Mexico to Canada. Its major food is rodents. Prairie rattlesnakes inflict more bites on people and livestock than any other rattler. People bitten by them usually survive.

Sidewinder. This desert rattlesnake is famous for traveling sideways, leaving curved parallel⁹ tracks in the sand. It hunts at night, mostly mice and lizards. Only 1½ to 2½ feet long, it is usually sand-colored to match the desert. It can be recognized by the small "horns" above its eyes. In daytime, it stays cool and avoids humans by burying itself in the sand.

Eastern Diamondback. This is the largest rattlesnake. Adults average 5 feet. However, giants more than 8 feet long have been recorded. Large enough to swallow a cottontail rabbit, these snakes also eat squirrels and birds. Their bite can be extremely dangerous. This giant reptile is native to the southeastern United States, especially Florida. The eastern diamondback snake is dark, yellowish-gray with large diamond-shaped patches on its back.

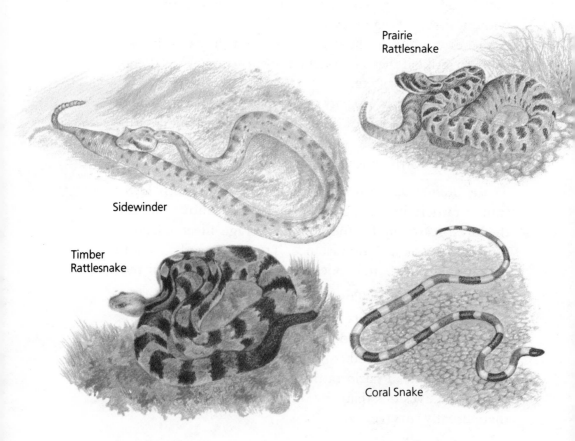

Prairie Rattlesnake

Sidewinder

Timber Rattlesnake

Coral Snake

Western Diamondback. Second only to its eastern cousin in size, this heavy-bodied rattler may reach lengths of more than 6 feet and weigh 8 pounds or more. The average adult is 4 to 5 feet long. The largest ones live in Texas and New Mexico. A western diamondback is often found in rocky canyons where it hunts rodents. It is quick to coil and strike if it is threatened.[c]

Water Moccasin. When threatened, this reptile displays the snow-white inside of its mouth. The "cottonmouth" lives in shallow water in southern states. Northern moccasins are non-poisonous. Cottonmouths may grow to 5 feet, are heavy-bodied, and are dark-colored with indistinct[g] markings. They are often aggressive[cg] and short-tempered. The cottonmouth carries a strong poison, although adult humans usually survive its bite.

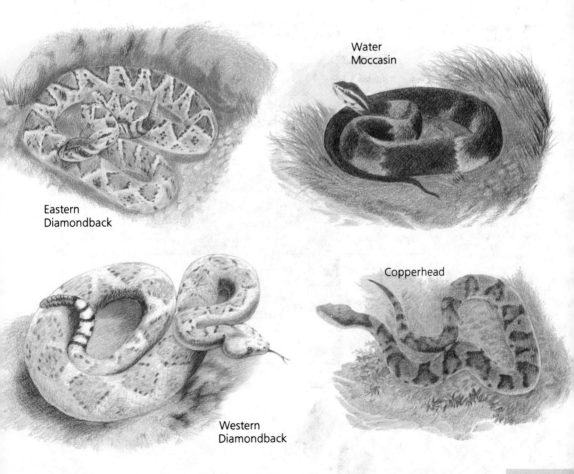

Water Moccasin

Eastern Diamondback

Copperhead

Western Diamondback

Copperhead. This pit viper lives in the eastern and southern states. Seldom more than 36 inches long, adults are brownish in color, with dark hourglass markings on the back. On hot days, they hide in rocky crevices and beneath logs. They eat frogs, snakes, and mice. The bite is seldom fatal to adult humans.

Coral Snake. These secretive beauties carry powerful neurotoxic⁹ poison. Instead of striking, they hang on and chew while poison flows into the wound. Eastern coral snakes reach 3 feet in length. Sonoran coral snakes, found in Arizona, New Mexico, and Mexico, are much smaller. Coral snakes resemble the colorful, non-poisonous scarlet snakes. But unlike scarlet snakes, the red and yellow bands of the coral snake touch each other. Coral snakes burrow°⁹in the ground and are seldom seen.

■ Remember that numbers on a graph can stand for different things. In the first graph you saw, the numbers 1, 2, 3, 4 stood for number of home runs. Here the numbers tell how many feet.

■ The key tells you that the lengths are shown in feet and that there are two kinds of measurements. Because some of the measurements are given in feet and inches, a bar may stop between numbers.

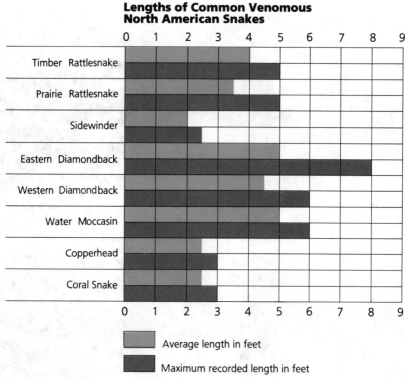

Lengths of Common Venomous North American Snakes

Average length in feet

Maximum recorded length in feet

Check the Skills

Understanding the Selection

1. How can you recognize a prairie rattlesnake? an eastern diamondback? What kind of snake would you be on the lookout for if you saw curved tracks in the sand?

2. Why do you think people should be able to recognize poisonous snakes? Is this a good example of the importance of understanding nature? Why or why not?

Study and Research Skills Parts of a Book

3. a. What information does the graph in this article give? What do the red bars on the graph stand for? the blue bars? What do the numbers across the top and bottom of the graph stand for?

   b. What is the longest poisonous snake ever found in North America? You should be able to tell at a glance by finding the longest blue bar. Follow it back to the label at the side. That label is the answer.

Literary Appreciation Skills Style and Intent

4. The author tells you directly that his purpose is to help you recognize poisonous snakes. Do you think, after reading the rest of the article, that he stated his purpose correctly? Do you feel you learned something about snakes from this article that you didn't already know?

Use the Skills

Understanding the Selection

1.   Read the next selection to find out how modern science has helped Sweden develop ways to conserve energy.

2.   Think about why it is important for all of us to conserve energy. How is an understanding of nature important before we can do this?

Study and Research Skills Parts of a Book

3.   Notice how some of the information in the article is summarized by the graph. Both compare the energy use of Sweden and the United States. The graph gives percentages.

Literary Appreciation Skills Style and Intent

4.   You know that the author's purpose in the first selection was to inform you. See if you think the author of the next selection had the same purpose.

CONSERVING ENERGY

Jack Myers

Of all the countries of the world, the United States is the biggest energy user. Now we are faced with the problem of getting enough energy. In spite of what we would like to think, the problem is not going to go away. It can only get tougher. It is easy to see that one of the things we must do is to use energy more carefully.

■ The author doesn't state his purpose directly. But you get the impression that he wants to convince you that the United States can use energy more carefully.

Although there is a lot of talk about it, we really have not done much about conserving[cg] energy. We have lived a long time with cheap and easy-to-get energy. We still haven't gotten used to the idea that energy is becoming harder and harder to get. It is as if we are beginning to play a new ball game with a new set of rules. The game does not even have a name yet. But we know how it must be played: How do we live best with the least use of energy? Sweden has been playing the game for a long time. Maybe we can learn from the Swedes.

The Swedes have about the same standard[g] of living that we do, yet their energy use is only about 60 percent of ours. How do they do it? Recently a number of studies have been reported comparing ways of life and energy use in Sweden and in the United States. No two countries are alike, so comparisons have to be made with care. Sweden is a much smaller country with only about 8 million people. So we had better make the comparison on a *per capita basis.*[c] That means comparing in terms of the average person.

There are many ways in which the Swedes have learned to play the game of energy conservation better than we do. For example, they use only about one-third as much electricity for lighting as we do. However, making all kinds of comparisons is just too much, so let's talk about three important uses of energy.

First, there is use of energy in homes, mostly for heating. Sweden has a colder climate and longer winters than most of the United States. The problem of heating homes is about like that in some of our northern states, such as North Dakota. Yet the Swedes spend only about three-fourths as much energy in homes as we do. Their houses are so much better insulated[cg] that they have half as much heat loss as our houses. Their houses cost more to build but use much less energy for heating.

A second big use of energy is industrial,[c] as in factories. Here again Sweden uses its energy more carefully. It uses more waste material for fuels. It saves waste heat from electrical power plants by using hot water to heat homes and factories.

The third big use of energy is for transportation, or moving people and freight. Transportation is less of a problem in Sweden because its cities are not so far apart. But here again the Swedes are more careful. They use smaller cars. They have built mass transit[g] systems with good service. All put together, they spend less than half as much energy for transportation as we do in the United States.

In learning to play the energy game, the Swedes have a head start. How did they get ahead? I think the answer is clear. For over a hundred years the United States has lived on cheap and easy-to-get sources of energy. Except for their hydroelectric[g] power from dams, Sweden's energy needs have had to be supplied from fuels bought from other countries and shipped in. Energy has been expensive and hard to get for a long time. No wonder Sweden is way ahead of us in learning to play the energy game. How do we live best with least energy? I think we can learn a lot about that game from the Swedes.

**Comparative Use of Energy Per Person
United States and Sweden**

■ The title tells you what the graph is about.

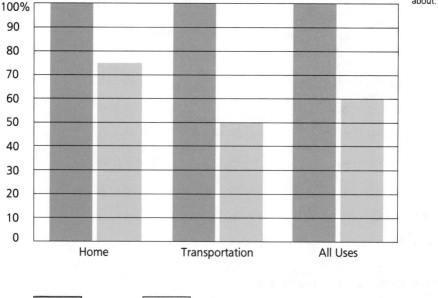

Home   Transportation   All Uses

■ U.S.   ■ Sweden

■ This key tells you which column represents each country.

Check the Skills

Understanding the Selection

1. How does Sweden conserve energy?

2. Why must we conserve energy? How can understanding nature help us learn to do this?

Study and Research Skills Parts of a Book

3. How did you figure out what the graph was about? How did you know which column represented which country? What do the figures on the left side of the graph stand for?

Literary Appreciation Skills Style and Intent

4. What was the author's purpose for writing this selection?

Selection 3

Use the Skills

Understanding the Selection

1. Read the selection to find out how the understanding of nature has helped people develop airplanes.

2. Discover how birds are so well designed for flight.

Study and Research Skills Parts of a Book

3. The graph with this selection uses percentages as did the graph in the last selection. But the information is presented here in the form of a circle. There are no bars or columns. Remember to read carefully the title and the label in each part of the circle.

Literary Appreciation Skills Style and Intent

4. Notice that this selection is written by the same person who wrote the first selection in this unit. Decide if his purpose for writing this article is the same as for the first selection. Note the humorous manner in which he presents some of the information.

DESIGNED FOR FLIGHT

George Laycock

Birds have been flying for millions of years. But people never really got off the ground in a heavier-than-air craft until the last century, when students of bird flight made the first successful gliders.

Since then we have made wonderful progress in flying. But the truth is that even in our fanciest multi-million-dollar aircraft we are still pretty clumsy^c compared with a blue jay. What we long dreamed of doing, birds do easily because from end to end they are designed for flight.

■ This gives a good idea of the author's purpose. It sets the tone for the rest of the selection.

Consider a bird's feather. All birds have them and only birds have them. That feather is a miracle of design that engineers envy.

But feathers do not make a bird lightweight. Taken together, a bird's feathers may weigh more than its skeleton. In Florida a scientist counted the feathers taken from an immature^g bald eagle and found that there were 7,182 of them. They made up 16 percent of the eagle's weight, more than double the weight of his skeleton.

These remarkable feathers help birds in several ways. They form a smooth surface over which air flows. They form a shield^c against injury. Besides, feathers insulate against the weather.

Birds must be lightweights if they are to get off the ground. A bird's mouth is a bill of tough material. This material is lightweight but strong enough to tear meat from bones and dig holes in trees. Birds may have skulls of paper-thin bone. Their bones are lightweight, nearly hollow. The bones may be stronger because of built-in struts, or braces. These struts are so efficient^g that engineers have borrowed the idea to add strength to bridges and the wings of airplanes.

Muscles also help the bird fly. The muscles of the bird's breast and shoulder may move the wings for hours, sometimes days, without rest. In fast-flying birds, these muscles may account for half the total body weight.

Wings also have remarkable design features.[c] They are so streamlined that air flows over them with minimum resistance.[g] And they can be folded back out of the way when not in use. Then they are fitted to the curves of the bird's body.

Feathers on the wing overlap and form a strong supporting surface. As with the wing of an aircraft, the thick leading edge tapers back to the thin trailing edge, producing a curved shape that provides lift.

Study of high-speed movies has shown that in flight a bird's wings move rearward[cg] slightly on the upstroke, forward on the downstroke. On the upstroke, the wing is rotated[g] so that air flows through slots between the feathers. Thus the wing makes a figure-eight motion.

These are some of the things that for ages made people on the ground envy the migrating[g] waterfowl and other birds sailing gracefully overhead.

The bird is a nearly perfect example of efficient flight design—and of nature's exquisite[c] beauty.

This circle graph gives you an idea of how a bird's total body is designed for flight.

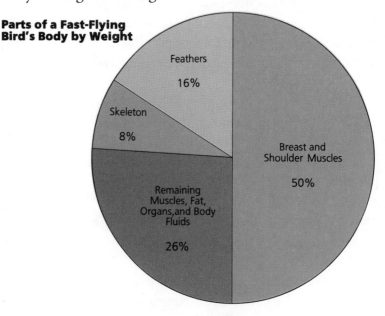

Parts of a Fast-Flying Bird's Body by Weight

Feathers 16%

Skeleton 8%

Breast and Shoulder Muscles 50%

Remaining Muscles, Fat, Organs, and Body Fluids 26%

■ A circle graph is used to show parts of a whole. The percentages, when added, should always equal 100 percent.

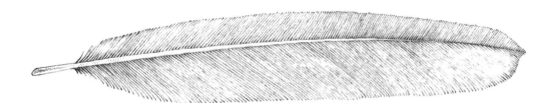

Check the
Skills

Understanding the Selection

1. What parts of a bird's body have people imitated in modern airplanes? Birds' bodies are designed for flight. How does understanding the details of this aspect of nature help people develop airplanes?

2. What makes birds so well suited for flying? Why can't people fly just by flapping their arms?

Study and Research Skills Parts of a Book

3. a. How did you know that the circle graph in this selection uses percentages? Why is the circle graph a good form to use for the information presented in this selection? What percentage of the bird's total body weight does this graph represent?

    b. Did you find this graph easier or more difficult to understand than the graphs in the first two selections? Give reasons for your answer.

Literary Appreciation Skills Style and Intent

4. Was Mr. Laycock's purpose the same for writing this article as it was for writing "Our Poisonous Snakes"? What is the author's purpose in this selection? How do you know?

Use the Skills

Understanding the Selection

This selection compares the height of some of the tallest mountains in the world. Several tall mountains are not included. But this article gives you a summary of some tall mountains of five of the continents.

1. As you read, think about how modern science has improved our ability to measure mountain peaks.

2. Find out why snow-capped mountains can't be measured exactly.

3. Discover how our understanding of nature tells us that we will probably never know exactly how high Mount Everest really is.

Study and Research Skills Parts of a Book

4. Use what you have learned to figure out the graph with this selection.

5. Think about how this graph compares to the graphs in the first two selections.

Literary Appreciation Skills Style and Intent

6. Decide what you think was the author's purpose for writing this article.

GRADING THE GIANT MOUNTAINS

Eric Shipton

The principles of surveying⁹ were known to the ancient Egyptians. But until modern scientific equipment was perfected,ᶜ surveyors could not measure distant summitsᶜᵍ with accuracy.ᶜ An 1836 chart depicts the world's topmost peaks rising one above the other like a huge ice cream cone. It gives first place to Dhaulagiri, which we now know is one of the lesser Himalayas. And it puts Everest in a minor position five peaks below Dhaulagiri. The graph below gives some major peaks of the world their correct order of height.

■ Can you figure out the author's purpose from this statement?

■ Remember to read the caption first to find out what the graph is about. Be sure to note what the numbers stand for.

■ Which is the highest mountain? What continent is it in?

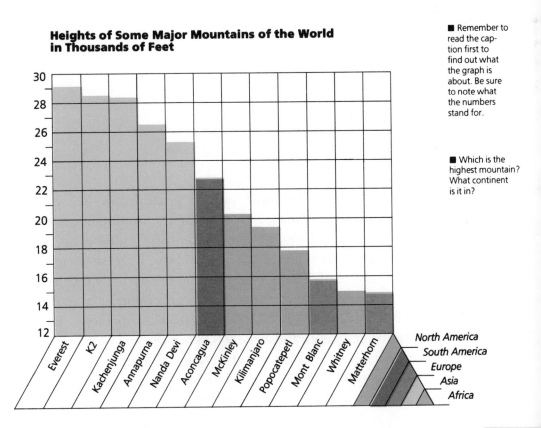

Heights of Some Major Mountains of the World in Thousands of Feet

But even with the most refined instruments, we can never establish a permanent height for any mountain under perpetual⁹ snow. Blizzards are continually building up or blowing away their crestsᶜ of snow and ice. Everest's height is still a subject of debate. Great Britain fixes it at 29,002 feet (8845.61 meters). But most European countries use the metric equivalent⁹ of 29,160 feet (8893.8 meters). The United States has established 29,028 feet (8853.54 meters) as Everest's height. Whichever it may be, Everest is the only peak that tops 29,000 feet (8845 meters). It is beyond doubt the highest mountain in the world.

Check the Skills

Understanding the Selection

1. How have we improved our ability to measure mountain peaks?

2. Why can't snow-capped mountains be measured exactly?

3. Why is there no exact measurement for Everest? How does our understanding of nature explain that we can't measure Everest exactly?

Study and Research Skills Parts of a Book

4. What do the numbers along the side of the graph stand for? How do you know? Which mountain peak is taller, K2 or Kachenjunga? Which continent has the most tall mountains?

5. How is this graph the same as the graph in the first selection? the second selection? How is it different from the graph in the first selection? the second selection? Was this graph easier or more difficult to figure out than the other two? Give reasons for your answer.

Literary Appreciation Skills Style and Intent

6. What do you think the author's purpose was for writing "Grading the Giant Mountains"? Why do you think as you do?

Use the Skills

A comet looks like a moving star with a long tail. Comets were once thought of as visitors from space. Some people thought they were signs that something disastrous was going to happen. But we now know what comets are like and how they behave. In the late 1600s, Edmund Halley discovered that the return of comets was regular and could be predicted. This is because comets travel around the sun in regular paths, or orbits, as planets do. As you read the next selection, you will find out what we have been able to learn about comets—what they look like, how they travel, how long it takes them to complete an orbit. Think about the author's purpose for writing this selection as you read. And use what you have learned about graphs to help you read the one on comets at the end of the selection.

You're on your own this time. There are no marginal notes to help.

HALLEY'S COMET

Willy Ley

The earliest definite date on record for Halley's comet is for the year 240 B.C.[g] The comet must have returned in 163 B.C. but there is no record that it was seen. The next appearance, in 87 B.C., and the one after that, in 11 B.C., are both listed in Chinese records. From then on every passage was recorded.

The most famous appearance of Halley's comet is that of 1066 because it coincided[g] with the Norman[g] conquest of England. Scientifically, a statement by Zonares, a Greek historian of that time, is important. The comet, he said, looked as large as the moon and had no tail at first. When the tail appeared the comet was "diminished in size."

Of course the comet must already have had a tail when it became visible to the naked eye. Zonares probably saw it head on, so that the tail appeared like a luminous cloud around the comet's head. Without a powerful telescope a comet is not visible when it is so far from the sun that it is tailless.

The normal performance of a comet that runs through the portion of its orbit near the sun consists of growing and losing its tail. While the comet is far from the sun, it cannot be seen.

When the comet is about three times as far from the sun as the earth is, it develops its coma.[cg] Its outline grows fuzzy and indistinct,[cg] and it looks like a cloud in space. When it comes still closer, say one and a half times to twice as far from the sun as the earth is, the tail begins to form. At that point a comet appears to consist of three parts: the coma, which is a cloud-like mass; the nucleus, a bright spot inside the coma; and the tail.

The closer the comet approaches the sun, the brighter it grows. There are two reasons for this. One is the simple one that it receives and reflects more and more sunlight. The other is that the coma actually grows larger, just as the tail grows longer. There have been comets whose tails were 30 million miles in length. The tail always points away from the sun. We now know that this is the result of something discovered less than a century ago—radiation pressure.

While the tail trails behind the comet during the approach to the sun like the smoke plume of an old-fashioned steamer, the tail points ahead like the landing lights of a jet as the comet travels away from the sun. After some time only the coma is visible. Then the comet disappears, until its orbital path brings it close to the sun so it becomes visible again. Halley's comet has been seen twenty-nine times during the course of recorded history. Its next approach to the sun is due in 1986. Its passage closest to the sun is predicted for 3:50 A.M., Eastern Standard Time, on February 5, 1986. These, however, are preliminary figures that can change. The comet may be a few days early or a few days late.

Of course it will be most carefully observed, and not only from telescopes on the ground. There will certainly be at least one telescope in orbit around the earth at that time. And we may even succeed in sending a rocket probe to the comet.

The graph below compares the regular appearances of Halley's comet to those of some of the other comets.

Number of Years Between Orbital Appearances of Comets

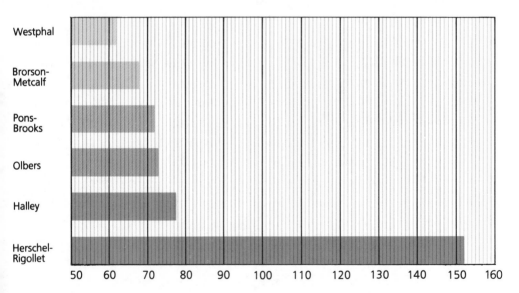

Check the Skills

Understanding the Selection

1. What does a comet look like? What happens when it passes by the sun?

2. How has modern science helped us understand comets?

Study and Research Skills Parts of a Book

3. What do the numbers across the bottom of the graph stand for? What do the words down the side of the graph mean?

4. How often does Halley's comet appear? How do you know? Which comet appears most often? least often?

Literary Appreciation Skills Style and Intent

5. What do you think is the author's purpose in this selection? Why do you think as you do?

Apply What You Learned in Unit 10

The Theme

Understanding Nature

1.   Through scientific study we have gained a vast amount of knowledge about nature. We know a great deal about the earth and the earth's creatures, as well as something about the solar system of which the earth is a part. But it has not been until the last few decades that people have come to realize that we have a responsibility for preserving nature. George Laycock tells us that we must preserve our poisonous snakes rather than kill them. Jack Myers strives to convince us that we must conserve our natural energy supplies.

•   Why do you think it is important for each of us to develop an understanding of our natural surroundings? What do you think each person can do to help preserve our natural surroundings?

The Skills

Study and Research Skills Parts of a Book

2. You found out in this unit that a graph often sum-
    marizes information in a way that is easy to read.
    Often you find graphs in newspaper or magazine
    articles. You find graphs, too, in materials you read
    in your math and science classes. Pay careful atten-
    tion to the graphs. They point out, in an easy-to-read
    fashion, certain facts and the relationship between
    these facts.

3. Remember to follow the steps at the beginning of
    this unit on "How To Read Graphs." See if your skill
    in getting information from graphs in your other
    classes improves.

Literary Appreciation Skills Style and Intent

4. Understanding an author's purpose for writing
    something can often help you read it better. If an
    author wrote to inform, you will pay attention to the
    facts. If the author's purpose is to entertain, you
    know you don't have to remember everything. You
    can just relax and enjoy it! Sometimes an author's
    purpose for writing may not be clear to you. When
    that happens, you can be sure that understanding
    the author's purpose is not terribly important to un-
    derstanding what you are reading. Nevertheless, it
    often helps to try to figure it out.

    What do you think was the author's purpose for
    writing this book? If you decide that it was to help
    you learn to read better, you're right!

Unit 11

Ability To Reason

Overview and Purposes for Reading

The Theme

Ability To Reason

1. Why is the ability to reason important to people?

The Skills

Study and Research Skills Reference Sources

2. What steps should you follow to find information in an encyclopedia?

Comprehension Skills Critical Reading

3. What is the difference between a statement of fact and a statement of opinion?

Learn About the Skills

Study and Research Skills Reference Sources

Pretend that you have a chance to go sailing. To get ready, you decide that you want to find out the names of the different kinds of sails on the boat. How would you find this information?

There are several resources possible. But most people would suggest an encyclopedia. That's probably the easiest to find. But once you have an encyclopedia, what do you do next? These steps should help.

How To Use an Encyclopedia

1. Decide what key word is likely to be the entry word you should look up.

2. Use your alphabetizing skills to find the volume and page where the entry is located.

3. Find the part of the entry that relates directly to the information you want. Do this by looking for the smaller titles, called subtitles, of sections of the article.

Try the Skill. Let's see how this works with the search for the names of the sails. What key word might be the entry word? You probably should start by looking up *Sailboats* or *Sailing.* First, find which volume of the encyclopedia contains these entries. To do this, look at the letters on the cover of each volume. Choose the volume whose cover letters show that it includes the letter *S*. Then look in this book at the guide words on each page or spread of facing pages. Find guide words close in alphabetical order to *Sailing*.

When you locate the entry, you don't need to read the whole article just to answer your question. Look at the subtitles. These are usually in darker type. In an entry on *Sailing*, the subtitles might include *The Parts of a Sailboat*, *Kinds of Sailboats*, *Sailing a Boat*, and *Sailboat Racing*. The names of the sails are most likely to be included in the section on *The Parts of a Sailboat*. So that is the section you should read.

Try another example. Suppose you want to find out how cold the water is in the Atlantic Ocean. Locate the entry labeled *Atlantic Ocean* in the A volume of the encyclopedia. Read the subtitles of the article to find one that seems related to how cold the water is. Would you find the answer in the section labeled *Location and Size* or the one with the subtitle *Temperature*?

The encyclopedia is a valuable reference source. You'll be able to think about how to use it as you read this unit.

Comprehension Skills Critical Reading

A fact is information accepted as true because experience or evidence supports it. It is a fact that the earth orbits around the sun. But whether there is human life anywhere besides the earth is opinion because it cannot be proved.

It is important to learn to tell fact from opinion so that you don't accept statements of opinion as fact. This is true with what you hear. It is also true with what you read. Some authors state their opinions as if they were facts. That makes it difficult. See if you can tell which of the following paragraphs states fact and which states opinion.

1. The mayor favors the building of a new expressway. The expressway would cost about $100,000,000, according to the mayor. It would probably take about five years to build. This includes the time needed for tearing down houses and other buidings to provide the best route for the highway.

2. The new expressway which the mayor favors is a great idea. It could help the downtown area a great deal. The cost is small. The city would have little trouble in raising the money. People who lose their homes can easily move somewhere else. We should lose no time in getting started on this highway. Progress demands it.

You're right if you recognized that the second paragraph is opinion. Some of the clues are judgment words, such as *should* and *could;* emotional words and phrases, such as *a great idea* and *help . . . a great deal,* that cannot be proved; statements which disagree with experience, such as *little trouble in raising the money.*

You'll use your skill in distinguishing between fact and opinion as you read this unit.

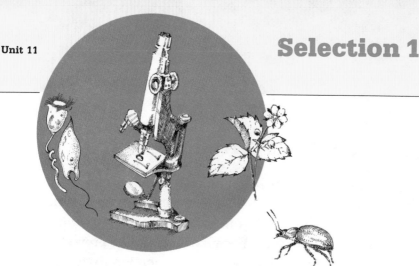

Selection 1

Use the Skills

Understanding the Selection

Suppose your science teacher refers to the system of classification of plants and animals. Curious about it, you look up Classification in the encyclopedia. You would find an article there like the following selection.

1. See how scientists used their reasoning ability to figure out this system. You don't need to read the entire article. The first section and the last section should be enough to read to find this out.

Study and Research Skills Reference Sources

2. Glance at the article. Which subtitle indicates the section you should read carefully if you are especially interested in how the system developed?

Comprehension Skills Critical Reading

3. Encyclopedias are carefully written so they give facts rather than opinions. See if that seems to be so as you read the first and last sections and skim the rest of this selection.

CLASSIFICATION, SCIENTIFIC

Classification, Scientific. Scientific classification is a method scientists have developed to arrange all animals and plants in related groups. It is the orderly arrangement of all living things. It indicates certain relationships among animal groups and among plant groups. Detailed classifications also show how ancient and extinct animals and plants fit into this arrangement. The classification of animals and plants is a science called *taxonomy* or *systematics*.

■ The guide word happens to be the same as the entry word.

Scientific classification is an interpretation of facts. It is based on the opinion and judgment a biologist forms after studying specimens of animals and plants. Most biologists use the same basic framework for classification. But not all biologists agree on how individual animals and plants fit into this scheme, and so classifications often differ in details.

■ It is a fact that biologists have differing opinions.

The Language of Classification. Latin and Greek words are used in scientific classification, because early scholars used these languages. Every known animal and plant has a two-part scientific name. Most of these names come from Greek or Latin words. We call this system of names the *binomial system of nomenclature,* or *binomial nomenclature.* These are Latin terms that mean *two-name naming.* The two names identify an animal or a plant in much the same way that your first and last names identify you.

Animals or plants are known by different common names in different regions. But each has only one correct scientific name, and scientists anywhere in the world can recognize an animal or plant by its scientific name. For example, the same large member of the cat family may be known in various parts of North and South America as a puma, cougar, mountain lion, panther, or león. The cat's scientific name is *Felis concolor.* Scientists can identify the animal by that name no matter what language they speak.

An international commission of scientists establishes the rules for adopting scientific names. Some scientific names are descriptive. The scientific name of the spotted skunk, for example, is *Spilogale putorius,* which means *smelly, spotted weasel.* But many scientific names have no descriptive meaning.

Groups in Classification. Seven chief groups make up a system in scientific classification. The groups are: (1) kingdom, (2) phylum, (3) class, (4) order, (5) family, (6) genus, and (7) species. The kingdom is the largest group, and the species is the smallest. Every known animal and plant has a particular place in each group.

Kingdom contains the most kinds of animals or plants. All animals belong to the animal kingdom, *Animalia.* All plants are members of the plant kingdom, *Plantae.*

However, some living things do not fit neatly into either the plant or the animal kingdom. Some organisms have features of both plants and animals. Others have characteristics that are not typical of either major kingdom. Most of these organisms consist of just one cell, or of colonies of one-celled members. Some scientists classify these organisms as a special kingdom called *Protista*. Other scientists separate them into two kingdoms: the *Protista*, or protists; and the *Monera*, or monerans. In this system, the monerans consist of bacteria and blue-green algae. These organisms differ in cell structure from all other living things. The protists in this system include other kinds of algae and single-celled organisms called *protozoans*.

Since the late 1960's, many biologists have used a classification system that recognizes five kingdoms. This system includes the plant, animal, protist, and moneran kingdoms. It adds the *Fungi* as the fifth kingdom. Fungi, which include molds, mushrooms, and yeasts, are traditionally classified as plants. Biologists who favor the five-kingdom system point out that fungi differ from green plants in the way they obtain their food. Also, fungi do not have the same kinds of tissues as do the multicelled green plants.

Phylum is the second largest group. The animal kingdom may be divided into 20 or more phyla. All animals with backbones belong to the phylum *Chordata*. The plant kingdom has 10 phyla. All plants that have tissues that transport materials from one part of the plant to another belong to the phylum *Tracheophyta*.

Class members have more characteristics in common than do members of a phylum. For example, mammals, reptiles, and birds all belong to the phylum *Chordata*. But each belongs to a different class. Apes, bears, and mice are in the class *Mammalia*. Mammals have hair on their bodies and feed milk to their young. Reptiles, including lizards, snakes, and turtles, make up the class *Reptilia*. Scales cover the bodies of all reptiles, and none of them feed milk to their young. Birds make up the class *Aves*. Feathers grow on their bodies, and they do not feed milk to their young.

Order consists of groups that are more alike than those in a class. In the class *Mammalia,* all the animals produce milk for their young. Dogs, moles, raccoons, and shrews are all mammals. But dogs and raccoons eat flesh, and are grouped together in the order *Carnivora*, with other flesh-eating animals. Moles and shrews eat insects, and are classified in the order *Insectivora*, with other insect-eating animals.

Family is made up of groups that are even more alike than those in the order. For example, wolves and cats are both in the order *Carnivora*. But wolves are in the family *Canidae*. All members of this family have long snouts and bushy tails. Cats belong in the family *Felidae*. Members of this family have short snouts and short-haired tails.

Genus consists of very similar groups, but members of different groups usually cannot breed with one another. Both the coyote and the timber wolf are in the genus *Canis*. But coyotes and timber wolves generally do not breed with one another.

Species is the basic unit of scientific classification. Members of a species have many common characteristics, but they differ from all other forms of life in one or more ways. Members of a species can breed with one another, and the young grow up to look like the parents. No two species in a genus have the same scientific name. The coyote is *Canis latrans,* and the timber wolf is *Canis lupus.* Sometimes groups within a species differ enough from other groups in the species that they are called *subspecies* or *varieties.*

Development of Classification. For thousands of years people have tried to classify animals and plants. Early human beings divided all living things into two groups: (1) useful, and (2) harmful. As people began to recognize more kinds of living things, they developed new ways to classify them. One of the most useful was suggested by the Greek philosopher and naturalist Aristotle (384–322 B.C.). Only about a thousand animals and plants were known in his time. He classified the animals as those with red blood (animals with backbones) and those with no red blood (animals without backbones). He divided the plants by size and appearance as herbs, shrubs, or trees. Aristotle's scheme served as the basis for classification for almost 2,000 years.

■ The best section to read to find out the history of the system.

The English biologist John Ray (1627–1705) first suggested the idea of species in classification. But the basic design for modern classification began with the work of the Swedish naturalist Carolus Linnaeus (1707–1778). Linnaeus separated animals and plants according to their *structure* (arrangement of parts), and gave distinctive names to each species. Biologists still rearrange classification, but today, our classification method is based on the principles that Linnaeus established.

Check the Skills

Understanding the Selection

1. Did it take logical thinking and the ability to reason to develop the system of classification of living things? Why do you think as you do?

Study and Research Skills Reference Sources

2. Why would you read the last section instead of the second one to find out how the system started?

Comprehension Skills Critical Reading

3. The statement about biologists' opinions is considered a fact. Why do you think this is so?

Selection 2

Use the Skills

Understanding the Selection

1.   The next selection tells about some odd statues. See how scientists have used their ability to reason to figure out the probable history of the statues.

Study and Research Skills Reference Sources

2.   As you read, think about the key words you could use if you wanted to find further information in an encyclopedia.

Comprehension Skills Critical Reading

3.   Even in an article that seems to be factual there may be statements of opinion. Be alert for them.

THE MYSTERY OF EASTER ISLAND

Gilbert Grail

It's a tiny spot on the map—an island in the Pacific Ocean, fourteen miles long and seven miles wide at its widest part. To the west, the nearest island is more than a thousand miles away. The continent^c of South America lies over 2300 miles to the east. It's a long way from anywhere. Yet Easter Island is famous the world over because of its mysterious statues.

■ A good key word. It should be in the E volume of an encyclopedia.

There are more than six hundred of these huge statues. The largest is thirty-seven feet high and weighs over eighty tons. The statues are unlike any in the world. Their heads are very long, with deep-set eyes, giving them a serious and thoughtful look. They have grim,^{g} disapproving mouths. They have exceedingly^g long ears. Some have a ten-ton block of stone balanced on their heads. Standing on lonely and windswept hillsides, the statues seem to be super-natural^g beings keeping a brooding watch over their island.

Only the heads remain of many statues, but these are often twelve feet high. Originally the statues had arms but no legs. This was because they stopped at the waist.

Most of the statues had been keeping their grim watches for hundreds of years before the first people from the out-side world saw them. On Easter Sunday in 1722, three Dutch ships under the command of Jacob Roggeveen reached the island. As the Dutch sailors approached the island, they were amazed to see that the coast was dotted with gigantic statues. Roggeveen estimated that there were a thousand of the forbidding^g figures.

■ Fact. It can be proved.

The Dutch visitors were more surprised when they got ashore. There was hardly any wood on the barren^g island. How had the enormous^c statues been raised without wooden levers?^{g} And where had the natives come from?

Somehow their ancestors[cg] had found this tiny island in the vast ocean, after voyaging over a thousand miles. Incredible!

The Dutch stayed only a few days at Easter Island, just long enough to give it its name. Then, for 150 years, few ships stopped there. It was not until the 1870s that scientists came to study the riddle of the statues.

It was a difficult task. Since the Dutch visit, civil war and disease had reduced the population[c] from thousands to a few hundred. The survivors[c] had little knowledge of the island's history.

Still, the search went on. Theories developed about the statues and the people who had created them. Scientists now believe that Easter Island was settled at least 1600 years ago by people from the islands to the west. And it seems possible that a people with the imagination and daring to make such a voyage would also be able to produce those amazing statues.

■ Two clues that opinions are stated.

Check the Skills

Understanding the Selection

1. Do you think that scientists have come up with a reasonable explanation for the mystery of the statues of Easter Island? Why do you think as you do?

Study and Research Skills Reference Sources

2. If you wanted to look up Easter Island in an encyclopedia, would you find the entry on a page with the guide words *earthquake* and *earthworm*? Why or why not?

Comprehension Skills Critical Reading

3. Is it fact or opinion that the first settlers of Easter Island came from islands to the west? Check the last marginal note for a clue if you need to.

Use the Skills

Understanding the Selection

1. As you read the selection, ask yourself how the trapper's ability to reason helped him figure out why the cave was so warm.

Study and Research Skills Reference Sources

2. Suppose you wanted to find out what hibernating is and if bears really hibernate. Think how you could use an encyclopedia to find out.

Comprehension Skills Critical Reading

3. After you finish reading, decide whether or not this selection is a factual report.

ROOMMATES

Maria Leach

One day a trapper got caught in a blizzard. It was cold, the wind was piercing, and the snow was coming so thick that he couldn't see his way more than a foot in front of him. He could not even find the trail for home. He kept stumbling up rough hills and slipping down into little icy hollows.

At last, exhausted, he decided to give up and look for some kind of shelter near at hand. He felt his way in the snow along the face of a huge boulder, thinking he might shelter^{cg} under some jutting ledge of rock. Suddenly he felt an opening—a big opening. He stepped into it and found himself in a cave. It was dark, but he was safe from the obliterating^g snow and piercing wind. There were dry leaves under his feet. This was wonderful! He lay down, rolled up in the position all hunters know, and went to sleep.

Suddenly he was startled from sleep by a great sound of thrashing around and grunting in the cave. He reached out his hand in the dark and felt something big and warm and rough and furry.

It was a bear. He had stumbled into the cave of a <u>hibernating bear</u>. Lucky me! he thought to himself, understanding at once the wonderful warmth of the place. But what was wrong with this old fellow—thrashing around and complaining in his sleep?

Suddenly he remembered the old tale that bears suck their paws during the long winter sleep. He felt around in the dark until he found a paw and stuck it back in the animal's mouth. "Mmm," said the bear and then was quiet. And they both went to sleep.

■ Entry words in an encyclopedia.

This story used to be a common hunters' tale all over the United States wherever there were bears and blizzards. It has been told for fact from Maine to Arkansas and the Rockies. It is a common European and legendary⁹ saints' anecdote. Various North American Indian groups have the tale also.

■ This paragraph is a clue to whether the selection is fact.

Check the Skills

Understanding the Selection

1. The trapper's ability to reason told him why the cave was so warm as soon as he realized there was a bear in the cave. It was the warmth of the bear's body that heated the cave.

Study and Research Skills Reference Sources

2. If you wanted to find out about bears hibernating, you could look up *Bear* in the encyclopedia. Would you read the section with the subtitle *Food* or the subtitle *Winter Sleep?* Why?

Comprehension Skills Critical Reading

3. Is this selection fact? How do you know?

Use the Skills

Understanding the Selection

1. The ability to reason is usually thought of as a human quality. But the following selection describes a true incident in which two birds seemed to be able to reason.

Study and Research Skills Reference Sources

2. Think how you could use an encyclopedia to find information about swamp sparrows.

Comprehension Skills Critical Reading

3. Remember not to accept statements of opinion as fact.

THE GIFT OF REASON

Walter D. Edmonds

I am not a scientist and cannot lay down rules for animal behavior any more than I can predict reactions in people. Human beings are supposed to be the only creatures on earth with the power to reason. But on their separate levels animals *do* reason. They have not the advantages of technology⁹ and science that give humans their power, but on occasion they overcome their basic fears, act against all instinct,⁹ and demonstrate what could be called the power to reason.

I am carried back to a sweltering⁹ midday in August many summers ago. I was fishing down Cold Brook. I used to fish it every summer, because a trout out of the icy water of Cold Brook was always prime.ᶜᵍ I also fished it because it was a very sporting stream.

I do not know when the two swamp sparrows discovered me. I was so preoccupiedᶜᵍ that it might have been several minutes before their insistenceᶜᵍ brought them to my attention. But then, there they were in the bush beside me, two small brown birds with dull rusty caps and undistinguished⁹ plumage.⁹ They were profoundly upset, spreading their wings, repeating over and over a rough single note.

■ If you wanted to find out more about sparrows, where in an encyclopedia would you look?

When I stopped fishing, they flew to another bush upstream and repeated their antics.ᶜᵍ I thought that perhaps they had new hatched babies somewhere nearby and wanted to lead me away from them. But as I had no intention of harming them, I resumed my fishing, passing around the next downstream clump of aldersᶜᵍ to try a new spot.

Immediately the two birds changed their tactics. In an instant they were in front of me, fluttering before my face, still uttering their distressed note. I stopped again to watch them. It would have been impossible to continue fishing with that flurry of wings going on almost in my face. Once more they flew to a bush upstream. But the minute I faced downstream again, they were back around my head.

I put my rod down, leaning it against a bush, and watched them. They quieted, but continued to flutter their wings. It came to me, how I do not know, that they were not trying to lead me *from* something. They wanted me to come *with* them.

As soon as I started back upstream in their direction, they fluttered on, much less noisily now. I followed them for perhaps a hundred feet, and then they led me away from the brook until they came to rest in another alder clump. Their voices were much quieter now; in an odd way they sounded reassuring.[g] I looked where they were looking.

There, its tiny leg caught in a vertical[g] cleft[g] of an alder stem, hung a sparrow nestling.[g] It gave no sign that it might

be alive when I went up to it, not even when I took the little body in one hand and with the other opened the cleft. I held it for several minutes cupped in my hands. Finally its eyes opened, and it stirred a little on my palm.

Only then did I realize that both birds had come close to me. They watched the young bird as intently as I. And in the end the little body gathered itself. The stretched leg moved under it. I put it on a branch two feet or so away from its parents. They had apparently no fear of me. They did not offer to move away. When I saw the toes of the baby take hold of the branch, I released it and left them so. I resumed my fishing, but nothing that happened that afternoon was as exciting as my encounter with the swamp sparrows. <u>Few things that have happened to me since have moved me more.</u>

■ Fact or opinion?

Check the Skills

Understanding the Selection

1. What did the birds do that made them appear to have the ability to reason? How does the title of the selection apply to both the author and the birds?

Study and Research Skills Reference Sources

2. Suppose you wanted to find out more about swamp sparrows. In an encyclopedia, you'd probably discover more information in an entry for *Sparrow* than you would in one for *Bird* or *Swamp*. Why do you think this is true?

Comprehension Skills Critical Reading

3. How did you know that the last sentence in the selection stated opinion?

Selection 5

Use the Skills

In this poem, someone asks about the sound of wind at night. Poems appeal to your imagination rather than to your ability to reason. But the poem may prompt you to want to find more facts about how wind is created and where the sound *does* come from. Decide how you could use an encyclopedia.

Before you read, you may want to check the glossary for the meanings of *ululation* and *threnody*.

ULULATION[9] ON THE NIGHT

Rosalind Clark

I woke
And heard a wail
Rising and falling
Through the empty cavern
Of the night.

Was it the world
Calling out
From its cross,
Weary of hate's scourge,
Of strife's thorn?

Was it the cry
Of the forlorn,
The oppressed,
The lonely?

Or was it only
The plaintive threnody[9]
Of the wind?

Check the Skills

Understanding the Selection

1. Could the ability to reason help answer the questions in the poem? Why or why not?

Study and Research Skills Reference Sources

2. If you wanted to find out about the wind, how could you use an encyclopedia?

Comprehension Skills Critical Reading

3. Are there any facts in the poem? How do you know?

Apply What You Learned in Unit 11

The Theme

Ability To Reason

1. In this unit, you read several examples of the ability to reason and why it is important. Because people have the ability to reason, they are able to solve problems, develop new ideas, and learn whatever they want to learn. The scientists in the first two selections used their reasoning ability to learn about the ancient world. One man used his ability to reason to figure out that swamp sparrows needed his help and they used theirs to get it.

*   Think about a time when you used your ability to reason. Do you think it is reasoning ability that often causes people to ask questions?

*   Do you think animals might have the ability to reason the way people do?

The Skills

Study and Research Skills Reference Sources

2. This unit gave you some help in learning how to rely on an encyclopedia as a source of information. You will need these skills as you do more and more research projects in school. Be sure you have the steps listed on page 287 clearly in mind.

Comprehension Skills Critical Reading

3. You were also reminded in this unit to be careful of accepting statements of opinion as though they are facts. Being aware of the difference can be important both in and out of school.

Creative Thinking

Overview and Purposes for Reading

The Theme

Creative Thinking

1.   People who think creatively come up with new ideas and projects. They use imagination as well as reason. What are some examples of creative thinking? How can you think creatively, too?

The Skills

Study and Research Skills Reading Techniques

2.   How do you read and study textbook assignments and informative articles?

3.   What steps can you follow to help yourself improve your comprehension of such materials?

Vocabulary Development Skills Dictionary

4.   How can context clues help you choose the right dictionary definition?

Learn About the Skills

Study and Research Skills Reading Techniques

There is a "sure-fire" way to improve your reading of textbooks! The method is called SQ3R, after the first letter of each of the steps listed below. If you follow these steps you are practically guaranteed to improve your understanding of the kinds of factual material you must study.

SQ3R

Survey	Look over the material first to see what it is about.
Question	Find out what questions you should be able to answer at the end of your reading.
Read	Read the selection to answer those questions.
Recite	After reading the selection, tell yourself the answers to all the questions.
Review	If there were questions you could not answer, review the appropriate section of the material to find the answers.

All the steps of SQ3R are important. But the Question step is the real key to your success. If you ask the right questions, you'll be successful. But how can you know what the right questions are? There are four ways to find out.

1.   Check to see if your teacher gives you questions to be answered. Of course your teacher is the best source. You should be alert for any questions she or he gives you. Sometimes these questions may be stated as directions. For example, suppose your science teacher tells you "Read the next chapter to find out how a lever works." The question you would then ask yourself would be "How does a

lever work?" If your teacher gives you ideas about what questions to ask before you begin reading, he or she is telling you "This is important. Be sure you get the answer to this when you read."

But you should be independent and learn to do this yourself. Several suggestions follow.

2.   Look in the textbook to see if it has questions to be answered. Often these are at the end of a chapter or unit. When you survey a chapter before you read it, find these questions and read them. You can use these as your SQ3R questions. The fact that they are there means that the textbook author feels that the answers are very important.

3.   Use the titles and subtitles to help yourself make up questions. Some textbooks or other materials you read for information do not include questions at the end of a chapter. In that case, make the chapter titles and subtitles into questions. These are usually set off in bigger and darker print. Suppose one of the subtitles is Egypt, Cradle of Civilization. You could ask "What is a cradle of civilization and why is Egypt called that?" If another subtitle is The Importance of the Aswan Dam, you can ask "Why is the Aswan Dam important?" Titles and subtitles usually give the main ideas. So they are a good source to use in finding the right questions to ask.

4.   Use illustrations to help you make up questions. The pictures, maps, tables, charts, and graphs in a book are important. Make up questions from the information and ideas in them.

You'll get some practice in using SQ3R as you go through this unit.

Vocabulary Development Skills Dictionary

Sometimes you find a word you don't know in your reading. You should first try to figure out what the word means by using the clues in the sentence. Sometimes, however, there are not enough of these context clues. Then you must look the word up in a dictionary.

However, skillful use of the dictionary also calls for the use of context clues. Suppose you read this sentence: *The pilot of the amphibian was looking for a place to land.* Context clues don't tell you exactly what an amphibian is. So you check a dictionary and find the entry below.

> **am phib i an** (am fib′ē ən), *n.*   1. any cold-blooded animal with a backbone and damp skin without scales, such as frogs and salamanders. The young live in water and the adults live on land.   2. an airplane designed for taking off and landing on both land and water.   3. a land vehicle that can move on land or water.

Which meaning of *amphibian* is the right one? You can tell by using the context clues around the word. In the sentence above, *pilot* and *a place to land* are clues that the second definition is the right one.

Which definition is appropriate in the following sentence? *The amphibian crawled up on the rock to sun itself.* The clue about "sunning itself" tells you that the first definition is the correct one for this sentence, since no machine would ever sun itself.

Some of the words in selections you'll read in this unit might be new to you. If context clues don't help enough, look the word up in the glossary of this book or in a dictionary. Remember to pick the meaning that fits the context.

Selection 1

Use the Skills

Understanding the Selection

1.   As you read this short article, ask yourself how young Africans are using creative thinking to help save the elephants.

Study and Research Skills Reading Techniques

2.   Use the SQ3R steps that you have learned. The notes in the margin will remind you what to do.

Vocabulary Development Skills Dictionary

3.   As you read you may find words whose meanings you don't know. Use context clues and the glossary or dictionary to figure out what they mean. Remember that words followed by a small letter *g* are in the glossary at the back of this book.

SAVING THE ELEPHANTS

Robert Gray

A few thousand years ago, there were many different kinds of elephants roaming the earth throughout Africa, Asia, and even North America. Today all but two of these species are extinct.^{cg}

What made them disappear everywhere but in Africa and Asia? Great changes in climate, perhaps. Experts do not know for sure. But they do know what dangers the elephants face today. People are competing^c with the elephants for land and are shooting the elephants who invade^g their farms. And people have long hunted elephants for ivory.

In some African and Asian nations it is now illegal to shoot elephants or to trade in ivory. But there are still people who hunt illegally and smuggle^g ivory.

Young people in African wildlife clubs are urging stricter enforcement of the laws and are also asking that more land be set aside for wildlife.

But how much land is enough for a herd of elephants? Some of Africa's young people want to help find out. To do this they will study Wildlife Management and then go out to the savanna^g to see if their ideas work. Let's hope these young scientists succeed, so there will still be elephants tomorrow.

- *Survey* by skimming the article to find out what it is about. Look at the pictures and read the captions. Check over the *questions* at the end. Keep them in mind as you read.

- The context clue word *illegally* should help you choose the first glossary definition for *smuggle.*

Study Questions

■ *Recite* or answer each question. *Review* the article if necessary.

1. On what continents do elephants live today?

2. What dangers do elephants face today?

3. What two things are wildlife clubs asking to be done to help protect elephants?

4. How will people decide what amount of land is necessary for a herd of elephants to live on?

The *African* elephant is larger and heavier than the Asian elephant. Its tusks can be 8 feet (2.4 meters) long and can weigh 80 pounds (36 kilograms). It has long ears. At the tip of its long trunk are two grasping knobs.

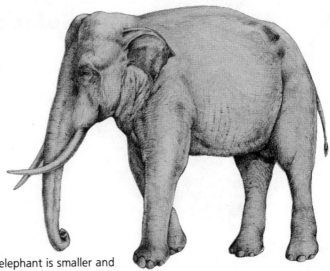

The *Asian* or *Indian* elephant is smaller and easier to tame than the African elephant. The tusks may grow to 5 feet (1.5 meters), but many have no tusks. The ears are half the size of the African elephant. There is just one grasping knob at the tip of its shorter trunk.

Check the Skills

Understanding the Selection

1.   What creative ideas are young people in Africa putting into effect in order to help save the elephants? Can you think of any other ideas that might work?

Study and Research Skills Reading Techniques

2.   a. Where did you find the questions you were to keep in mind as you read the article? Did you form some questions of your own from looking at the pictures and reading their captions?

     b. What is the answer to each of the study questions on page 316? If you don't know, how can you find out?

Vocabulary Development Skills Dictionary

3.   Explain the meaning of the word *smuggle* as it is used in this selection. Use the note in the margin and the glossary. How did context clues help you to choose the correct definition?

Use the Skills

Understanding the Selection

The first step in SQ3R is *Survey,* which means to look something over in a general way. As you read the next selection, context clues will tell you that in the article the word *survey* is used with a more specific definition. Here it means a careful measurement or study of public opinion.

1. Read the article to find out how both creative thinking and reasoning play a part in developing the way surveys are taken.

Study and Research Skills Reading Techniques

2. Remember to *survey* the article to find out what it is about. Find the *questions* you should be able to answer after reading. Then *read* the article. *Recite,* or answer each question, and *review* the article if necessary.

Vocabulary Development Skills Dictionary

3. Remember to let context clues help you choose the right glossary or dictionary definition of words you don't know.

DO YOU LIKE SPINACH?

John Weiss

You are sitting at home, watching the evening news on television. During the program an announcer makes this statement: "A survey indicates that 75 percent of all Americans like spinach." Then she comments on how this news is affecting the spinach growers.

But how did they find out how many Americans like spinach when they didn't ask you? You are an American, and you don't like spinach. Everyone you know hates spinach.

They did it by conducting⁹ a survey.

To take a survey or a <u>poll</u>ᶜ means to question a certain group of people about a topic or an issue. This certain group of people is called a <u>sample;</u>ᶜ it was picked from a larger group of people called a population.ᶜ A sample can be taken of the population of a state, a city, or even a neighborhood. In the announcer's statement, the population would be all of the people in America, but the sample is only certain Americans.

<u>A sample is normally taken at random;ᶜ that is, each person in the population is given an equal chance of being picked for the sample.</u> Imagine that you are in a dark room, holding up a bunch of grapes. You cannot see or feel all the grapes at once, but you want to know if the bunch is ripe or rotten. So you pick some from the top of the bunch and some from the bottom and some from the sides, taste them, and you get a pretty good idea of what the whole bunch is like. You have just taken a random sample. Now you can say, for example, that the bunch is ripe or rotten, or that the grapes on the top are okay but the ones on the bottom are rotten. Yet you haven't seen or eaten the whole bunch of grapes, only certain ones picked at random.

Mathematically, this process of picking certain things at random (certain Americans, certain grapes, and so on) and

■ After *surveying* the article, you know that it is about the study of public opinion. The *questions* you should keep in mind as you *read* are in the Check the Skills section on page 323.

then making statements about all of the things (Americans, a bunch of grapes, or whatever) is based on the laws of probability,[9] first explained by a seventeenth-century French scientist, Blaise Pascal. At first not many people used the laws of probability when they sampled a population. The 1936 American Presidential election is often used to illustrate what happens when people are not surveyed correctly.

In 1936, a magazine called the *Literary Digest* sent out 10 million survey forms to all the people on its mailing list to try to find out who would win the presidential election between Democrat Franklin D. Roosevelt and Republican Alfred Landon. Based on almost 2½ million returns, the *Literary Digest* predicted that Alfred Landon would win with 57 percent of the popular vote. But when the election votes were counted, Alfred Landon had only received 38 percent of the popular vote. The *Literary Digest* poll was not even close!

If you go back to the example of the grapes, you can see why the poll was so wrong. When you examined the grapes in the dark, you took some from all over the bunch—a random sample. If you had picked only from the top or only from the bottom, you could not have said for sure if the whole bunch was ripe or rotten. And when the *Literary Digest* received survey forms back from the people on its mailing list, the magazine realized that the people were not a random sample of Democrats and Republicans at all. In fact, the people who subscribed to the magazine were mostly Republicans who later voted for the Republican candidate, Alfred Landon.

Since that time, survey researchers[c] or pollsters,[c] those who conduct surveys or polls, have found better ways to sample a population. The two most famous polls in use today are the Gallup Poll and the Harris Poll—named for the men who started them. On certain questions these two polls survey the entire United States population—over 210 million people—using a sample of only 1,500 people.

The results of these national surveys are correct to within three percentage points. If, for example, 75 percent of Americans say they like spinach, that percentage could be as low as 72 percent or as high as 78 percent, but it is most likely to be 75 percent. This difference one way or the other is called the margin⁹ of error.ᶜ The survey researchers could decrease the margin of error by increasing the number of people surveyed—just as you could pick more grapes to test the ripeness of the bunch. But the margin of error decreases only slightly as larger numbers of people are surveyed. It would require a survey of 4,000 people instead of 1,500 to lower the margin of error to two percentage points.

■ Is this space at the edge of a paper?

What determines if you will be among those surveyed? Simply, where you live. For the Gallup Poll, five people are selected within 300 randomly chosen areas of the United States, for a total of 1,500 interviews.

But don't feel bad if you are never asked to fill out a survey form. It would take the Gallup Poll, which changes survey locations every four months, over 400 years to interview every adult in America just once.

In the meantime: Do *you* like spinach?

Mr. Gallup   Mr. Harris

Check the Skills

Understanding the Selection

1. Creative thinking about the mistaken results of the magazine poll in 1936 helped survey researchers develop better ways of sampling. What was wrong with the 1936 sample?

Study and Research Skills Reading Techniques

2. You should be able to *recite* the answers to the following questions. *Review* the article if you need help. Hints have been underlined for you.

   a. What is a poll? a sample of the population?

   b. Explain what a random sample is.

   c. What does margin of error mean? What is the margin of error in a national survey?

   d. What determines if you will be surveyed?

Vocabulary Development Skills Dictionary

3. Look up *margin* in the glossary. What context clues told you that the second definition fits the sentence on page 322?

Selection 3

Use the Skills

Understanding the Selection

This selection is from a textbook you might read in a social studies class.

1. Use your own creative thinking ability to decide why a ten-year-old would need more calories than an adult woman does.

Study and Research Skills Reading Techniques

2. Remember to use the SQ3R steps listed on page 311. The table and the questions at the end of the selection can help you with the Question step.

Vocabulary Development Skills Dictionary

3. Often terms in textbooks are explained right in the context. So you probably won't need to use your dictionary skills with this selection.

WHERE DO YOU GET ALL THAT ENERGY?

Gasoline provides energy for automobiles. When a car runs out of gas, it just won't go. Human beings also need energy to operate. Without energy you could never push a pencil, sing a song, or pedal a bicycle. Even your heart, brain, and lungs need energy to do their jobs.

Which one needs more calories?

The energy you need comes from the food you eat. Food energy is measured in calories.ᶜ A calorie is not a substance like carbohydratesᵍ and fats. Rather it is a unit of measurement, like *gallon*, or *centimeter*, or *ounce*. Calories are used to indicate the amount of energy that you get from food.

The number of calories you need depends on how old, large, and active you are. Generally, people who live in hot climates need fewer calories than those who live in cooler climates.

The table on this page shows the number of calories health experts recommend for people who live in middle-latitude[9] climates.

■ If you do SQ3R correctly, you should read these questions *before* you read the article.

1. Using the table, figure out how many calories you need daily.

2. How many calories should your parents get?

3. How many calories should your sister or brother get?

4. Why is the number of calories recommended for women in an age group less than the number recommended for men in the same age group?

■ What questions could you make up from this table?

FOOD ENERGY

Recommended Daily Allowances for Normally Active Persons

Children	Calories	Girls	Calories	Boys	Calories
1-2 years	1,100	10-12	2,250	10-12	2,500
2-3	1,250	12-14	2,300	12-14	2,700
3-4	1,400	14-16	2,400	14-18	3,000
4-6	1,600	16-18	2,300		
6-8	2,000				
8-10	2,200				
		Women	Calories	Men	Calories
		18-35	2,000	18-35	2,800
		35-55	1,850	35-55	2,600
		55 and older	1,700	55 and older	2,400

Which one needs more calories?

Check the Skills

Understanding the Selection

1. Why do you think a ten-year-old needs more calories than an adult woman? The answer isn't in the selection. You'll have to use your creative thinking to figure it out.

Study and Research Skills Reading Techniques

2. a. Did using SQ3R help you get information from this selection? How?

   b. How could the table help you make up questions to ask?

   c. Finish SQ3R by answering the questions at the end of the article. What should you do if you don't remember an answer?

Vocabulary Development Skills Dictionary

3. Did you need to use the glossary or dictionary for any of the words in this selection? If so, how did context clues help you choose the right definition?

Use the Skills

Understanding the Selection

The game lacrosse is played today with a ball and long-handled racket by two teams of ten players each. The players try to send the ball into a goal. This selection tells about an incident in the early history of the game.

1. Find out how lacrosse and creative thinking by American Indians helped them get into a French fort.

Study and Research Skills Reading Techniques

2. You won't need to survey the selection because the section above has already told you what it is about. Follow the other steps of SQ3R, though. As you read, think of the meaning of the question in the title. Decide what it has to do with the story. Remember to find other questions, too.

Vocabulary Development Skills Dictionary

3. Remember, if you cannot determine the meaning of a word from context alone, use the glossary or dictionary *and* the context.

WHO'S MINDING THE FORT?

Howard Liss

When European explorers first came to Ontario, Canada, they found the Native Americans there playing a peculiar game called *baggataway*. It was played with a kind of ball and a net made of strips of animal skin on a stick. Because the stick looked like a bishop's cross, the French explorers called the sport *lacrosse*.

■ What questions should you read to answer?

In a way baggataway wasn't a game at all, but a way to prepare for future hand-to-hand combat. Teams sometimes consisted of all the young men of a tribe. Sometimes they even wore war paint. Goals were various kinds of markers, and could be any distance apart. Occasionally the game was played on horseback. The referees were medicine men whose decisions were final.

Soldiers watching the American Indians play thought they were slightly crazy, because they suffered painful injuries and broken bones playing that violent game. But it turned out to be the soldiers who were foolish, because baggataway helped the Native Americans win an important battle.

In 1763, Chief Pontiac of the Ottawas planned to capture Fort Michilimackinac (now called Fort Mackinac). But the French garrison was too strong. However, Pontiac knew that the French soldiers liked to watch baggataway being played. He asked permission to play a game on a large open field near the fort and invited the French soldiers to watch.

■ Context clues can help you decide the best glossary definition.

As the game got under way, the soldiers opened the gates so that they could see the game better. During the wild play, the ball was thrown near the gates of the fort and some of the players chased after it. That was the secret signal!

The older Indians were sitting at the edge of the field quietly watching the game. But they were concealing tomahawks under their blankets. The young Ottawa braves grabbed the weapons and stormed the fort.

Historians do not agree on the final outcome of that battle. Some versions⁣ᶜᵍ say the garrison was overwhelmed,ᶜ beaten by an early sporting event. Others state that the attack was beaten off. But no matter which ending is true, the fort soon fell into the hands of Chief Pontiac and the Ottawas. And two hundred years later, the game of the Ottawas is still played.

Check the Skills

Understanding the Selection

1. a. What creative idea was used by the Native Americans to enter the strong French fort?

    b. Use your own ability to think creatively to give reasons why you think we do not call the game *baggataway,* which was its original name.

Study and Research Skills Reading Techniques

2. a. What do you think the title of the selection means? What does the title have to do with the story?

    b. Who invented the game of lacrosse?

    c. Why did the French name the game *lacrosse?*

    d. What was the real purpose of baggataway?

Vocabulary Development Skills Dictionary

3. Which glossary definition fits *garrison* as it is used on page 329? How did you decide?

Selection 5

Use the Skills

You might read the following article in a social studies textbook. It describes the Egyptian pyramids and guesses at the creative thinking that prompted the building of them. Make sure you follow the SQ3R steps as you read. Make up your own questions using the clues in the titles and subtitles. Remember to use context and the glossary or dictionary to get the meaning of any words you don't know.

Do it yourself this time, without marginal notes to help.

THE EGYPTIAN PYRAMIDS

Tourists marvel at the pyramids, and engineers add them to lists of great engineering feats.[9] But the Egyptians did not build the pyramids to surprise tourists or engineers. They built them to house the dead bodies of their kings. The pyramids are tombs.

First Tombs

The early kings of Egypt had been buried in simple flat tombs called mastabas.[c] Made of mud brick, the mastabas were built far from the Nile's banks, so the summer river-flood would not wash them away.

This picture shows the ruins of an ancient mastaba.

Sometime around 2700 B.C., a king named Zoser asked his royal architect, Imhotep, to build him a tomb. Imhotep used stone instead of mud bricks. At first he built a regular mastaba. Then he changed his mind and made it square. Finally, he made it bigger by piling more mastabas on top of the first one, each smaller than the one below. The result was a pyramid of mastabas. From the side, it looks like steps. Because of this, people call it a step pyramid.

Some historians think Imhotep had a special reason for building the step pyramid. About that time, the Egyptians were adding a new idea to their religion: the idea that after death the king went to live with the sun-god. One of their religious writings said, "A staircase to heaven is laid for him so that he may climb to heaven thereby." Could the step pyramid have been a "staircase" to heaven?

Real Pyramids

Around 2600 B.C., the pyramid-builders got another idea. They did away with the "steps" and made pyramids that had slanting sides. No one knows exactly why they did this. But again, some historians think the reason has something to do with the sun-god religion. The rays of the sun shine down through the clouds at about the same slanting

angle as the sides of these pyramids. Maybe the slanting sides of the pyramids stood for the rays of the holy sun.

The biggest and most famous of these pyramids is the Great Pyramid. King Cheops ordered it built for him. He wanted to top any pyramid built before or after him, and he did. Another king tried the trick of building his pyramid on higher ground, but few were fooled.

It took thousands of men to build the Great Pyramid. During the three-month flood season in summer, when no one was able to farm in the valley, some archeologists⁹ believe that as many as 100,000 men worked on the Great Pyramid. The rest of the year, about 4,000 men did the work. Those men—replaced by fresh ones every three months—worked for 20 years on this one pyramid. They had to make and move 2,300,000 blocks of stone. Each block was usually about 2½ tons, but some weighed as much as 16 tons. Engineers still wonder how the Egyptians did it.

Building with Numbers

The pyramid-builders had to measure the square base for the pyramid. They had to figure out how to make the sides of the pyramid equal. They had to cut the stone blocks even and straight. Foremen[9] had to keep track of thousands of workers—quarrymen,[9] boatmen, toolmakers, and other laborers. They had to know how long each man worked and what wages to pay him. Scribes[9] recorded the number of stone blocks cut, hauled, and laid in place each day.

To help do these jobs the Egyptians used a number system. It looked like this:

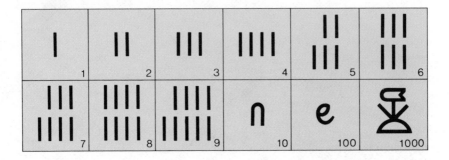

They wrote the number 43 like this:

Do you think the Egyptians could have done the jobs mentioned above without a system for counting and measuring?

Check the Skills

Understanding the Selection

1. How did creative thinking contribute to translating religious ideas into types of pyramids?

2. Do you think it must have taken creative thinking to invent a number system? Why or why not?

Study and Research Skills Reading Techniques

3. How did you use SQ3R as you read this selection? What questions did you form from the title and subtitles?

Vocabulary Development Skills Dictionary

4. How did context clues help you choose the second glossary definition of *foremen* as the one appropriate to this selection?

Apply What You Learned in Unit 12

The Theme

Creative Thinking

1. In this unit you read about creative thinking. Creativity may be simply making something new. It may mean having an original idea. What is your definition of creative thinking? What does it mean to you?

• Do you think creative thinking is as important to human beings as the ability to reason is? Why or why not?

The Skills

Study and Research Skills Reading Techniques

2. As you read each selection in this unit, you discovered how SQ3R can help you read and study. You saw its importance in reading textbooks and informative articles.

3. Remember to use the SQ3R steps as you read assignments in your classes at school. Use them, too, whenever you read an informational article.

Vocabulary Development Skills Dictionary

4. In this unit you have seen that context clues are often important in choosing the right dictionary definition. Remember this whenever you look up a word and try to decide which definition is the appropriate one.

Apply the Skills As You Do Your Schoolwork

The study and research skills you have learned in this section will be very useful when you read materials assigned in school. For instance, the selection on the next five pages is from a textbook used in many social studies classes. Read it to find out why a graph is used to show certain information in a clear form.

The study and research skills you have learned will help you to read this selection more efficiently. You can see how the skills work with the questions below. Read them. Then read the selection, keeping the questions in mind. Afterward answer the questions.

1.   **Following directions.** Materials needed for the project at the end of the article are not listed, but what are they? To follow the directions, what steps would you take?

2.   **Graphs.** What is a bell-shaped curve? What do the numbers along the side of each graph in the article show? What information does each graph give you?

3.   **Encyclopedia.** Suppose you wish to learn more about what the Congo Pygmies look like. In what volume of the encyclopedia would you look? (Be careful!) Suppose the article has two subtitles, *Characteristics* and *Way of Life*. Which would probably contain information on the physical appearance of the pygmy?

4.   **SQ3R.** The questions above can be used for your SQ3R questions as you read the article. Skim the article to find out where else you can find SQ3R questions for it. How can the graphs help you make up questions? What is the answer to each question you made up? If you don't know, what can you do?

Getting Information from Graphs

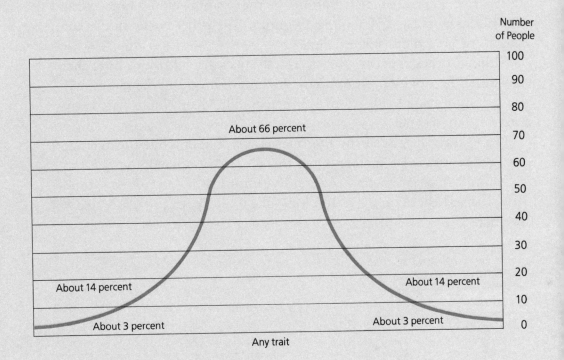

Number of People

About 66 percent

About 14 percent

About 14 percent

About 3 percent

About 3 percent

Any trait

A trait is a special quality, or feature, of living things. Common sense and blue eyes are examples of some human traits.

Study the graph on this page. How does the number of people who have a trait change as the red line curves upward? How does it change as the red line curves downward? People who work with graphs like this have called the red line a *bell-shaped curve*. Does it look like a bell to you?

When most people in a group have a trait, then that trait is said to be *normal* for the group. A curve that shows this is called a *normal curve of distribution*. This is another name for the bell-shaped curve. At the top of the curve are shown the people who have the normal trait. At each end are shown people whose traits are different in some way from the normal trait. Of course, "normal" does not mean it is *good* to have the trait. It just means that most people have it.

As you can see from the graph, if about 66 percent of the people in a group share the same trait, then it can be called normal. What percent of the group will have traits that differ from the normal?

USING CURVES OF DISTRIBUTION

A curve of distribution shows how a trait varies within a group. Look at the two curves of distribution on the graph below. One curve shows the heights of 98 Congo Pygmies. The other curve shows the heights of 119 Nilotic tribespeople.

Although these curves are not exactly bell-shaped, they show that most members of each group share the trait of height in the same way. Most Pygmies are from 1.3 to 1.5 meters tall. Most Nilotics are from 1.6 to 1.9 meters tall.

The average height of the Pygmies is 1.4 meters while the average for the Nilotics is 1.8 meters. Does this mean that none of the Nilotics are shorter than 1.8 meters? Are all Pygmies 1.4 meters? What would the left-hand curve on the graph look like if all Pygmies were actually 1.4 meters?

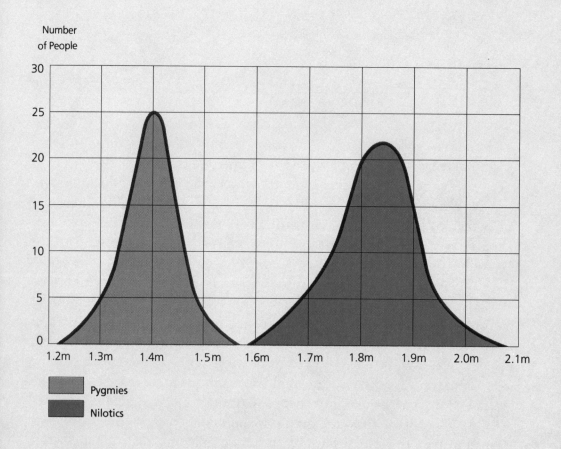

These Pygmy girls are members of the Wachimbiri tribe in Uganda.

Graphing is a clear way of showing data. By glancing at the graph, you can see that Pygmies vary in height among themselves, as do Nilotics. Perhaps you can also see, however, that height varies very little within each of the two groups.

The graph shows that there is also a great difference in height between the two groups. The probable height for a Nilotic—that is, how tall he or she is likely to be—is not the same as for a Pygmy. None of the Pygmies is as tall as the shortest Nilotics. No Nilotic is as short as the average Pygmy height—1.4 meters.

Curves of distribution are used to compare the way the same trait is distributed in different groups. The graph, in this case, shows that two groups—Pygmies and Nilotic tribespeople—differ greatly in the trait of height.

A Project To Do

Count the number of people in your classroom. Next count the number of those people who have brown eyes. Blue eyes. Green eyes. Hazel eyes. Now draw a graph from your data. You can use the graph on page 345 as a model. Label the side of the graph **Number of People**. Label the bottom **Eye Colors**. In the center bottom of your chart write the eye color that *most* people in the room have, such as Brown. On either side write Hazel, Blue, and Green. Then place a dot on the graph where the number of people who have blue eyes meets the column labeled Blue. Do the same with the other eye colors. Then connect the dots with a line. Do you have a bell curve?

The graph on page 345 shows the distribution of eye colors in one classroom. How does this graph compare to the one you made of your classroom?

Now remember to reread the questions on page 340 and answer them.

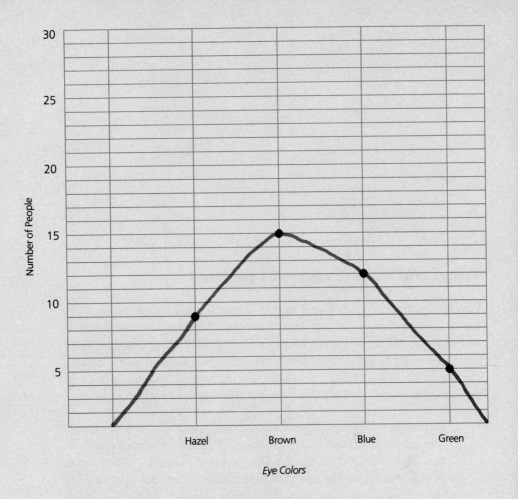

Apply the Skills As You Deal with the World

You'll find that you will need to use these study and research skills when you read material outside of school, too. The following advertisement for three summer camps is an example. Suppose you were reading it to find out more about the camps. See how to use the skills by reading the questions below first. Again keep the questions in mind as you read. Then answer the questions afterward.

1. **Following directions.** The directions provided here are the travel directions for getting to each camp. The selection does not list materials needed to follow the travel directions. What does your common sense tell you is necessary? By following any of these directions, what would be the end result?

2. **Graphs.** What information does the picture graph give you? What do the labels along the top and side tell you? Which camp would you prefer? Why?

3. **Encyclopedia.** If you wanted to learn about the sport of archery, how could you make use of an encyclopedia?

4. **SQ3R.** How can you use SQ3R as you read this selection?

Going to Camp

Summer is right around the corner. It's time to be thinking of the type of summer camp you want to go to. Below are listed three excellent (but not real) camps and what each has to offer. Which camp is the most appealing?

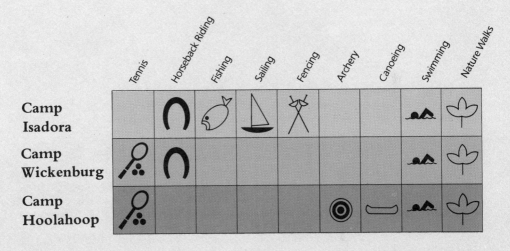

	Tennis	Horseback Riding	Fishing	Sailing	Fencing	Archery	Canoeing	Swimming	Nature Walks
Camp Isadora		♘	🐟	⛵	⚔			🏊	🍃
Camp Wickenburg	🎾	♘						🏊	🍃
Camp Hoolahoop	🎾					◎	🛶	🏊	🍃

Where It Is and How to Get There

Camp Isadora
P.O. Box 49
Watervliet, Michigan

From Chicago or Gary, take a bus to Benton Harbor. From Grand Rapids or Detroit, take a bus to Kalamazoo. Arrange in advance for the camp station wagon to meet your bus at either Benton Harbor or Kalamazoo.

Camp Wickenburg
P. O. Box 78
Wickenburg, Arizona

The camp is 60 miles northwest of Phoenix. Every Monday at 3:00 P.M., during camping season, the camp bus leaves the Phoenix airport with new campers aboard. This bus also stops at the bus stations in Phoenix and Glendale.

Camp Hoolahoop
216 Sand Drive
Evanstown, Georgia

From Charleston, Savannah or Jacksonville, take the train to Brunswick, which is 25 miles from the camp. From Atlanta, Macon or Augusta, take a bus to Brunswick. Arrange for the camp station wagon to meet your train or bus in Brunswick.

Now go back and answer the questions on page 346.

Section 4 Literary Appreciation Skills

Learning

Overview and Purposes for Reading

The Theme

Learning

1. Why is learning important? How do people gain knowledge and information?

The Skills

Literary Appreciation Skills Types of Literature

2. Why is it necessary to distinguish between fiction and nonfiction? What is the difference between them?
3. What are some kinds of nonfiction?

Study and Research Skills Parts of a Book

4. How can you get information from tables, schedules, and charts?

Learn About the Skills

Literary Appreciation Skills Types of Literature

Most of what you read is either fiction or nonfiction. **Fiction** tells about imaginary characters and imaginary events. Sometimes fiction seems very real. But if it was "dreamed up" by its author, it's still fiction.

Nonfiction is based on fact. It tells about real people, things, and events. There are many, many kinds of nonfiction. Descriptions of some of them follow.

Newspaper articles. These describe what is currently happening in the world.

Magazine articles. Frequently longer than those in newspapers, these may give more detail or explanation.

Essays, editorials, special newspaper "columns." These are fairly short, usually center on a single topic, and describe the writer's opinion or thoughts about the subject.

Biographies. These are descriptions of all or part of someone's life, written by someone else.

Autobiographies. These tell the story of someone's life or part of it, written by that person.

Diaries, journals. A person's account of what he or she thought, said, felt, or did on a day-by-day basis.

Reference materials. Dictionaries, encyclopedias, indexes and other sources of factual information. These are organized in such a way that you can easily find what you want to know. You use them to find out certain facts, but you do not read them straight through.

Informational materials. The textbooks you use in your classes at school are a good example. But there are many other informational articles and books. Almost any topic you are interested in can be found in informational books or magazine articles. There are cookbooks, car repair books, music and art books, books about games and hobbies, books about animals, cities, planets and movies.

You'll meet some examples of various kinds of nonfiction in this unit.

Study and Research Skills Parts of a Book

As you read informational material, you will often find various types of **charts, tables and schedules.** These organize many details and facts very briefly and easily into lists or columns.

Suppose your cousin is coming to visit you. She will arrive at the airport about 11 A.M. From there she will take the next bus. Then you will meet her at the Hotel Clarence. What time will she arrive at the hotel? Find out by checking the schedule below.

AIRPORT BUS SCHEDULE

Leave Airport	Pines Hotel	Lee Square	Hotel Clarence
8:15 A.M.	8:50 A.M.	9:05 A.M.	9:20 A.M.
10:15 A.M.	10:50 A.M.	11:05 A.M.	11:20 A.M.
12:15 P.M.	12:50 P.M.	1:05 P.M.	1:20 P.M.
2:30 P.M.	3:05 P.M.	3:20 P.M.	3:35 P.M.
4:30 P.M.	5:05 P.M.	5:20 P.M.	5:35 P.M.
6:30 P.M.	7:05 P.M.	7:20 P.M.	7:35 P.M.
8:30 P.M.	9:05 P.M.	9:20 P.M.	9:35 P.M.

First read the titles of the columns. The first column tells when the bus leaves the airport. Look down that column for the earliest time your cousin could get on the bus. Since she is arriving at 11 A.M., the next bus she could get leaves at 12:15 P.M. Put your finger on the line that says 12:15. Staying on that line, move to the column headed Hotel Clarence. There you see that the bus that leaves the airport at 12:15 arrives at the Hotel Clarence at 1:20 P.M. Now you know when you should be at the hotel to meet her.

Use these techniques as you get information from the charts, tables, and schedules in this unit.

Selection 1

Use the Skills

Understanding the Selection

1.   Here is a true story of two football coaches who try to trick each other. As you read, ask yourself what you think each coach learned as a result of the experience.

2.   Decide if you think what they did was fair.

Literary Appreciation Skills Types of Literature

3.   Be on the lookout for clues that tell you this is nonfiction—about real people and real events. Remember to use the notes in the margin for help if you need it.

4.   Decide if this is biography or autobiography. Keep in mind that an autobiography is written by the person whose life it describes.

Study and Research Skills Parts of a Book

5.   There is no schedule, table, or chart with this selection. This is because the information in the story doesn't need to be organized that way in order for you to locate it easily.

NOT AGAINST THE RULES

Howard Liss

Two of the smartest football coaches were Percy Haughton of Harvard and "Pop" Warner, who coached at Carlisle.

In 1908 Carlisle was scheduled to play Harvard. The week before, Warner had used a trick to help win against Syracuse. Carlisle players had pads sewn to their uniforms. Each pad was the size, shape, and color of a football, making it difficult to tell which player had the real football. When Carlisle practiced on Harvard's field the day before the game, Haughton saw the pads.

"That's not fair," said Haughton mildly.

"It's not against the rules," laughed Warner. "I can put anything I like on my players' uniforms."

But Haughton knew a few tricks, too. Just before kick-off, the coaches met to pick out the game football. Warner reached into the bag of balls and pulled one out.

It was red! Haughton had dyed all the balls crimson, the color of Harvard's jerseys.

"It's not against the rules," Haughton smiled. "A football doesn't have to be brown, does it?"

Harvard won the game, 17–0.

■ These are facts that could be checked. They are clues that the selection is about real people.

■ The subject and the conversation help make this an entertaining biographical sketch.

Check the Skills

Understanding the Selection

1. What do you think each coach learned from this experience?

2. Do you think the tricks were fair? Why or why not?

Literary Appreciation Skills Types of Literature

3. What clues tell you this is nonfiction?

4. Is this biography or autobiography? How do you know?

Study and Research Skills Parts of a Book

5. If this football game took place today, you could probably check the score in a table in the sports section of the newspaper.

Selection 2

Use the Skills

Understanding the Selection

1.   A good source of facts and information is an encyclopedia. Suppose you have a chance to travel to Greece. You want to know what kind of clothes to take along. You could read the following part of an encyclopedia article to learn about the climate.

Literary Appreciation Skills Types of Literature

2.   Look for clues that tell you this is nonfiction rather than fiction. Marginal notes will help you. Remember that nonfiction is about real places, people, or events.

Study and Research Skills Parts of a Book

3.   Included with the selection is a table that gives some details about the weather in Athens, the capital of Greece. Athens is located in the southeastern part of Greece. Decide how you could use the table to find out what the weather will probably be like when you visit Athens in January.

ENCYCLOPEDIA ARTICLE

The Climate of Greece

Greece has a so-called Mediterranean⁹ climate, with mild, wet winters and hot, dry summers. The climate may vary sharply from area to area because of differences in altitude⁹ and location. Temperatures average about 40°F. (4°C.) in winter and above 75°F. (24°C.) in summer. In much of Greece, about three-fourths of the total rainfall occurs in winter. Snow is rare in the lowlands, but falls in the high mountains. During the summer, skies are nearly cloudless, and cool breezes blow along the coasts every day.

■ Greece is a country on the Mediterranean Sea. These are facts about the climate of Greece.

Most of Greece's rivers dry up in summer because of the lack of rain. Many wells also dry up. The people in villages where the wells dry up—or where there are no other sources of water—must either have water pumped to them, or carry water from several miles away. Many of Greece's trees and plants have especially large roots that extend deep into the earth to reach water during the long dry periods.

Westerly winds bring much moisture to western Greece. There, the winds lose most of their moisture after they reach the mountains and are forced to rise to cool air. As a result, most of eastern Greece is much drier. The *precipitation*ᶜ

AVERAGE MONTHLY WEATHER IN ATHENS

	Temperatures F°		C°		Days of Rain or
	High	Low	High	Low	Snow
JAN.	54	42	12	6	7
FEB.	55	43	13	6	6
MAR.	60	46	16	8	5
APR.	67	52	19	11	3
MAY	77	60	25	16	3
JUNE	85	67	29	19	2
JULY	90	72	32	22	1
AUG.	90	72	32	22	1
SEPT.	83	66	28	19	2
OCT.	74	60	23	16	4
NOV.	64	52	18	11	6
DEC.	57	46	14	8	7

■ If you want to find out about the weather in Athens in January, you only need to find the line with the title *January*.

(rain, snow, and other forms of moisture) decreases from the northwest to the southeast. It ranges from more than 60 inches (150 centimeters) a year in northern areas to less than 15 inches (38 centimeters) on the southern island of Kéa. The rain usually falls in heavy but brief showers.

Check the Skills

Understanding the Selection

1.   If you were going to the lowlands of Greece in the winter, would you need a heavy winter coat? Why or why not?

Literary Appreciation Skills Types of Literature

2.   How do you know that this selection is nonfiction?

Study and Research Skills Parts of a Book

3.   Use the table to find out the average low temperature in Athens in January. Look only for the information you need.

Use the Skills

Understanding the Selection

1. Studying and learning were thought to be unsuitable for women during much of the past. Read this selection to find out why Maria Mitchell, a famous astronomer, was able to overcome these unfortunate limits.

Literary Appreciation Skills Types of Literature

2. Use what you know about types of nonfiction to help you decide whether this is a biography or an autobiography.

Study and Research Skills Parts of a Book

3. This selection has no chart, table, or schedule. Decide why you think none was included.

MARIA MITCHELL, ASTRONOMER 1818–1889

Charlene Lundell

■ What information in the title signals that this is nonfiction?

In 1905, Maria Mitchell was named to the Hall of Fame for Great Americans for her important work in astronomy.[g]

■ Using these clues, you should already be able to tell that this is *not* an auto-biography.

Maria was born on Nantucket Island in 1818. In those days most people did not believe business and study were suitable for a lady. Girls were taught to sew, paint, and take care of a home. Boys were sent to school. But Nantucket Island was isolated[g] from the rest of the country. It was a whaling[g] community. While the men were at sea with the whaling fleets, the women took care of the business and spent their spare time reading and listening to lectures. On Nantucket Island a bright young girl like Maria Mitchell could learn all she wanted without anyone telling her it wasn't proper for a girl.

William Mitchell, her father, made astronomical observations for the United States Coast Survey. He had a small telescope on the roof of their home. Maria loved to watch her father work. The observatory[g] became her favorite spot. Her father quickly noticed how Maria detected[g] small differences in color between different stars. He began to teach her all he knew about astronomy.

While her father scanned the sky, Maria carefully recorded each finding he made. Sometimes Maria used the telescope, and her father wrote down notes. When she was twelve, she recorded the exact moment that the annular[g] eclipse of the sun began while her father observed it through his telescope. It was a day she remembered all her life.

When Maria was sixteen she entered a school for young ladies. Her teacher found she had a quick mind for mathematics. He gave her one difficult mathematical assignment after another. Soon she knew all her instructor could teach her, and she longed to know more.

Two years later a wonderful opportunity was presented to her. She was offered a job as the librarian at Nantucket's new library.

The new library had many books about mathematics and navigation.⁹ She began to study all the library had to offer. At night she joined her father in his observatory and put her new knowledge to work.

One evening Maria Mitchell hurried to the observatory on the roof to scan the stars while her father visited with friends downstairs. As usual she lost herself in her work, peering through the telescope and jotting down notes.

Suddenly her telescope showed a new, fuzzy object. She knew no object belonged in that part of the sky. Quickly she checked her notes and maps. Her heart raced with excitement. She looked through the telescope again. It was a ghostly object, faint and hazy with a bright center. Its head pointed down and its great tail flared upward. Immediately she wrote down the exact time—10:30 P.M., October 1, 1847.

She dashed downstairs and whispered in her father's ear. He jumped to his feet and followed her to the observatory.

Carefully he adjusted the telescope and viewed the heavenly body never before seen. He smiled at her, then opened his notebook and recorded Maria's new discovery.

King Frederick VI of Denmark had established an award of a gold medal to be given to the first discoverer of a telescopic comet.⁹

After some confusion, Maria Mitchell's discovery was finally established. She became the first American astronomer to discover a telescopic comet. She not only discovered it, but also computed⁹ its orbit,⁹ an extremely difficult task. She made a major contribution to the science of astronomy.

It was the first time Denmark's gold medal was awarded to an American.

■ Charts showing the positions of the stars are available. Why do you think one wasn't included here?

The discovery brought Miss Mitchell worldwide recognition. Through the years that followed she made many more important astronomical discoveries. She compiled astronomical data for the *Nautical Almanac,* a publication of the United States Naval Observatory, and became professor of astronomy at Vassar College.

Maria Mitchell described her view of science with these words: "It is not ALL mathematics nor all logic; it is somewhat beauty and poetry."

Check the Skills

Understanding the Selection

1. Why was Maria Mitchell able to overcome the attitude that studying and learning were unsuitable for women?

Literary Appreciation Skills Types of Literature

2. How do you know that this selection is a biography?

Study and Research Skills Parts of a Book

3. There is no chart, table, or schedule with this selection because none of those would provide further information about Maria Mitchell. But if you wanted to learn about the various groups of stars, or constellations, you could probably find a chart in a reference book such as an encyclopedia.

Selection 4

Use the Skills

Understanding the Selection

Pretend that you and your parents are staying in a hotel in downtown Chicago. From Chicago's O'Hare International Airport you will fly home to Boston on Saturday. However, you don't have tickets yet. You don't even know when the flights leave on that day.

1.   Think what kinds of information you would need to learn before you could take the plane to Boston.

Literary Appreciation Skills Types of Literature

2.   The following selection is an airline schedule that you might use to find the information you need. This is a very specialized kind of reference material. Decide if it is a better source of flight information than a newspaper travel column written by a person who visited Boston.

Study and Research Skills Parts of a Book

3.   Remember that to find information in a schedule, you should *not* read everything in it. Instead, look for labels and titles of columns that tell you where you'll find certain facts. Remember, too, to look for a key to abbreviations or symbols.

AIRLINE SCHEDULE

CHICAGO	Leave	Arrive	Flight No.	Stops or Via	Meals	Equip.	Freq.
To Albany, N Y	9:45a	12:27p	564	NON-STOP	☕	727	Daily
F$113.00 Y$87.00	8:00p	10:45p	402	NON-STOP		727	Daily
From Albany	10:00a	10:59a	109	NON-STOP		727	Daily
	7:29p	8:30p	567	NON-STOP	X	727	ExSa
To Boston	6:40a	9:44a	206	NON-STOP	X	707	Daily
F$129.00 Y$99.00	10:00a	1:03p	454	NON-STOP	X	707	Daily
	1:50p	4:58p	362	NON-STOP		727	Daily
	3:55p	7:05p	28	NON-STOP		D10	Daily
From Boston	7:00a	8:22a	321	NON-STOP	X	727	ExSaSu
	7:40a	10:07a	415	ONE-STOP	X	707	Daily
	9:45a	11:11a	105	NON-STOP	X	707	Daily
	2:45p	4:14p	307	NON-STOP		727	Daily
To Buffalo	7:00a	9:19a	270	NON-STOP	X	727	Daily
F$87.00 Y$67.00	1:55p	4:12p	108	NON-STOP	☕	727	Daily
	8:05p	10:29p	192	NON-STOP		D10	Daily
From Buffalo	7:40a	8:09a	181	NON-STOP	X	D10	Daily
	1:40p	2:09p	319	NON-STOP		727	Daily
	7:55p	8:26p	227	NON-STOP		727	Daily

Symbols	X Meal	☕ Snack	F—First Class	Y—Coach

■ Which column tells what time this flight arrives in Boston?

■ Will you be given a meal during the 10 A.M. flight to Boston?

Check the Skills

Understanding the Selection

1. What kinds of information would you need to learn before you could take a flight home to Boston? Would the airline schedule tell you everything you need? Why or why not?

Literary Appreciation Skills Types of Literature

2. Which source probably has more dependable information, this schedule or a newspaper travel column? Why?

Study and Research Skills Parts of a Book

3. If you take the plane that leaves Chicago at 10 A.M., what time will you arrive in Boston?

Use the Skills

By reading this factual magazine article you will learn how astronauts eat in outer space and what kinds of food they eat. You will also learn how the preparation, the serving, and eating of food has improved through the years for astronauts. Be aware of clues that tell you that this is nonfiction.

No table, chart, or schedule accompanies the article. But as you read you may think of information that you could find in table, chart, or schedule form that would give additional facts about astronauts.

This time there are no notes in the margin to help you.

FOOD FOR SPACE

When astronauts have to spend many days in space, they must eat good, nourishing food so that their duties can be well performed. Scientists began their research into space foods with the first Mercury flight.

Space meals must undergo many conditions that are not common on Earth. Weight and space limitations in the spacecraft make it necessary for astronauts to take food that is lightweight and easily stored. Food must also be taken directly from sealed containers. Weightlessness during space flight makes it difficult to keep solid food on an ordinary plate or liquid in an open cup.

The requirements for feeding people during long space flights began to be studied before the Mercury missions. Astronaut Scott Carpenter reported that crumbs from his bite-size cubes floated freely in his cabin.

Many astronauts had problems with crumbs, unappetizing taste and texture. Some had difficulty adding water (rehydrating^c) to the freeze-dried^g foods. However, they found the actual act of eating in space to be relatively simple.

During the Gemini missions the food was improved. The bite-size cubes of fruit, meat, bread, and dessert foods were coated with an edible^g gelatin to cut down on the crumbs. Rehydratable foods were increased so that the astronauts would have more variety in their menus.

The meals were nicely packaged. The cubes were vacuum-sealed^g in clear plastic. The rehydratables came in laminated^g plastic bags with a one-way valve on one end and a tube on the other. The astronaut would insert a gun-type water dispenser into the bag and add a squirt or two to the dry contents. After the mixture was kneaded it could be squeezed through the tube into the astronaut's mouth. A typical meal included shrimp cocktail, chicken, vegetables, toast, butterscotch pudding, and apple juice.

The Apollo foods were similar to Gemini foods, but more rehydratables were added for variety. However, the astronauts were still not impressed with the rehydratables because the appearance was not particularly appetizing, and the result was a very thick lukewarm soup.

The Apollo 8 crewmen got a surprise on Christmas 1968. They opened a beautiful dinner which included turkey chunks, gravy, and all the trimmings of a Christmas dinner on Earth. They were able to heat this in their food heating system. It was the first "home-cooked" meal in space. They also demonstrated that space food can be eaten with a spoon.

The 173-day Skylab program provided the crewmen with freezers, refrigerators, and warming trays. Their foods were packaged in aluminum cans with pull-out lids. At mealtimes, the crew members assembled these cans into a magnetized food warmer/retainer tray. They ate this food with spoons, forks, and knives.

The Space Shuttle crew will eat a 3,000-calorie-a-day diet that will range from pot roast to scrambled eggs. They'll even have wafers and snacks. Hot and cold liquids will be put on board in dry forms, and the astronauts will add water to them before drinking. They will eat their meals from a warming tray which is specially designed to hold food, utensils, and moisturized towels in a weightless environment.

Check the Skills

Understanding the Selection

1. As space travel has developed, so have space foods. How did scientists learn to improve food for astronauts?

2. What did you learn from this article?

Literary Appreciation Skills Types of Literature

3. What clues helped you decide that this is nonfiction?

Study and Research Skills Parts of a Book

4. Suppose you are interested in finding out the names of space missions and the astronauts who participated in each. You could look for a chart or table with that information in a reference book such as an encyclopedia.

Apply What You Learned in Unit 13

The Theme

Learning

1.   You gained some knowledge and information as you read this unit. You learned about some reading skills and how to use them. You also were asked to think a little about learning. You may have thought that people learn only in school. But you now know that learning goes on anywhere. People learn at home, on their jobs, and through reading they do on their own. Why do you think learning is important?

•   Reading is one way to gain knowledge and information. What are some other ways?

The Skills

Literary Appreciation Skills Types of Literature

2.   It is necessary to know whether what you're reading is fiction or nonfiction. You must do this mainly so you know whether the information is dependable. Remember that fiction is imaginary and nonfiction is based on fact.

3.   Because nonfiction is factual, it is the kind of writing you can use to find information. You may want to review the short description of some kinds of non-fiction given at the beginning of this unit. Keeping those in mind can help you choose an appropriate source for what you need.

Study and Research Skills Parts of a Book

4.   Remember that tables, schedules, and charts are a type of nonfiction, too. They summarize information in a way that makes it easy to find only the exact details you need to know. Use tables, schedules, and charts efficiently by reading titles of columns and by noting any key to symbols or abbreviations.

Unit 14

Changes

Overview and Purposes for Reading

The Theme

Changes

1. What effects do changes have on people's lives?

The Skills

Literary Appreciation Skills Story Elements

2. As you read a story, how can you figure out the characters and the setting?

3. Are these elements always important?

Vocabulary Development Skills Word Structure

4. How can knowing about suffixes help you figure out some words you don't know? What are some common suffixes?

Literary Appreciation Skills Story Elements

Fictional stories have three major elements—characters, setting, and plot. This unit focuses on characters and setting.

Characters are the people or animals in the story. The **setting** of a story is where and when it takes place.

Characterization means the way an author tells you about the characters in a story. Of course you learn about the characters from the author's description. But you also learn what the characters are like from what they do and say.

Read the following very short story. Think about the setting and the personalities of the characters.

> Once a fox saw a crow fly by with a delicious-looking piece of cheese in its beak. Hungrily, the fox watched as the crow settled on the branch of a tree.
>
> "That's for me," said the fox to himself.
>
> "Good day, Mr. Crow," he called up. "How fine you look today. How glossy your feathers are! How bright your eye! Surely your voice must be more beautiful than any other bird's. Let me hear a song so I may salute you as the King of the Songbirds."
>
> Pleased, the crow cawed his best. But the moment he opened his mouth, the cheese fell to the ground and the fox snapped it up.
>
> "Thank you," the fox said. "Now, in exchange for your cheese, let me give you a bit of advice—never trust flatterers!"

What are the personalities of the two characters? Nowhere does the story describe the fox as clever and the crow as stupid. But what they do tells you that they are.

The place in the story is a meadow. But the time is not given. The time isn't even important to the story.

Sometimes the setting of a story can be very important. For example, a story about people living on the moon would have to be set in the future. The time and place of that story would be very important to understanding what the story was about.

Try the Skill. Read the part of a story that follows. Decide what the setting is and if it is important to the story. Also figure out from the characters' attitudes and thoughts what kind of people they are.

> Suzanne and Joan often went to Joan's apartment after school. The apartment overlooked one of the busiest streets in the city. Suzanne, who lived on a quiet street, enjoyed the view. Joan had seen it all her life and was bored. Usually they played records. Suzanne didn't have a record player, so this was a treat for her. She wished she had a room of her own, like Joan. She admired the entire apartment, with its spacious rooms and large picture windows. Suzanne could not understand why her friend was not excited about living in such a pleasant apartment.

The place is important in this story, because the story is really about the girls' attitudes towards the apartment. Although the story doesn't say so, you know that the story is set in modern times. The clues are the mention of the record player, school, picture windows, and so on.

How could you describe Joan and Suzanne? What kind of people do you think they are?

You'll learn more about characterization and setting as you read this unit.

Vocabulary Development Skills Word Structure

You know that a suffix is one or more syllables added to the end of a word. Many suffixes have meanings of their own. So adding the meaning of the suffix to the base word can help you figure out many words that contain suffixes. A suffix also gives a clue to how the word is used in a sentence.

Remember that sometimes the spelling of the base word changes a little when a suffix is added. For example, the final e of *love* is dropped in *lovable,* and the final y in *happy* changes to i in *happiness.* Also, sometimes a suffix is spelled in several ways, as in *-ation, -ion, -ition,* and *-tion.*

Here's a chart you can refer to as you read this unit.

Suffix	Common Meaning	Examples
-er, -or	one who; that which	container, informer, director
-ish	like; something like; about	foolish, childish, yellowish, fortyish
-ity, -ty	state, quality, or condition of being	reality, sincerity, safety, loyalty
-less	without; free from	careless, endless
-ly	in a way like	carefully, happily, exactly
-ly	appropriate to; like; happening every time	friendly, orderly, beastly, cowardly, weekly, daily
-ness	state, condition, quality of	brightness, thickness, readiness
-ous, -ious	full of; having; like	adventurous, courageous
-ry	things together; work of; result of	pottery, scenery, robbery, carpentry
-y	full of; like	cloudy, squeaky

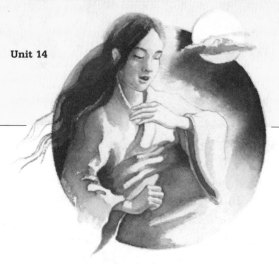

Use the Skills

Understanding the Selection

Here is an unusual modern ghost story from Taiwan, a large island off the coast of China. It doesn't really have an ending, so you are free to imagine your own.

1. As you read the story, think about the way the two main characters are affected by change in their lives.

Literary Appreciation Skills Story Elements

2. One of the characters in the story is a lonely young man. The author never describes him that way, however. As you read the story, notice how the man's actions reveal his loneliness.

3. Decide if the setting is important or not. Notes in the margin will help.

Vocabulary Development Skills Word Structure

4. Use the notes in the margin to help you figure out the meaning of some words that have suffixes.

A STORY FOR POETS
A Folk Tale for Today

Cora Cheney

High on a mountain near the city of Taipei there was once a graveyard with a fine view. Na-Tao trees and willows sifted the sunshine by day and the moonlight by night. Altogether it was a most fortunate⁹ place for one's ancestors.

But nowadays young people forget. Some people have even ceased tending the graves of their ancestors.ᶜ⁹ Some of the graves became neglected and shabby, rundown homes for lonesome spirits.

And then the very worst happened. Someone bought the land and moved the tombs and built a college over the old cemetery.

Wise old people on the neighboring farms had advised against moving the graves. Ghosts hoveredᶜ over the land, anxious and watchful. Who wants to harm students with their fresh faces and their bright minds, but then who wants to disturb tired ghosts?

One night a young student, a poet, was weary, yet unable to sleep or write. He was trying to write a poem. Laying aside his papers, he walked out into the cool night to breathe the fresh air.

It was very late and no one was about. A dim winter moonlight skimmedᶜ the campus. He walked to the edge of the cliff to sit alone on the mountain slope, thinking long sad thoughts of youth and poetry.

He was sitting there when he first heard the singing. It was a simple melody, a song he had always known but had never known. Who was singing? He looked behind him. The dormitory⁹ windows were dark. He stood up and looked around, but there was no one in sight. Could he be imagining things?

■ The suffix –ry can mean "the work of." So you know poetry means "the work of the poet."

■ Taking away the –ry at the end of dormitory doesn't leave you with any base word. So here the letters –ry are not a suffix.

He settled down again, and the singing continued, clear as the song of a baby bird at dawn.

"Where are you? Who are you?" he whispered.

With that, a slight girl in a white silk robe slipped from behind a Na-Tao tree and sat down beside him. Her robe was an old style such as he had seen on ancient scroll⁹ pictures.

Had he met her before? It seemed he had always known her but he had never known her.

"Who are you?" he asked, grasping her pale hands.

"I am Ah-Leah," she whispered. "I have come to sing you to sleep."

"Are you a music student?" he asked.

"Yes, you might call me that," she laughed with laughter that sounded like wind on a harp. "Shh," she said. "The night is too still and beautiful for talking," and she put a cool finger over his mouth to quiet his questions.

How long he sat there he never knew. He only knew that she was gone when he woke the next morning, a little stiff from sleeping on the ground in the cool dew.

As soon as he had washed and eaten his breakfast he went to the desk at the girls' dormitory.

"I would like to see Miss Ah-Leah—I'm sorry, I don't know her family name."

"Ah-Leah?" said the girl on duty. "I don't think we have a student with that name."

"But you must," insisted the boy. "She is a music student."

"No, there is no one by that name enrolledᶜ here."

The boy rubbed his head and frowned. He must see her again, the misty girl in white with the heavenly voice.

An old man, the floor scrubber, paused and looked at the boy.

"Was she white and slender with a voice like wind blowing through the strings of a viol?"⁹

"Yes, yes," said the boy. "Do you know her?"

"I know about her," said the old man with a faraway smile. "She died fifty years ago, and her grave was on the

■ The young man's search for Ah-Leah is one action that shows his loneliness.

hillside before they tore it up and moved her body. Sometimes she walks here at night, singing for special people. They say she likes poets, young poets. Perhaps she died of love for a poet. Did you see her? You are lucky if you did."

"Lucky?" said the young poet. "I wonder. I shall never feel lucky until I meet her again."

■ Now you know that the place is very important. The story had to happen where the graveyard had been. The time is less important, although it had to be sometime after the graveyard was moved.

Check the Skills

Understanding the Selection

1. How did the changing of the graves affect Ah-Leah? Ah-Leah's appearance was a change in the poet's life. How do you think he was affected by it? Why do you think as you do?

Literary Appreciation Skills Story Elements

2. The author gives hints that the poet is lonely earlier in the story. The poet is described as "thinking long sad thoughts." Then his first thought when Ah-Leah appears is that he has always known her.

3. This story takes place "high on a mountain near the city of Taipei." Could it occur anywhere else? Why do you think so?

Vocabulary Development Skills Word Structure

4. In the story, you read the words in the list below. Look at the underlined letters in each word. Those letters form a suffix in the words in the first column. But the underlined letters in the words in the second column do not form suffixes in those words. Why not?

watchful	anxious
misty	unable
heavenly	winter
scrubber	melody
lucky	slender

Use the Skills

Understanding the Selection

Old Ramon is a shepherd. He has worked for the same family for most of his life. He is used to tending the sheep with the help of two dogs. This summer the owner of the ranch has sent his young son out to help Old Ramon and learn from him.

1. A great change would come about in a shepherd's life if all coyotes disappeared. That is not likely to happen. But many shepherds probably wish it would. As you read this story, find out Old Ramon's surprising opinion of that imaginary change.

Literary Appreciation Skills Story Elements

2. Notice what you learn about the old shepherd from what he says about loneliness and about coyotes.

3. The setting is very important to this story. See if you can decide why.

Vocabulary Development Skills Word Structure

4. Use your knowledge of suffixes to help yourself figure out several words you may not know. Notes in the margin and the list on page 373 will help.

OLD RAMON

Jack Schaefer

The hills rose dark and rounded in the night toward the far heights of the mountains beyond. At their edging where a smattering⁹ of grass began and a small spring fed a small pool the flockᶜ was bedded. The last embersᶜ of the little fire nearby made a tiny pinpoint of living spark in the immensity⁹ of the big land. Old Ramon sat close, wrapped in his blanket, and watched the glowing of the embers fade. A few feet away the boy lay on the ground, a shapeless roll in his blanket.

■ If you don't know the meaning of the base word *immense*, check the glossary.

The boy stirred and he too sat up, holding the blanket about him. "It is very late," he said. "And yet I cannot sleep. How is that?"

"It is often so after a long day and into the night," said Old Ramon. "The man then is too tired to sleep right away. His head is full of the long journeying and his muscles are tight. He must sit quiet and let the tightness slip away and then between a word and a wink of the eye the sleep creeps on him."

Slow moments moved and from beyond the flock came a long low howling that seemed a part of the dark vastness⁹ around, that climbed in tone and intensity and broke off in a series of short yappings.ᶜ The boy sat up straighter and looked around toward the packs and the loaded rifle leaning against one of them.

"There is no need of the gun," said Old Ramon. "It is only the coyote.⁹ I think that he is saying things about us and our using his water hole. I do not think they are nice things. But he will not harm the flock. Pedro is there."

The howling came again, long and long-drawn. It died away and was followed by barking from close by the flock, barking angry and challenging.⁹

"That is Sancho," said Old Ramon. "He is young. He talks back. But it is useless. That is what the coyote wants, to insult the dogs and make them angry. That is his game now. He would make no noise if he thought that he could get one of the sheep. I think that already he has tried and that now he knows. Pedro is there."

The howling came again and broke into many short barks and yappings. It was several sounds at once seeming to come from several places.

The boy sat up straight again. "There are more of them!"

Old Ramon chuckled, a reassuring sound in the night. "There is only the one. Ah, he is smart, Don Coyote. That is one of his little tricks. To throw his voice and sound like many. I think there are as many stories about him as there are hairs in his own tail. When we are settled on in the hills for a time I will tell some of them to you. . . . Ai, he is a nuisance and a thief and an <u>insulter</u> of good dogs. But he is Don Coyote. Ramon would miss him if he were gone, if his kind were all killed. He is like a voice of the land and of the night over the land. . . . Ai, ai, he is smart. He is not big but he is very clever. I have known him to sneak to a flock in the bright light of the day and pick a sheep too stupid to know he is not a dog and take hold of her wool and pull and lead her away far enough so that the noise of her killing would not be heard. And that with a lazy dog asleep close by. . . . And he knows the gun, even the pistol that is small and carried at the belt. A man walks with a gun and the coyote sees him but he never sees the coyote. He walks without a gun and Don Coyote may not move much more than to get out of the way unless a dog is there to chase him. Ai, he is cunning and full of tricks. But my Pedro knows them all. . . ."

The howling came again, farther away and fading, and then there was only the soft cool silence of the night. The boy shifted a little in his blanket. "Ramon. Is it not sometimes lonely, tending the sheep?"

"I suppose it is so for some men," said Old Ramon slowly. "For those who are accustomed⁹ to the towns and the clutterᶜ and the clatterᶜ of many people about. It has never been so for Ramon. It is never so for the true herder

■ Here is the suffix –er.

■ Ramon's respect for the coyotes and for his dogs is clear.

■ Ramon really likes being a shepherd.

of sheep, for the man with the feel of the flock born in him. . . . I have thought much about that. I think that it rests upon what a man is in himself, on the inside of him. I think that to be alone is one thing and that to be lonely is another thing altogether. I have felt the loneliness when I was in a town with many people around me. I think that is because it was a strange town to me and I did not know the people. But I have never felt the loneliness when I was alone with my flock even in the far valleys of the mountains and no other people within many miles. I think perhaps that is because I know this land and its people that are the wild

■ There are two suffixes here. They are –ly and –ness.

things living in it and nothing of it is strange to me. . . . I do not see how a man can be lonely when the good God's world is open around him, when there is the sun that shines by day and the stars that look down by night and the wind that blows and the mountains that watch all and everything and the grass that grows, when there are the sheep that need him to care for them and the dogs to help him and Don Coyote to call him names and the owl to ask him questions from hidden places. . . ."

"I think," said the boy, "that my father is right. There are many things that are not in the books."

Check the Skills

Understanding the Selection

1. Ramon says that he would not want all coyotes to disappear. Why not? What effect does Ramon think that kind of change would have on himself?

   You might enjoy reading the book that this selection was taken from. It's *Old Ramon* by Jack Schaefer, published in 1960 by Houghton Mifflin Company.

Literary Appreciation Skills Story Elements

2. The author tells you about Ramon mainly through what Ramon says. You know that Ramon cares about nature. You know that he likes being a shepherd. What clues in his conversation helped you realize these things about him?

3. This story could not take place in a city. Why not? Could it take place in the daytime? Why or why not? The time and the place affect this story very much. So you know the setting is very important in this story.

Vocabulary Development Skills Word Structure

4. What is the base word in *immensity? insulter? loneliness?*

Use the Skills

Understanding the Selection

1. A sudden accident has a tremendous effect on the actions of the girl in this story. Find out how she handles the situation. Think, too, how she changes because of it.

Literary Appreciation Skills Story Elements

2. Note what the author reveals about Peggy at the beginning, as the story unfolds, and at the end.

3. This is another story in which the setting is extremely important. You'll see why as you read. You'll notice that the setting requires some special terms and words that probably are not familiar to you. Don't worry too much about their exact meaning. They are not too important to the story. Peggy's feelings and her reasons for acting are the main things to note as you read.

Vocabulary Development Skills Word Structure

4. Remember to use what you know about suffixes for help with some words. Use the chart on page 373, or a dictionary, if you need to.

THE SAILOR'S DAUGHTER

R. G. Coates

The wind was gusting,^c and Peggy's face and shoulders were getting wet from the spray that came over the bow^c of the Sunfish. In her left hand she nervously held the tiller.^g With her right she pulled in the mainsheet,^c the rope that controlled the sail.

■ The opening two paragraphs set the scene and tell you something about Peggy.

Her father had started taking her sailing when she was only five years old, and now at ten she was an experienced^c sailor—except for one thing. She had never handled the boat alone before. Now she had to muster^g all of her sailing ability to save her father's life.

Shaking from the cold wind, Peggy thought about her father. They had sailed to Sand Key this morning, and after lunch they had hiked the cliffs. But while he was scaling a steep face, her father had suddenly slipped and fallen to a rocky ledge below. He was unconscious when she reached him, his right leg bent at an odd angle. There was no way to get him back to the Sunfish, so Peggy had made the desperate^c decision to leave her father and go for help. Even though they had sailed across the bay together hundreds of times, the thought of doing it alone terrified her. But she was a sailor's daughter, she told herself. She would make it. She *had* to make it.

As she pulled in the mainsheet, Peggy watched the front edge of her sail. It was luffing^c—flapping in the breeze—so she pulled harder. When the ripples in the canvas were gone, she knew her sail was getting the right amount of wind. The boat began to skim the waves like the flat stones she had skipped across the water that morning. Sailing with her father, the speed had been exciting. Alone, it was scary.

Peggy kept watching the sail. The gusts grew stronger, and the boat began to bounce. She knew it would be safer to go slower, but she had to get help quickly. So, holding the tiller steady, she tucked her toes under the hiking straps^g

and shifted her weight to the side of the boat. Leaning out with her head and shoulders over the water now, she could balance the boat despite the strong wind. The Sunfish barely touched the waves.

After what seemed ages, Peggy spotted the lighthouse and aimed directly for it. Suddenly the sail began to flap violently back and forth, and the boat stopped. She had done something wrong. In her mind, Peggy raced over all the instructions her father had given her. How could she get moving again?

■ The suffix –or can help you here.

She looked at the red ribbon tied to the mast. The homemade wind indicator was flying straight back now; by aiming for the lighthouse, Peggy had turned directly into the wind. That was wrong. To correct her mistake, she moved to the center of the boat. When the Sunfish began to drift backwards, she gently pushed the tiller away from her body. The bow turned obediently,ᶜ and the boat picked up speed.

Soon the wind was pressing on the sail so hard that the mainsheet burned Peggy's palm. To give it some rest, she fastened the rope to a cleatᶜ mounted in the center of the boat and let her hand drag in the water. It was a dangerous thing to do with the wind blowing like this, but it relieved the pain.

Clouds covered the sun, the air grew much colder, and Peggy—most of her clothes damp—grew colder, too. She had left her windbreaker on Sand Key, wrapped around her father's shoulders, and she missed its protection now. To take her mind off the biting wind, she looked for the lighthouse again. In panic she saw that instead of pushing her towards it, the wind was blowing her away from it! Peggy quickly realized that she couldn't sail in a straight line. She would have to tackᶜ—setting a zigzag course—to get anywhere at all, and it would be tricky in this high wind.

The waves grew choppier, and the Sunfish began to take on water. Peggy's jeans got soaked as she knelt in the center of the boat. Gently, she pushed the tiller away from her.

The bow began to turn, and the mainsheet went slack. Slowly the boom rolled across the boat. Ducking under it, Peggy shifted to the windward side to balance the boat. She adjusted the mainsheet, the sail filled, and the Sunfish was off again.

Pushing the wet bangs from her forehead with an even wetter sleeve, she looked for the lighthouse. At this course, she would be west of it and would have to tack several more times. Peggy cleated the mainsheet again and looked at her raw hand. Suddenly she felt ashamed of her selfish concern. It was her father who was in real pain, lying alone and

■ The setting of the boat is what is important. Don't get too concerned about the exact meaning of the specialized terms.

■ Here is more characterization of Peggy.

helpless back on Sand Key. Ignoring her hand, she un-cleated the sheet, pulled it tighter, and sailed as close to the wind as possible. The lighthouse seemed nearer now.

Soon Peggy was ready to tack again. In her hurry, she made the turn much, much too fast, and the wind suddenly lifted the boat like a teacup, spilling its contents into the sea. Peggy hit the water so fast she barely had time to hold her breath. She surfaced, grateful that her life jacket popped her up so quickly and relieved to see that the boat had managed to stay upright. Gasping and sputtering, she swam for the stern. Getting aboard wouldn't be easy. In the past, her father had always given her a boost.

Peggy grabbed for the boat and kicked the cold water furiously, trying to hoist herself over the edge. It didn't work. She felt her muscles begin to stiffen and knew she had to get into the boat quickly—before all her body heat was gone. Holding her breath, pulling and kicking, she tried again, and again she fell back into the cold bay.

She took a few seconds to rest, then tried once more. Finally, kicking as hard as possible, she managed to lift her shoulders and chest onto the edge of the boat, grab for the hiking straps, and haul herself aboard.

For a few minutes she lay in the bottom of the boat, too numb and exhausted to move. Then she looked around. Except for what was dripping from her clothes, there was no water in the Sunfish. It must have spilled out when the boat tipped. Grateful that she didn't have to waste time bailing, she set sail again.

The sun was gone now, and the wind began to die down. Peggy knew time was running out. If the wind stopped completely, she would be stranded. But somehow the wind did hold up. Peggy tacked twice more to reach the shore. Then, her body almost frozen, she pulled up the center-board and beached the Sunfish. She didn't bother to lower her sail, but raced for the lighthouse, running awkwardly in her wet clothes. Breathlessly she explained what had hap-pened, and while the lighthouse keeper radioed the Coast Guard, Peggy called her mother.

Together they reached the hospital just after her father had been admitted to the emergency room. His leg was, indeed, broken, but he had regained consciousness and was going to be all right.

The next morning, the doctors finally allowed Peggy to see her father. Kissing her face, he thanked her for her bravery. "Did you have any trouble?" he asked her with concern.

"Nothing a sailor's daughter couldn't handle," she answered, giving him a reassuring⁹ hug.

"Nothing a good *sailor* couldn't handle," he said proudly.

Check the Skills

Understanding the Selection

1. How does her father's accident affect Peggy? Do you think Peggy changed because of it? Do you think she'll have more confidence in herself? Why do you think so?

Literary Appreciation Skills Story Elements

2. There is little conversation in this story. You learn about Peggy mainly from the descriptions of what she does. What kind of person is she? Why do you think as you do?

3. Why is the setting so important to this story? Could the story have happened somewhere else? Why or why not?

Vocabulary Development Skills Word Structure

4. The following words from the story all include suffixes. Use what you know about suffixes. See if you can explain what the words mean. Look back at page 373 only if you really have to.

sailor	indicator	breathlessly
nervously	selfish	bravery

Selection 4

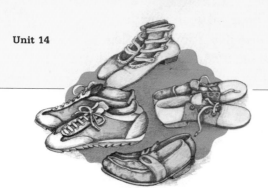

Use the
Skills

Understanding the Selection

1. Here's a poem about changes—present and, probably, future.

2. What is the poet's attitude toward these changes?

Literary Appreciation Skills Story Elements

3. Find out what the girl talking in this poem is like. What hints does the poet give you about her?

4. Decide if the setting is important to this poem.

Vocabulary Development Skills Word Structure

5. The meanings of the words in this poem are clear. You probably won't need to use your knowledge of suffixes here.

CLOTHES

Elizabeth Jennings

My mother keeps on telling me
When she was in her teens
She wore quite different clothes from mine
And hadn't heard of jeans,

T-shirts, no hats, and dresses that
Reach far above our knees.
I laughed at first and then I thought
One day my kids will tease

> ■ Here's a hint about the time the girl is describing.

And scoff^c at what *I'm* wearing now.
What will *their* fashions be?
I'd give an awful lot to know,
To look ahead and see.

Girls dressed like girls perhaps once more
And boys no longer half
Resembling us. Oh, what's in store
To make *our* children laugh?

> ■ What do you learn about the girl?

Check the Skills

Understanding the Selection

1. What are the changes mentioned in the poem?

2. What does the poet think of changes in fashion and the effects of those changes?

Literary Appreciation Skills Story Elements

3. How would you describe the girl? Why?

4. The time being described is when very short dresses were fashionable. Is this setting important? Do dresses that are that short look funny now, as the poet expected?

Vocabulary Development Skills Word Structure

5. Remember that knowing about suffixes won't help you with all new words you meet. But it's always worth a try!

Use the
Skills

Our fortunes often change from day to day. We have good days and bad days. Ludell, the girl in the next story, goes to a small country school in Georgia. She is expecting a good day. But she is due for a surprise. You learn something about Ludell in this excerpt from a recent novel. Read to find out what it is, and decide how important the setting is. There are no marginal notes this time. You're on your own!

LUDELL'S AMAZING PAPER

Brenda Wilkinson

Miss Stevanson was reading off portions[c] of different people's book reports to the class, complaining about how poorly they'd all done.

"I tell you," she said, "I'm beginning to wonder if any of you ever picked up a book that wasn't forced on you!"

Ludell beamed with pride, knowing that she didn't fall into that category.[g]

"You're gonna pay for wasting your time, I tell you! Some of these reports sound like first graders wrote them!" she continued, thumbing through the papers.

Ludell sat, going, "Let her get to mine, let her come cross mine. I know it's good! I just know it!"

She'd spent two weeks on that paper, and when she'd finally completed it, had sat reading it over and over, amazed at herself. Each time she read it, she liked it better and better. All week she'd been wondering when Miss Stevanson was going to get around to checking the reports.

Suddenly Miss Stevanson had stopped fussing and flipping papers and was staring silently at this particular[g] one. Then she read out slowly.

"Ramona."

"It's mine, it's mine!" Ludell cried out silently.

"*Ramona* is another of Helen Hunt Jackson's splendid[g] works wherein she preaches[c] the doctrine[g] of humanitarianism,"[g] read Miss Stevanson. "Uh-uh," she went, stopping and shaking her head. "You didn't write this!" she said, shaking the paper.

"Yes mam, I did," Ludell said in a soft tearful voice.

"I'm sorry Ludell, but I know what every student is capable[c] of, and I don't feel you could have written this. I think perhaps you copied this out of the front of the book. Are you sure that you didn't?" she asked smiling and drawing laughter from some.

"No mam, I wrote that myself. I've read a lot of books by Helen Hunt Jackson, and in them she always—" Ludell was saying when Miss Stevanson cut her off and said, "Well I know you do read a lot.

More than anyone in here as a matter of fact," she added, rolling her eyes around at the rest of the class.

"Maybe you—I tell you what," she said. "I don't have time to go through it all now, but what I'll do is take the book home and evaluate⁹ the whole thing by tomorrow. I'm not accusing you of cheating, but I feel I must check out the introduction to the book, because this just sounds so professional."ᶜ

At that point Miss Stevanson left it alone. Ludell felt humiliated⁹ and angry, but at the same time a deep sense of pride for she knew that she had indeed written every word of the paper. "And tomorrow," she told herself, "tomorrow they'll all know!"

Obviously⁹ sensingᶜ her frustration,⁹ her friend Willie touched the person next to him and asked him to touch the person next to him, and on and on it went until the person next to Ludell had touched her for him. Answering his call, she looked in his direction and read his lips saying, "I believe you," and smiled.

On the way home, she kept going over how she'd written the paper from her own thoughts and Willie kept telling her that it would be cleared up tomorrow, so she shouldn't be worrying about it. She finally hushed, but couldn't turn it off in her head. All afternoon it stayed with her.

Miss Stevanson apologized to her the following day. Miss Stevanson went on and on with her praise for her, and she relishedᶜ it all, remembering how ashamed she'd felt with people laughing yesterday. "Now THEY look foolish!" she thought.

Check the Skills

Understanding the Selection

1. In these two days of Ludell's life, what changes occurred? How did she react to these changes?

Literary Appreciation Skills Story Elements

2. How does the author use Ludell's thoughts, talk, and actions to show you the kind of person she is?

3. Is the setting of a small schoolroom important to the story? Why or why not?

Vocabulary Development Skills Word Structure

4. Chances are that you did not need your skill with suffixes with most of the words in this story. Words like *finally* and *tearful* you already know. You don't have to stop and think about their suffixes and bases. But noting the suffix *-ion* might have helped you decide the meaning of *frustration.*

   Would you like to read the book from which this selection was taken? It's entitled *Ludell* and was published in 1975 by Harper & Row.

Apply What You Learned in Unit 14

The Theme

Changes

1.   It has been said that there is nothing permanent in life except change. The selections in this unit described some examples. Peggy in "The Sailor's Daughter" had to deal with a frightening change in her life. But in the poem the change described was amusing, not scary. Other changes can be comfortable or happy ones. Sometimes change is easier to accept when you know it's coming. But growing up is a big change that can be very hard. And everybody knows it will happen. You probably want to decide for yourself what *you* think about changes and their effects.

The Skills

Literary Appreciation Skills Story Elements

2.   You can enjoy reading stories more, and you can understand them better. One way to do this is to look for the setting and characterization. Remember that setting means the time and place of a story. Characterization is the way the author helps you get to know the people in the story.

3.   Remember, though, that characterization and setting do not have the same importance in every story. In "Old Ramon," the kind of person Ramon was, the time, and the place were all important. You could tell because the whole story would have been different if any of those elements had been changed.

Vocabulary Development Skills Word Structure

4.   You know that one way to try to figure out a new word is to check it for suffixes. Copy the list on page 373 if you want to keep it for easy reference. But there are many more suffixes than are on that list. And suffixes can get so tricky that some college professors spend years studying them! So don't try to remember them all.

    Just make sure there is a real base word left after you subtract what you think is a suffix. And always depend on your own common sense about how the word is being used in the sentence.

People and Animals

Overview and Purposes for Reading

The Theme

People and Animals

1. What are some of the ways people and animals relate to each other?

The Skills

Literary Appreciation Skills Style and Intent

2. What makes a selection entertaining to read?

3. Is it possible to get something besides entertainment from reading you do just for fun?

Comprehension Skills Interpretive Reading

4. Getting involved with what you read can make reading more fun and more useful. How can you help yourself do this?

Learn About the Skills

Literary Appreciation Skills Style and Intent

An author who writes in an interesting, pleasing, or even funny way can be described as having an **entertaining style.**

You can find entertaining selections in some newspaper and magazine columns and cartoons. You can find many entertaining books. If you're especially interested in something, you might even decide that an encyclopedia article about that topic is entertaining!

Reading fiction can entertain you by showing you another view of the world. It can give you different experiences that you would never have unless you read about them.

You will probably find reading entertaining if it includes something unusual or unexpected. In fiction, there may be surprises in the characters, the situations, the settings, or in the events.

One example of an **unusual character** is the mouse named Amos who appears as the main character in the book *Ben and Me* by Robert Lawson. Amos lives in Ben Franklin's old fur hat. Amos is convinced that it is he and not Ben Franklin who is really responsible for most of Ben's accomplishments. You'll meet Amos in an excerpt from the book later in this unit.

An **unusual situation** is described in the book *Watership Down* by Richard Adams. Here the reader enters a rabbit civilization. Rabbits are the main characters. They talk, think, and have feelings. Yet they remain rabbits. The author describes the way rabbits really live. This unusual situation helps make the book entertaining. You'll discover this when you read a few pages taken from the book, appearing as the last selection in this unit.

An **unusual setting** is created in a book called *Catseye* about a boy who lives on a faraway planet. He saves the lives of animals who talk to him. The description of the place, as well as the very idea of living on another planet, is entertaining. The book was written by Andre Norton.

Author Emily Neville in her book *It's Like This, Cat,* creates a series of **unusual events** about a teen-aged boy and a cat. At one point the boy is caught in the middle of a robbery just as he tries to rescue his cat!

You can probably find all four of the books mentioned in your school or public library.

Fiction is entertaining when written by skillful authors who weave good stories around unusual characters, situations, settings, and events. Nonfiction can be entertaining for similar reasons. As you read the selections in this unit, decide why they are entertaining. What makes them so? Is it the characters? the situation? the place? the events? or something else?

Comprehension Skills Interpretive Reading

To make reading truly fun and useful, you must get involved in what you read. Sometimes you need to make a real effort to become involved. You need to force yourself to think beyond what you are reading to figure out how to extend it into your life.

You can help yourself do this by asking yourself questions like the ones below.

Following Up and Extending What You Read

1. What message or information is here?
2. How do I feel about this message? Do I agree? Does it interest me?
3. Do I want to learn more about this? If so, where can I get more information?
4. How can I use what I have learned? How can it help me?

Ask yourself questions like these. You will find that you become much more involved in what you are reading. Your reading will become more interesting. You'll discover that reading can help you understand yourself and your world. This will happen when you actively look for exciting and useful ideas.

Try asking the questions listed above as you read the selections in this unit. See if you get more out of them as you become more involved.

Use the Skills

Understanding the Selection

Momo has left her mountain home in Tibet to find her pet dog, Pempa. The dog is a valuable Lhasa terrier. It has been stolen and taken to the distant city of Calcutta, in India, to be sold. Momo is determined to rescue Pempa.

1. As you read this selection, find out how Momo feels about Pempa.

2. Momo's way of living is very different from yours. But some things are the same. See if her feeling about her pet reminds you of anyone you know or have read about.

Literary Appreciation Skills Style and Intent

3. Watch for unusual characters, situations, setting, or events that help make this selection entertaining. Notes in the margin will help.

Comprehension Skills Interpretive Reading

4. Think how an atlas, globe, or encyclopedia might help you get more involved in this selection.

DAUGHTER OF THE MOUNTAINS

Louise Rankin

"What is the matter?"

Momo opened her eyes upon a tall British⁹ gentleman standing before her. He was studying her with keen⁹ blue eyes. And he was speaking to her in her own Tibetan⁹ tongue.ᶜ Even at that moment this filled her with astonishment. Momo gulped back a rising sob. She stuck out her tongue at him. Even in her misery and astonishment, she remembered her manners enough to make him this, the most respectful greeting a poor Tibetan can give to one of high rank.ᶜ

"Do you want to get on this train?" asked the gentleman. Momo nodded. She gasped out one word, "Calcutta!" Then the tall gentleman looked off to where the station master was watching him and raised his right hand. The station master nodded and ran up toward the engine to talk to the engineer,ᶜ who could see everything from where he stood in his open cab.

"Now," the gentleman went on, turning again to Momo. "Tell me, child, Why are you traveling to Calcutta? And where are your father and mother?"

By this time Momo had control over her voice. She replied, "I am Momo, and I live near the top of the Jelep La pass. My father carries the mails. My mother keeps a tea shop in Longram. And I go down to Calcutta to get back my dog Pempa, who was stolen from our house."

■ Unusual character and unusual situation.

"You have come all this way alone?" asked the man.

"Yes, I have come alone," Momo answered. "The last two days I have followed those ten traders, because my friend Little Dorje told me they go to Calcutta. They know that great city, and they speak my tongue. So I thought they might help me find Pempa when we get down to Calcutta. But"—and her face puckeredᶜ up again, the tears flowed down her cheeks—"I have no money, and cannot buy a *tikkut* to get on the *te-rain*."

The tall gentleman looked at her in silence. Finally he said, "My child, you have courage. Do you love this Pempa of yours enough to brave the dangers of that great, strange city of Calcutta? Enough not to fear getting lost?"

"Oh, yes, yes," Momo replied. "I am not at all afraid. The Holy One will keep me from all harm. I know that. And I thought He was going to put me on this *te-rain* today. But," she gulped back another sob, "He has not done so."

The blue eyes that looked searchingly into her black ones were very bright. The gentleman said, "Ah, but your faith is rewarded, little Momo. The Blessed One is even now going to put you on this train."

He took her by the hand and walked with her up to the ticket window. He laid down some money and took up the red ticket the agent handed him. This he put into Momo's hand.

■ The man's unusual kindness is an unexpected and interesting situation. The setting in Tibet is unusual, too.

"There is the ticket," he said. "Hold to it tightly, Momo. Do not let it out of your hands till you pass out of the gate on the station platform at Siliguri. There you must follow the other travelers and buy still another ticket for Calcutta. Just stand before the window, lay down this money"—he put some silver in her hand—"and say these words, 'One ticket to Calcutta.' Can you do that, do you think?"

Momo's hand closed tightly over the money, and she nodded her head. "Yes, yes, I can. One *tikkut* to Calcutta. That is easy," she said. Her face was shining like the sun after a rain.

"Good," said the gentleman. "Now listen carefully, Momo. When you come to the city of Calcutta, you will need more money. Take this." He handed her more silver and one paper note. "Tie this into your scarf, and *tell no one that you have any money*. Do you understand? Do not open your scarf and show your money where you may be watched by strangers. For in Calcutta there are many quick and clever thieves." Again he repeated, "Do you understand?"

"Yes, yes," Momo nodded. "I do understand, and I will remember your warning, great sir." Her fingers worked quickly as she tied the money into a corner of her red scarf. She tucked the scarf into the fold of her robe.

■ A map or globe could help you see just how far Momo was going.

"Very well," said the gentleman. "You now have money enough, Momo, to take you down to the city. It will also give you food and lodging^c there in some Tibetan hostel,^g and help you make inquiries^c about your dog. There is also money for your return ticket back to the hills. So if you are wise and careful, you should have no further trouble—only the finding of your dog."

"And the Blessed One Himself will do that, when I get to the city," answered Momo happily.

"We must in any case leave that to Him," replied the tall gentleman with a smile. He led her along the platform, looking into the carriages as they passed.

"Where are those ten traders you spoke of?" he asked her. Momo looked and said, "There they are, in this, and this carriage. And here," she added, "here is Big Dorje, whom Little Dorje told me to follow." She pointed to where he sat among other people in a closed carriage.

"In with you, then," said the gentleman. "Stick closer to Big Dorje than his shadow. Be secret and careful of your money. And the Holy One will find your dog for you." He laid his hand upon the carriage door handle.

Momo looked up at him with all the thankfulness of her heart in her eyes. She bowed her head and clasped her hands. "Great and merciful sir, I thank you. May the Blessed One deliver you from all distress! May you be rich and may good health dwell in your house forever!"

The British gentleman answered politely, "It is my good fortune to be chosen as the unworthy agent of the All Merciful." And he added with a smile, "When I was your age I too had a dog that I loved very much."

He opened the door, and leaning toward the people sitting within said, "Make room there for this child, and see, all of you, that she comes to no harm on her journey down to the plains."

The men and women within jumped to their feet and bowed, their arms full of bundles. They nodded their heads, and smiled and spoke eagerly all together, like a chorus.

Check the Skills

Understanding the Selection

1. How does Momo feel about Pempa? How do you know?

2. Do people in our country often love their pets, too? What examples can you think of?

   If you want to read more about Momo's experiences, read the book *Daughter of the Mountains* by Louise Rankin. It was published in 1948 by the Viking Press.

Literary Appreciation Skills Style and Intent

3. This story is entertaining partly because its characters, situations, and setting are unusual. Is Momo unusual because she loves her dog or because she is willing to go so far to rescue it? What are the unusual situation and setting?

Comprehension Skills Interpretive Reading

4. Suppose you looked at a globe or world map to see just where the country of Tibet and the city of Calcutta are. How would doing that help you understand better what Momo was trying to do?

Use the Skills

Understanding the Selection

Anglers—people who like to fish—will tell you that theirs is the greatest of all sports. In this true story, a young Scottish lad has hooked his first salmon, one of the hardest-fighting of all the big fish. The author's fishing guide, Donald, gives instructions from his own experience.

1. As you read, learn how the young angler and the salmon react to each other.

2. Discover how the author, Donald Sutherland, feels about this fish.

Literary Appreciation Skills Style and Intent

3. The exciting events make this story very entertaining. Watch for an unusual character who adds interest, too.

Comprehension Skills Interpretive Reading

4. Think about how you feel about fishing. Do you find yourself favoring the fish or the angler? Why?

MY FIRST SALMON

Donald Sutherland

It is a wild, narrow pass there and the river runs fast and deep through the gorge. The brown water creams round points of jagged rock which break the surface here and there.

We went to work in the same way as before. Donald was some feet above me and behind, looking down into the water. Suddenly he gave a shout and came tumbling down the brae.⁹

"Try you there again," he said. "Just below the big rock. I could not be sure of it, but I think there was movement under the water."

I cast again and dropped the fly⁹ in the same place as before. There was a boil⁹ in the water and a sharp tug at the line. There was no need to strike. The fish did it for me.

"Take in your line," said Donald. "Quickly, now."

The fish headed towards us, thought better of it, turned back, and the fight was on.

■ Here is the unusual character in the story.

Anglersᶜ should give thanks nightly for the fact that salmon⁹ do not know their own strength. If they did, they would never be taken by rod and line.ᶜ I was reasonably strong for my age. The rod was a fifteen-foot split cane, a powerful thing, most beautifully balanced. Yet at first I had the sensation⁹ of being caught by something far more powerful than I was. Then the salmon dived and sulked at the bottom of the pool for a few minutes.

"Keep the strainᶜ on him," said Donald. "Just keep the strain and by and by we will see what he will be after."

So far, neither of us had seen our enemy. Then, suddenly, the strain was gone, the line went slack, and my heart leaped into my mouth. The fish jumped clear out of the water.

"Lower your point!"ᶜ shouted Donald.

For a split second the great fish hung in the air, then fell back into the water with a crash and a splash of spray. Next second the rod was nearly torn out of my hands. He was still hooked.

Luck held, the line held, but soon my arms were aching and I had no reason to believe that the salmon had begun to tire.

"Look you, son," said Donald. "This is a fish we must not lose. Maybe you will never see his like in all your days." He spoke prophetically,⁹ although he knew it not. "If you become too tired I will take the rod from you if you wish. But I am thinking you would prefer to bring the fish to bank by yourself. Don't be giving him too much of the butt, now. Just a steady strain, and rest yourself when you can."

■ The actions of the salmon are unexpected.

That salmon fought like a demon.⁹ He tried quick, short rushes. He skulked⁹ at the bottom of the pool. He nearly as possible broke me on a rock. It took all my strength and

Donald's know-how to stop him from getting out of the pool into a shallow, stony run⁹ which linked it with the pool below. Twice again he jumped, and each time he looked bigger, and fresher, than before.

Forty-five minutes—they felt like as many hours—passed before Donald's strategy⁹ began to take effect. For the first time in that afternoon, I began to feel that I and not the fish was in control. Twice I brought him in to the bank, but not close enough for Donald's gaff.⁹ But the third time the gaff flashed, quick and sure. Two minutes after that he was dangling on Donald's pocket-scales, all thirty-five and a half pounds of him, a great fish, fresh from the sea. Thirty-five and a half pounds. Mere numerals do not do justice to such a fish. For fifty years since that day, from time to time, in various waters, I have tried to catch his like, but never came within twenty pounds of him. I never shall.

■ Think about whether you agree or not.

Check the Skills

Understanding the Selection

1. How did the salmon and the author react to each other?

2. Does Sutherland respect the salmon? What makes you think so? How would you have felt?

Literary Appreciation Skills Style and Intent

3. Who is the unusual character in this story? You probably didn't expect the salmon to fight so hard and so cleverly. Do these unusual actions help make the story entertaining?

Comprehension Skills Interpretive Reading

4. How do you feel about fishing as a sport? Did your opinion change at all after you read this story? Why or why not?

Use the Skills

Understanding the Selection

The next selection is a fantasy—a story that could not possibly take place. In it, a mouse named Amos tells of his friendship with the great Benjamin Franklin.

1.   As you read, you will discover that, in a fantasy, the relationship between people and animals can be quite amusing.

Literary Appreciation Skills Style and Intent

2.   Amos the mouse is an unusual character who makes this selection entertaining to read. Notice how the author has Amos think and talk like a person. How does this add to the entertaining qualities of the story? Watch for any other unusual elements, too.

3.   Suppose the author had chosen an ordinary person instead of the famous Benjamin Franklin as a main character. Would the story be as entertaining? Think about it as you read.

Comprehension Skills Interpretive Reading

4.   When you read something you enjoy, you can sometimes extend that reading by finding other material to read that is similar. Think how you might do that with this selection.

BEN AND ME

Robert Lawson

Adapted from the original.

As the hot summer weather came on we often took long walks in the country which were, to me, most enjoyable. One unusually warm day, when we had come to a secluded^g spot on the banks of the Schuylkill River,^g Ben suddenly stripped off all his clothing. He donned^c a silly-looking striped garment^c which he called "bathing trunks," and plunged into the water.

It was only my sudden scream and sharp nip on the ear that prevented him from diving in cap and all.

He disported^g in a most ridiculous fashion, snorting and floundering^c about. I, in the cap, was left perched on his heap of clothing. There I was the prey^c to any wandering cat, dog, hawk or snake that chanced to come along.

As we walked home that evening, I spoke my mind fully on this ridiculous habit and the dangers to which it exposed me.

"In addition," I said, "your hair is soaking wet. I shall no doubt contract a frightful cold."

Ben was stubborn about it, though. He was rather proud of his skill as a swimmer and insisted that nothing would happen to me.

Nothing did, for some time. Until one afternoon, as I watched Ben diving, snorting and splashing like an overgrown grampus,^g the thing I dreaded came to pass.

Along the bank came trotting a half-grown mongrel dog. It was seeking mischief, as is the usual habit of such brutes.

I looked wildly for Ben. But at the moment only the soles of his feet were visible. Fortunately, there were many bushes and small trees thereabout. So I lost no time in scurrying^g up a small sapling.^c Here I settled in comfort to watch the proceedings.^g

The cur,ᶜ spying Ben, rushed to the bank, barking furiously. Ben *shoo-ed* and shouted as he floundered franticallyᶜ toward shore. The pile of clothing next attracted the dog's attention. Nosing it over, he selected the cap—and trotted off with it just as Ben, dripping and panting, slitheredᶜ up the muddy bank.

■ Here is an unexpected event. Note that Ben thinks Amos is still in the cap.

With a wild cry of "Amos! Amos!" Ben charged after him.

Apparently, this was just the sort of frolicᵍ the dog had been seeking. So for a full quarter-hour he had a jolly rompᶜ with Ben. Poor Ben coaxed, pleaded and threatened, but to no avail. Had I not been in such a temper, his ridiculous anticsᵍ would have been most amusing.

At length, tiring of the game, the mongrel picked up the cap and trotted off up the riverbank. He was hotly pursued by Ben—who dashed through thickets and over rocks with utter disregard of his ill-clad person.

Scarce had they disappeared around a curve in the riverbank when two fellows appeared on the scene. Noting the pile of clothing and failing to discover its owner, they became greatly excited. Their excitement increased on discovering Ben's silver watch engraved with his name.

"The great Dr. Franklin!" they shouted. "Drowned! Drowned!" They took to their heels in the direction of Philadelphia, carrying Ben's clothes with them.

It was warm and sunny in my tree, and very quiet now. Far up the river I could still hear occasional sounds of barking. These finally culminatedᵍ in a terrific outburst of yelps and howls. Then all was silent, and I dozed.

I was wakened by the footfalls of an approaching figure which I took to be Ben. But few could have recognized in that ludicrousᵍ and bedraggledᵍ apparitionᵍ the famous Dr. Franklin! His legs were muddied, bruised and scratched, his bathing trunks torn, his glasses missing. His wet hair, which hung in long disordered wisps, was surmountedᵍ by the fur cap, worn at a rakishᵍ angle.

As he approached, limping, he kept up a continual sound of finger-snapping, whistling and clucking. "Amos,

Amos," he called, "Amos, where are you?" All the while he was peering nearsightedly into the bushes along the way. Touched as I was by his fondness for me, I could not help a chuckle at his appearance.

I was about to relieve his anxiety^c when my attention was caught by the approach of a great crowd of people from the direction of Philadelphia. Among them I could discern^c the Governor, the Mayor and many other prominent citizens, as well as Ben's First Volunteer Fire Brigade.

Ben looked frantically about. But there was no escape save in the water, and of that he had had plenty. So, folding his arms, he attempted to appear as dignified as possible, and awaited their arrival. As he did so, he leaned against the tree in which I had taken refuge.^c Without a moment's loss I slipped into the cap so gently as to be entirely unnoticed.

■ It will extend your enjoyment of this story to know that Franklin really did start this in Philadelphia.

As the crowd beheld Ben, everyone broke into shouts of relief and joy, accompanied, however, by not a few snickers. He was surrounded by a milling throng all bent on shaking his hand and congratulating him. Various articles of clothing were loaned and he was soon decently garbed.

Through it all, however, Ben preserved an appearance of the utmost despondency.[9]

The Governor approached offering his hat, a very elegant[c] affair trimmed with lace and gold braid.

"Permit me, Dr. Franklin," he said, most courteous. "Pray do me the honor to wear this. Your present headgear appears—er—slightly disheveled."[9]

"Never," cried Ben angrily. "This cap shall never again

leave my head!" And he reached up both hands to settle it more firmly.

I bit his thumb.

"Amos!" he exclaimed happily.

"Beg pardon?" said the Governor.

"Yes, Amos," I whispered fiercely. "And if you don't get us home quickly you'll hear from me. Your hair is soaking and this cap smells so strong of dog I'm half-suffocated!"

Ben brightened up at once. By the time the procession reached home he was as pleased with himself as though he had done something really smart—instead of just scaring half the town to death.

Check the Skills

Understanding the Selection

1. How did Ben Franklin and Amos feel about each other? Why do you think this is amusing?

Literary Appreciation Skills Style and Intent

2. a. Amos thinks, talks, and has strong opinions. Is this unusual character entertaining to read about? Why or why not?

   b. What other unusual elements were in the story? Notes in the margin will give you some hints.

3. Do you think the story would be as entertaining if the human being in it was *not* a famous person? Why do you think as you do?

Comprehension Skills Interpretive Reading

4. Did you like this story? If so, you may want to follow up by reading the rest of the book. Look in the library for *Ben and Me* by Robert Lawson. It was published by Little, Brown and Company in 1939.

Selection 4

Use the
Skills

Understanding the Selection

In coal mines in many parts of the world, ponies are still used to pull
tubs of coal along the narrow tracks hundreds of feet underground.
Many of them spend their entire lives in the dark mine pits. Wilfrid
Gibson has written a poem about an unexpected event in the dull
lives of some of these mine ponies.

1. Find how the ponies react to the unexpected.

2. Think about the relationship between these ponies and people.

Literary Appreciation Skills Style and Intent

3. Who are the unusual characters in this poem? What is the
    unexpected situation? See how these add up to an entertaining
    picture as you read the poem.

Comprehension Skills Interpretive Reading

4. This is the first selection in this unit about the fact that people
    sometimes use animals to the animals' disadvantage. Decide
    how you feel about this message of the poem.

THE PONIES

Wilfrid Gibson

During the strike, the ponies were brought up
From their snug stables, some three hundred feet
Below the surface—up the pit's main shaft
Shot one by one into the light of day;
And as each stepped, bewildered, from the cage,
He stood among his fellows, shivering
In the unaccustomed freshness of free air,
His dim eyes dazzled by the April light.
And then one suddenly left the huddled group,
Lifted his muzzle, snuffed the freshness in,
Pawed the soft turf and, whinneying, started trotting
Across the field; and one by one his fellows
With pricking ears each slowly followed him,
Timidly trotting: when the leader's trot
Broke into a canter, then into a gallop;

■ Unusual
characters?
Unexpected
situation?

And now the whole herd galloped at his heels
Around the dewy meadow, hard hoofs, used
To stumbling over treacherous stony tramways
And plunging hock-deep through black steamy puddles
Of the dusky narrow galleries, delighting
In the soft spring of the resilient turf.
Still round and round the field they raced, unchecked
By tugging traces, at their heels no longer
The trundling tubs, and round and round and round,
With a soft thunder of hoofs, the sunshine flashing
On their sleek coats, through the bright April weather
They raced all day. . . .

■ Why are
the animals
so excited?

Check the Skills

Understanding the Selection

1. How did the ponies react to being outside in the field?

2. People aren't mentioned in the poem. But if you think "between the lines" you'll know that the ponies belonged to people. What do you think the relationship between these animals and people was like? Why do you think as you do?

Literary Appreciation Skills Style and Intent

3. Mining ponies are certainly unusual characters to read about. And the unexpected situation of their being let outside is the action of the poem. Were you entertained by the picture of the ponies racing happily around the field? Why or why not?

Comprehension Skills Interpretive Reading

4. One message of the poem is that the ponies rarely are allowed outside. In that sense, people are using the ponies in a way that is unfair to the animals. How do you feel about this message?

Selection 5

Use the Skills

The last selection is from the beginning of a famous novel of the 1970's—*Watership Down.* It is about a rabbit civilization. The animals in this story have a different attitude toward people than the animals do in any of the other selections in this unit. Read to see if you can figure out what it is. Think, too, why so many people have found this book to be so entertaining.

WATERSHIP DOWN

Richard Adams

The May sunset was red in clouds, and there was still half an hour to twilight. The dry slope was dotted with rabbits. Some were nibbling at the thin grass near their holes. Others were pushing further down to look for dandelions or perhaps a cowslip that the rest had missed. Here and there one sat upright on an ant heap and looked about, with ears erect and nose in the wind. But a blackbird, singing undisturbed on the outskirts of the wood, showed that there was nothing alarming there. And in the other direction, along the brook, all was plain to be seen, empty and quiet. The warren⁹ was at peace.

At the top of the bank, close to the wild cherry where the blackbird sang, was a little group of holes almost hidden by brambles.⁹ In the green half-light, at the mouth of one of these holes, two rabbits were sitting together side by side. At length, the larger of the two came out, slipped along the bank under cover of the brambles and so down into the ditch and up into the field. A few moments later the other followed.

The first rabbit stopped in a sunny patch and scratched his ear with rapid movements of his hind leg. Although he was a yearling⁹ and still below full weight, he had not the harassed⁹ look of most "outskirters." Outskirters are the rank and file of ordinary rabbits in their first year who, lacking either aristocratic⁹ parentage or unusual size and strength, get sat on by their elders and live as best they can—often in the open—on the edge of their warren. This rabbit looked as though he knew how to take care of himself. There was a shrewd, buoyant⁹ air about him as he sat up, looked round and rubbed both front paws over his nose. As soon as he was satisfied that all was well, he laid back his ears and set to work on the grass.

His companion seemed less at ease. He was small, with wide, staring eyes and a way of raising and turning his head which suggested not so much caution as a kind of ceaseless, nervous tension. His nose moved continually, and when a bumblebee flew humming to a thistle bloom behind him, he jumped and spun round with a start that sent two nearby rabbits scurrying for holes before the nearest, a buck with black-tipped ears, recognized him and returned to feeding.

"Oh, it's only Fiver," said the black-tipped rabbit, "jumping at bluebottles⁹ again. Come on, Buckthorn, what were you telling me?"

"Fiver?" said the other rabbit. "Why's he called that?"

"Five in the litter, you know. He was the last—and the smallest. You'd wonder nothing had got him by now. I always say a man couldn't see him and a fox wouldn't want him. Still, I admit he seems to be able to keep out of harm's way."

Fiver came closer to his companion, lolloping on long hind legs.

"Let's go a bit further, Hazel," he said. "You know, there's something queer about the warren this evening, although I can't tell exactly what it is. Shall we go down to the brook?"

"All right," answered Hazel, "and you can find me a cowslip.ᶜ If you can't find one, no one can."

He led the way down the slope, his shadow stretching behind him on the grass. They reached the brook and began nibbling and searching close beside the wheel ruts of the track.

It was not long before Fiver found what they were looking for. Cowslips are a delicacyᶜ among rabbits. As a rule there are very few left by late May in the neighborhood of even a small warren. This one had not bloomed and its flat spread of leaves was almost hidden under the long grass. They were just starting on it when two larger rabbits came running up.

They were both Owsla. Nearly all warrens have an Owsla. This is a group of strong or clever rabbits, all second year or older. They surround the Chief Rabbit and they have authority over the rest of the warren.

"Cowslip?" said one of the Owsla. "All right—just leave it to us. Come on, hurry up," he added, as Fiver hesitated. "You heard me, didn't you?"

"Fiver found it, Toadflax," said Hazel.

"And we'll eat it," replied Toadflax. "Cowslips are for Owsla—don't you know that? If you don't, we can easily teach you."

Fiver had already turned away. Hazel caught him up by the culvert.⁹

"I'm sick and tired of it," he said. "It's the same all the time. 'These are my claws, so this is my cowslip.' 'These are my teeth, so this is my burrow.'⁹ I'll tell you, if ever I get into the Owsla, I'll treat outskirters with a bit of decency."

"Well, you can at least expect to be in the Owsla one day," answered Fiver. "You've got some weight coming and that's more than I shall ever have."

"You don't suppose I'll leave you to look after yourself, do you?" said Hazel. "But to tell you the truth, I sometimes feel like clearing out of this warren altogether. Still, let's forget it now and try to enjoy the evening. I tell you what—shall we go across the brook? There'll be fewer rabbits and we can have a bit of peace. Unless you feel it isn't safe?" he added.

The way in which he asked suggested that he did in fact think that Fiver was likely to know better than himself, and it was clear from Fiver's reply that this was accepted between them.

"No, it's safe enough," he answered. "If I start feeling there's anything dangerous I'll tell you. But it's not exactly danger that I seem to feel about the place. It's—oh, I don't know—something oppressive,ᶜ like thunder. I can't tell what; but it worries me. All the same, I'll come across with you."

They ran over the culvert. The grass was wet and thick near the stream and they made their way up the opposite slope, looking for drier ground. Part of the slope was in shadow, for the sun was sinking ahead of them. Hazel, who wanted a warm, sunny spot, went on until they were quite near the lane. As they approached the gate he stopped, staring.

"Fiver, what's that? Look!"

A little way in front of them, the ground had been freshly disturbed. Two piles of earth lay on the grass. Heavy posts, reeking of creosote and paint, towered up as high as the holly trees in the hedge. The sign they carried threw a long shadow across the top of the field. Near one of the posts, a hammer and a few nails had been left behind.

The two rabbits went up to the sign at a hopping run and crouched in a patch of nettles on the far side, wrinkling their noses at the smell of a dead cigarette end somewhere in the grass. Suddenly Fiver shivered and coweredᵍ down.

"Oh, Hazel! This is where it comes from! I know now—something very bad! Some terrible thing—coming closer and closer."

He began to whimperᶜ with fear.

Check the Skills

Understanding the Selection

1. Who are the "outskirters"? Who are the "Owsla"? To which group of rabbits do Hazel and Fiver belong?

2. Fiver senses that "some terrible thing" is coming. Have you ever noticed that animals can sometimes sense changes? Later, the author reveals that the sign announces the building of a housing project. How would a sense of this bring fear to Fiver? What does this tell you about the relationship of these rabbits to people?

Literary Appreciation Skills Style and Intent

3. What do you learn about the rabbit civilization in *Watership Down* from this brief excerpt? How does the author make the situation seem real? What makes this story entertaining?

Comprehension Skills Interpretive Reading

4. Of course no one really knows how rabbits think. The author has used his imagination for that. But the descriptions of the rabbit warren and the lives of the rabbits are based on fact and research. How could you follow up or extend this knowledge about what you read in this selection?

Apply What You Learned in Unit 15

The Theme

People and Animals

1.　People and animals relate to each other in many different ways. When animals are pets, the relationship may be based on affection. Hunters and anglers think of animals for sport. Sometimes the work people do requires the help of animals, as the ponies in the mines.

- What are some other ways in which people and animals relate to each other?

- What kind of relationship might there be between people and animals in a zoo? between a horse and rider? between birds and the people who put out a winter bird feeder? between the audience and the animals in a circus?

- How about animals raised to be food, such as cattle, hogs, and chickens?

The Skills

Literary Appreciation Skills Style and Intent

2.   Many things can make a selection entertaining to read. If you're really interested, chances are you'll find it entertaining, no matter what it is!

One element of an entertaining style, however, is the unusual or unexpected. Authors may write about surprising characters, situations, events, or settings. Because people's opinions and tastes are different, you may not find a selection as entertaining as someone else does.

•   Look back through this book. Which selections did you find the most entertaining? Which the least? Was there something unusual or unexpected in the ones that entertained you the most?

•   Think about other kinds of reading you have done. What things did you find entertaining? Why?

3.   Even when you read just for fun, you may find that you are learning something new. Reading about something unfamiliar can expand your view of the world. Did any of the selections in this unit describe something you had never thought of before? Which ones? What in them was new to you?

Comprehension Skills Interpretive Reading

4.   Remember that you can get more out of your reading by putting more into it. In other words, get involved. Make an effort to decide how what you're reading can be useful. Figure out how you feel about it.

Friendship

Overview and Purposes for Reading

The Theme

Friendship

1.   What is friendship? Why is having friends impor-
       tant? Are a person's friends always human beings?

The Skills

Literary Appreciation Skills Figurative Language

2.   What is an idiom? Why is it necessary to understand
       idioms when you read?

3.   How can you figure out the meaning of an unfamiliar
       idiom?

Comprehension Skills Literal Meaning

4.   How can you determine the correct sequence, or
       order of events, in what you read?

Learn About the Skills

Literary Appreciation Skills Figurative Language

Have you ever said, "I'm so hungry I could eat a horse"? Did you plan to sit down to a dinner table filled with horse? Of course not. What you really meant was that you were very, very hungry. You were using an idiom when you spoke. All languages have idioms. English is no exception.

An idiom is a phrase or expression whose meaning cannot be figured out by knowing the definition of each word in it. Idioms have special meanings all their own. So when you say you are "in the doghouse," it means that you are in bad trouble. When you say you are "hanging around," it means that you are going to spend time doing nothing. And "catching cold" doesn't mean running after something until you grab it! You understand these idioms because you've heard them used often enough to have learned their special meanings.

You often meet idioms in your reading, too. Some of them may be new to you. Remember that you can identify a phrase as an idiom if the usual meanings of the words don't make sense in the sentence. How can you figure out what an unfamiliar idiom means? First, use the context, or the words around the idiom, as clues. If that doesn't help, you might check a large dictionary. Many dictionaries include some idiomatic expressions in the entry of a key word of the idiom. For example, the idiom "in the doghouse" is at the end of the entry for *doghouse* in some large dictionaries. Not all idioms are included in dictionaries, though. You should always first try using the sense of the words around the idiom.

Try the Skill. What's the idiom in the following sentence?

When I heard the thunder, I nearly jumped out of my skin.

You're right if you decided the idiom is "jumped out of my skin." If you had taken the usual meaning of these words, you certainly would have had a weird-looking person in mind! The rest of the sentence helps you know that the idiom really means being very scared or startled.

Look for two idioms in the following excerpt.

Tom had to stay home that night because he was up to his neck in homework. Joe said, "You should have done it last night. Then you could have come to the movie with us tonight."

"I know, I know," Tom groaned. "Don't rub it in!"

Did you figure out that "up to his neck in homework" was an idiom? If you hadn't heard that before, you still could decide it means "very busy with much to do." The sense of the rest of the paragraph tells you that. What's the other idiom? You're right if you think it's "don't rub it in." What do you think that means?

So the next time a big thunderstorm comes along and someone tells you it's raining cats and dogs outside, don't go running outside to get a new pet. Instead, just nod knowingly to yourself and say "Aha! An idiom!" Watch for idioms in the selections of this unit. See if you can identify them and figure out what they mean.

Comprehension Skills Literal Meaning

When you're reading, it can be very important to understand the **sequence,** or the order in which things happen. This can be fairly easy to do when there are certain words that are clues.

Common words that are clues to sequence include *first, next, afterwards, then, finally, before,* and *last.* When these appear in your reading, you know that a separate event is being described. You also know when it took place in relation to other events. For instance, note how clue words signal the sequence of events in the paragraph below.

> Kathy and Lisa had a busy day. *First* they went window shopping. *Then* they went to the new golf course. *Next* they rode their bikes to the record shop where they talked to friends. *Afterwards* they got some ice cream. *Finally* they rode home, happily making plans for the next day.

Clues like these are easy. Others are less obvious. For instance, the words *while* and *meanwhile* tell you that several things are going on at the same time. Read the following examples.

> *While* Annie was at school, Sue was busy making plans.
> Annie was at school all day. *Meanwhile,* Sue made plans.

To help yourself understand the sequence of events in what you read, watch for the clue words. The selections in this unit will give you a chance to practice this skill.

Use the Skills

Understanding the Selection

This is a funny story about a woman who has a special problem with idiomatic language.

1. See if you think her husband is a good friend of hers.

Literary Appreciation Skills Figurative Language

2. Idioms are an important part of this story. Watch for them. Notes in the margins will help you.

Comprehension Skills Literal Meaning

3. Remember that words such as *next*, *afterwards*, *then*, *finally*, *before*, and *last* are clues to sequence. Be on the lookout for those words. They will help you figure out the order in which things happen.

THE DAY IT RAINED CATS AND DOGS

Linda Allen

It was a curious thing about Mrs. Jenkins, but every once in a while her words had a strange way of coming true.

"Oh, *blow!*" she said to Mr. Jenkins one day after she had stumbled over something in the road. Immediately the wind began to blow so hard that they had to cling to a tree until it stopped.

■ The rest of the sentence tells you she meant only to express annoyance.

"My dear," said Mr. Jenkins, straightening his clothes, "you really will have to be careful what you say when these moods come over you. Let's go home, and I will make you a nice cup of tea."

As Mrs. Jenkins sipped her tea, Mr. Jenkins said, "You just sit here quietly, and I'll do the housework today."

"Thank you," said Mrs. Jenkins gratefully. "I'll do as you say, although it does seem a shame to leave all that work to you. The kitchen is quite full of dirty pots and pans."

No sooner had she spoken than they heard a great clatter in the kitchen. When Mr. Jenkins opened the door, he found that he could scarcely get into the room for all the pots and pans. They were piled up on the table and on the shelves, in the sink and on the chairs, from the floor right up to the ceiling. It was late in the evening by the time poor Mr. Jenkins finished washing them all.

The next day Mrs. Jenkins was her usual self. As the weeks went by, she quite forgot to be careful about what she said. Then one morning, after she had done the washing and hung it outside to dry, she began to feel rather peculiar again. She didn't like to mention it to Mr. Jenkins. I'll just sit down quietly, she thought to herself. Perhaps it will pass.

■ These words tell you that some time passes before the next event occurs.

She was just about to go into the sitting room when she happened to glance out of the window. "Oh!" she shouted angrily. "Look at that! The washing was almost dry, and now look what's happening. It's raining cats and dogs!"

Immediately the black clouds parted, and out of the sky there came an absolute downpour of cats and dogs. Big dogs and little dogs, nice cats and nasty cats—dozens of them falling everywhere—barking and meowing and fighting among themselves as they landed. Some of them splashed into the goldfish pool, and others twanged up and down on the clothesline. They ran up the trees and along the fences. They sat on the window sill and stared in at Mr. and Mrs. Jenkins.

"It's that Mrs. Jenkins again!" cried the neighbors. "She's had one of her spells⁹ again. Why can't she be more careful when she feels them coming on? Shoo! Shoo! Go away!"

"It's only a shower," called Mr. Jenkins from an upstairs window. "It will be over in a minute or two."

But it wasn't. All the rest of the morning it rained cats and dogs around the Jenkins's house, until there wasn't a patch of ground or an inch of fence that wasn't being sat upon.

"You've done it this time," said Mr. Jenkins, shaking his head. "You've really done it. Pots and pans were bad enough, but at least we were able to give them away to our friends. Who on earth would want so many damp cats and dogs?"

Just after noon a policeman came to the door. "Are you the owner of these animals?" he asked Mr. Jenkins. "We've had a complaint."

"I'm sorry," apologized Mr. Jenkins. "You see, it's Mrs. Jenkins. She's had one of her spells again."

"I can't help that," said the policeman. "Just keep these animals under control, or we shall have to take action."

"Oh, dear!" wailed Mrs. Jenkins when he had gone. "What can I do? I shall be seeing pink giraffes next!"

■ This idiom means that she will think she sees something that is not really there.

There were two great thumps. When Mr. and Mrs. Jenkins looked out of the kitchen window, they saw two pink giraffes sitting on the lawn, looking rather dazed. The cats began to spit, and the dogs put their tails between their legs and howled. For a moment the giraffes just looked at them; then suddenly they trumpeted⁹ loudly and began to chase the cats and dogs.

Round and round the garden they went, and out of the gate, and up the road, and the last that Mr. and Mrs. Jenkins saw of them they were disappearing over the hill.

Mrs. Jenkins went out into the garden and brought in her wash. "I hope I never see anything like that again in the whole of my life," she said. Which was a good thing to say, because she never did. And from that day to this she hasn't had another spell.

Not yet.

Check the Skills

Understanding the Selection

1. Is Mr. Jenkins a good friend to his wife? What does he do that is like what good friends do for each other?

Literary Appreciation Skills Figurative Language

2. The humor in this story comes largely from idioms becoming literally true. What is the idiomatic meaning of the following phrases from the story?

    raining cats and dogs
    seeing pink giraffes

Comprehension Skills Literal Meaning

3. In the following sentences, what words are clues to sequence?

    The next day Mrs. Jenkins was her usual self.
    Then one morning she began feeling peculiar again.

Selection 2

Use the Skills

Understanding the Selection

1. The next selection is about an unusual friendship. Find out what it is.

2. Notice how the main character feels when he is faced with the threat of losing his friend.

Literary Appreciation Skills Figurative Language

3. Be on the lookout for idioms. Try to determine their meanings from the context. Marginal notes will give you some hints. If necessary, look up in the glossary or a dictionary the key word in the idiom.

Comprehension Skills Literal Meaning

4. Look for words that are clues to the sequence of events. Remember that some clues to sequence are less obvious than others.

HAROLD AND BURT
AND SUE AND AMY, ETC.

Casey West

This girl, Jill, walked up to me in the hall and said, "Do you like plants?"

"No."

"Good," she said. "Take this one home."

I said, "I don't want it."

"Go on," she said, holding the pot out to me. "It's an *Aralia Spinosa.*^g That's Latin. Just keep it for me, for a science experiment."

Larry, beside me, laughed. "He wouldn't know what to do with a plant. Actually, that's rather a nice specimen^g of *Spinosa.* Why are you giving it to Mark?"

"It's a secret experiment."

"Mark'll fail, whatever it is."

I put out my hand. "I'll take it," I said.

"What are you going to do?" Larry asked. "Eat it for lunch?"

"Just water it twice a week and put it in an east window," she said.

"Yeah, yeah," I said. "OK." I took the damp-feeling clay pot. The few little leaves were shiny, and there were thorns on the stems.

So I took the *Aralia Spinosa* home with me, walking hunched over so that every Tom, Dick, and George wouldn't see me with this plant and start asking funny questions.

I put it on my windowsill and started my records and put on my earphones. I like my sound loud, man, and my mother has other ideas. She got in such a habit of saying, "Turn that thing down, Mark," that pretty soon she was saying it before I even turned it on. So she gave me the 'phones. Now it's in one ear and *in* the other, too, and the

■ *Every Tom, Dick, and George* doesn't really mean word for word what it says.

■ Here's a clue word to the order of events.

guitars meet in the middle right over the percussion⁹ and that is where I *live*.

One day I found this article about plants and it had a picture of my own *Aralia Spinosa* in it, so I read on. It also said some plants like to be talked to, as long as you talk nicely.

This is when I decided to do my reading out loud. It wouldn't bother me—I would be inside the groovy sound from my 'phones and Old Spiny would be out there taking advantage of all this knowledge. If I came to any bad parts, like wars or famines, or—especially—forest fires, I wouldn't read them aloud.

So every night I plugged myself in and read to Old Spiny. And I watered him on Mondays and Thursdays. I noticed that he had grown a couple of new leaves and a third was ready to uncurl. And his stems were growing very, very tall.

Sometimes Jill asked me, "How's the *Aralia?* Still alive?"

"Sure."

"I bet," she said.

Well, he was not only alive, he was thriving,⁹ but I wasn't going to argue with her.

Old Spiny and I really communicated. Naturally he didn't talk back, or even groan and sigh like a dog, but it was nice to have company. Even when I didn't have anything to read I still talked out loud to him. He just sat there and grew.

Leaves, sprouts, stems seemed to pop out from him. He must love geometry was all I could say, and history and—very probably—science. I was also taking this poetry course. I needed something third period and it was that or dressmaking.

The first few days I sat in the class with my chin in my hands and stared out the window. I was not going to like poetry and no one could make me like it. But then some of the sounds started to creep into my ears and my brain opened up and let them in. And they were cool.

We had to memorize poems and dissect them like frogs in

■ Mark's brain didn't really open up. What did happen?

biology, and even write some of our own. So at home I had to read poetry out loud to hear the rhythms. Old Spiny loved it. He grew to Whitman and Poe all right, but I could almost see him expanding to the rhymes and rhythms of Longfellow.

"You're getting to be a long fellow yourself," I told him one Thursday when I was watering him.

His branches had shot upward and outward and so many new leaves had appeared that I could hardly keep up with the names. The first three he had come with were Harold, Nancy, and Stephanie. But then after Burt appeared and Louise and Sue and Amy and James and Virginia and Matthew, I couldn't keep track, so I talked to them collectively.ᶜ

"Leaves," I said, and then I told them what the history assignment or poem was for that night, and they listened and they grew.

■ A clue word to sequence.

I had to move the pot to the bookcase—it was too tall for the windowsill. Then, finally, to the floor.

Near the end of the year Jill said to me, "Can you bring the plant to school tomorrow? First period."

My heart thumped. I hadn't thought about giving Old Spiny back. "I don't know," I said.

"Listen, I need it. It's mine, you know."

"OK," I said. "Don't get excited."

"Just wait in the hall until I call you," she said.

My mom and I wrapped a sheet of plastic around him and I sat with the pot between my knees and the long stems bent over at the top.

I waited with Old Spiny outside the science room and then the door whooshed open and Jill came out.

"OK," she said. "You can bring it in now." Then she stopped and threw up her hands. "Good grief!" she hollered. "What have you done?"

"Me?" I said. "What?" I looked around.

"Look at that plant!"

I did. There stood Old Spiny, tall as I was, leafy and green, holding out Nancy and James and Virginia, and the others, and just unrolling Albert and Frank. I didn't see anything wrong with it.

"You've ruined my experiment."

"Look, I don't understand your problem, but I'm going in there to find out." I picked up Old Spiny and carried him, swaying over my head, into the room.

The whole class started to laugh. Some even clapped. What was happening? So then they told me.

Jill had given Old Spiny to me to neglect. She had given another to Larry to care for. And she had taken one home to care for herself. Those were the two scrawny‍ undersized plants on the table. She and Larry, since they were conscientious types, would take such good care of their plants that they would thrive. While Old Brown Thumb (me) would ignore mine and the poor thing would wither.

So I told them about the reading, the earphones, and the poetry, and about how sometimes I had even put the 'phones on Old Spiny and let him listen directly to the sounds.

■ Here's an idiom. Context indicates it means someone who neglects plants.

"Actually," I said, "I think I proved your experiment. You will probably get an A. If you talk to plants, play them some music, then they grow. Especially if you love them. I love this plant."

Jill did get an A and she told me I could keep Old Spiny.

I told him on the way home, "Not so much poetry next semester, Spiny, or you'll grow too much and I'll have to send you to a greenhouse." But then I told him I didn't mean it.

"In fact," I said, "I'll get you a nice fern to keep you company. That's a *Filicales,*^{cg} you know."

He knew.

Check the Skills

Understanding the Selection

1. What is the unusual friendship in the story? How did the plant become Mark's friend?

2. How did Mark feel when he thought he had to give Old Spiny back to Jill?

Literary Appreciation Skills Figurative Language

3. Someone who has great success growing plants is often described as having a green thumb. Is this an idiom? Why? What is the connection between this popular idiom and "Old Brown Thumb," as Jill expected Mark to be?

Comprehension Skills Literal Meaning

4. What happened first in each of the following sentences from the story? What clue word helped you decide?

    Pretty soon she was saying it before I even turned on the stereo.

    "Leaves," I said, and then I told them what the history assignment or poem was for that night.

Use the Skills

Understanding the Selection

As a joke, Katie John replaces a football with a big ball of twine. The results are tangled and hilarious. Afterward, Katie John and Edwin discover that they really want to continue their friendship.

1. As you read this excerpt from the book *Honestly, Katie John!*, you'll find an example of something very important in a friendship—shared interests.

Literary Appreciation Skills Figurative Language

2. Remember to watch for idioms. Make sure you understand their meaning.

Comprehension Skills Literal Meaning

3. Help yourself sort out the sequence by noticing words that signal it.

HONESTLY, KATIE JOHN!

Mary Calhoun

Everybody went into gales⁹ of laughter.

Katie John saw that Edwin on the sidelines was laughing too. Say, that's right, he hadn't been in the game. As a matter of fact, Edwin was often doing something alone when the other kids were playing. Oh, he messed around with them sometimes, but he was pretty much of a lone wolf.

■ This can't really describe Edwin, so you know it is an idiom.

Katie John grinned wholeheartedly at Edwin. And Edwin, still laughing, grinned back.

In fact, everyone was still laughing at the efforts of the football players to unsnarl themselves from the twine.

"Trust Katie John to do something like this," somebody said.

"Yeah," said Howard half in disgust, half in admiration. "Only Katie John would think of a thing like this."

Katie John walked up to Edwin. And then she didn't know what to say.

■ The sequence is clear because of the clue word.

"That was fun," she said, trying to carry along on the strength of the game's excitement.

But Edwin wasn't laughing now. He looked as awkward as Katie John was beginning to feel. For a minute she thought he wasn't going to speak.

Then he said, "I thought you hated boys."

"Well, I don't," she said firmly. "I guess—boys are just people."

"Huh." He poked his toe at a pebble, watching it carefully as if the pebble might get away. "Huh—I thought you weren't ever going to speak to me again."

"Well—I'm sorry and I—that is—Now look, Edwin Jones, I'm trying to be friends, so you just quit being so hard to get along with!"

Katie John watched him anxiously.

Finally Edwin looked up and grinned. "Okay, Katie John."

Abruptly he stuck out a dirty hand. Katie John looked at it, then understood. She put out her own hand, and they shook on it.

To get over the embarrassment of the moment, Katie plunged into talking.

"I saw that trench⁹ you dug out at the deserted farm. What are you digging for?"

"Indian stuff!" Edwin's face lit up even more. "Katie John, I think I've found an old Indian burial mound!"

Eagerly he told how he'd come across a stone hatchet in the gully⁹ bank. Now he was digging the trench, carefully picking away at the earth so as to find things just as they lay, the way archeologists⁹ dig. Already he'd found an earthen pot with only a few pieces broken off. But he hadn't come to any bones yet.

"Buried treasure!" Katie John exclaimed.

Edwin hurried on as if he'd been storing up words for two months.

"It could be the burial mound of some of the Sac and Fox Indians. I've been reading up on them, and they were the tribes that lived around here mostly. When I've got more to go on, I'm going to tell Mr. Boyle, and maybe he'll notify the archeology professor at the state university. But first I've got to dig some more to be sure."

"I could help!"

"Yeah, I could use you. We've got to hurry before the ground gets too frozen this winter to dig. Just think, Katie John, maybe next spring the man from the university might bring his students over here. We could watch a real dig!"⁹

"Yes!" But Katie's sigh was really a great big breath of relief. Things were going to be all right between her and Edwin.

Just then a familiar chant sounded. It was Howard.

"Katie's got a boy friend! Katie's got a boy friend!"

Casually Edwin shouted back, "Aw, go climb a tree."

"Go chase yourself!" Katie John called out at the same moment.

They looked at each other in surprise at expressing the same idea at once. And then the two friends began to laugh together as the school bell rang.

■ Do Edwin and Katie John really expect Howard to do these things?

■ A sequence clue word.

Check the Skills

Understanding the Selection

1. What shared interests seemed to help Katie John and Edwin be friends? Why do you suppose liking similar things is important in a friendship?

Literary Appreciation Skills Figurative Language

2. a. What do you think "being a lone wolf" means?

   b. Do the idioms "go climb a tree" and "go chase yourself" mean the same thing? What do they mean?

Comprehension Skills Literal Meaning

3. Read the following sentences from the story. What action happened first? How do you know?

   > Katie John walked up to Edwin. And then she didn't know what to say.

Use the Skills

Understanding the Selection

Robert was campaign manager for his friend Soup when Soup ran for class president. Soup, whose real name is Luther, ran against Norma Jean, who was also a close friend of Robert's. Robert and Soup had done a crazy trick to draw attention to Soup's campaign.

1. Find out what they did, as you read this excerpt.

2. Look for another friendship developing between Robert and someone who may surprise you.

Literary Appreciation Skills Figurative Language

3. You'll need to use your skill in understanding idioms. Watch the context for clues to their meanings.

Comprehension Skills Literal Meaning

4. You should have no trouble keeping the sequence of events straight. Just remember to pay attention to signal words.

SOUP

Robert Newton Peck

"I saw it," said Miss Kelly.

"You did?" I asked her.

"Yes, I certainly did. Miss Boland came for lunch on Sunday, and in the afternoon, we took a drive in her car."

Miss Kelly had asked me to stay after school. I knew she wasn't mad or anything like that. It was sunny, so Miss Kelly and I walked out behind the school. Some of the red and gold leaves had come down and our feet rustled through a fallen October. We sat on a jigsaw fence of long gray rails and talked. She brought up the subject of paint.

"We did it," I said. "Soup and I."

"As soon as I saw that paint on Mr. McGinley's barn, I remembered the red I had seen on your hands. So I put one and one together and concluded that you and Luther had tested your hand at exterior decoration."

"What are you going to do, Miss Kelly?"

"Robert, I'm not quite sure the question you just asked is the main issue. I believe the situation can best be mended by my asking you. What do you and Soup intend to do?"

"I believe we ought to go face Mr. McGinley and tell him that Soup and I were the ones who put red paint on his barn."

"Is that all?"

"Well, I don't guess we ought to stop short of making it right."

"How will you do that?"

"Best we scrape off the paint."

"That," said Miss Kelly, "is what I hoped to hear."

"Soup feels the same way. Actually it wasn't Soup's fault as much as mine. He didn't paint the barn. I did."

Miss Kelly lifted her eyebrows. "So you're saying the whole idea was yours?"

■ What is the idiom here?

■ Here's a clue to sequence.

"Not exactly."

"I thought not. Having observed one Luther Vinson for several years, I would conclude that he had a hand in everything . . . except the paint."

"Seeing as I put the paint up, maybe old Soup ought to take it down, while I lie under a tree and eat a Jonathan."

"Best apple there is," said Miss Kelly.

"Uh, did Miss Boland see the barn, too?"

"Come now, Robert. One would have to be blindfolded *not* to see it."

"What did Miss Boland say?"

"I can't repeat her exact words," said Miss Kelly. "But I was there when she stopped the car to crank down the window so that we could both take a better look."

"We painted the barn so Soup would win."

"So I presumed. Miss Boland and I both laughed, tears rolling down our faces, until we suddenly became aware of *who* owns the barn."

"Mr. Cyrus McGinley," I said.

"Indeed he does."

"Maybe he doesn't understand politics."

"Do you?"

"Yes," I said. "Campaign managers do all the work."

Miss Kelly smiled. "Incidentally," she said, "the poster you made was very amusing. And creative."

"Do you think we picked up any votes?"

"Well, now," said Miss Kelly, twisting the stem of a yellow maple leaf in her fingers so that the hand of the leaf spun round and round in an autumn waltz, "I would predict at this very moment that the election is going to be a close tally.⁹

"I believe I could name *one* boy who'd like to vote twice—once for Norma Jean and once for Soup."

"You mean *me?*"

"I do."

"By the way, I'm sure glad you didn't make me read that note in school, the note that Norma Jean Bissell wrote me."

"Looking back," said Miss Kelly, "I am rather ashamed of myself for even *asking* you to read it aloud. Teachers make mistakes, too, you know."

"They *do?*"

"Certainly we do. I saw you reading her letter instead of your geography book. So temper took hold of me."

■ What do you think this idiom means?

"You didn't *look* real mad."

"An inner temper. So, in that one moment of haste, I ordered you to read a letter. Something I should not have done, as it was personal. And when you chose the ruler, as opposed to reading the letter aloud, you made me feel more than a little ashamed."

"Honest?"

"Honest and truly." Miss Kelly tapped the top of my head with the leaf. "In spite of my being petty^cg and vengeful,^cg *you* were noble. You acted with honor."

"Sort of like Ivanhoe?"^g

"Yes, very much like Ivanhoe."

"But he had a horse and a sword." I picked up a stick and began to jab away at an imaginary enemy.

"As you mature, Robert, you will learn that being honorable is far more shining than either a sword or a horse."

"You're right about all that."

Miss Kelly smiled. "How rewarding it is to learn that, upon occasion, I am right about *something*."

"I didn't mean it like that."

"No, you didn't."

"It just sort of . . . popped out."

Miss Kelly nodded. "In the same way I popped out my order to you to read Norma Jean's note. I apologize for that."

"You don't have to apologize. I started it."

"I wanted to tell you that I was sorry," said Miss Kelly, "just to put things right once again. Did you ever do something wrong, and want to undo it?"

"You mean like painting the barn?"

"Yes. Like the barn."

"Me an' Soup'll fix it."

Check the Skills

Understanding the Selection

1. What had Soup and Robert done that they shouldn't have?

2. Do you think Miss Kelly and Robert were becoming friends? What were some of the things they said to each other that helped you decide? Does it surprise you that a teacher and a student can be friends? Why or why not?

Literary Appreciation Skills Figurative Language

3. a. What does the idiom "having a hand in everything" mean? How do you know?

    b. Did temper really take hold of Miss Kelly? What does that idiom mean?

Comprehension Skills Literal Meaning

4. How do you know that the two actions in the following sentence would take place at the same time?

    Soup ought to take it down while I lie under a tree.

Use the Skills

Island of the Blue Dolphins is a famous book about an Indian girl who survived alone on an island for many years. Although the book is fiction, it is based on fact. The girl tamed a wild dog. He was her constant companion for years. The depth of their friendship is clear in the following excerpt.

Use your skill with idioms and sequence as you read. This time you're on your own, though. There are no marginal notes to help you.

ISLAND OF THE BLUE DOLPHINS

Scott O'Dell

It was late in the summer that Rontu died. The days since spring, whenever I went to the reef to fish, he would not go with me unless I urged him to. He liked to lie in the sun in front of the house and I let him, but I did not go so often as in the past.

I remember the night that Rontu stood at the fence and barked for me to let him out. Usually he did this when the moon was big, and he came back in the morning, but that night there was no moon and he did not return.

I waited all that day for him until almost dusk and then I went out to look for him. I saw his tracks and followed them over the dunes and a hill to the lair where he had once lived. There I found him, lying in the back of the cave, alone. At first I thought that he had been hurt, yet there were no wounds on him. He touched my hand with his tongue, but only once and then he was quiet and scarcely breathed.

Since night had fallen and it was too dark for me to carry Rontu back, I stayed there. I sat beside him through the night and talked to him. At dawn I took him in my arms and left the cave. He was very light, as if something about him had already gone.

The sun was up as I went along the cliff. Gulls were crying in the sky. He raised his ears at the sound, and I put him down, thinking that he wished to bark at them as he always did. He raised his head and followed them with his eyes, but did not make a sound.

"Rontu," I said, "you have always liked to bark at the seagulls. Whole mornings and afternoons you have barked at them. Bark at them now for me."

But he did not look at them again. Slowly he walked to where I was standing and fell at my feet. I put my hand on his chest. I could feel his heart beating, but it beat only twice, very slowly, loud and hollow like the waves on the beach, and then no more.

"Rontu," I cried, "oh, Rontu!"

I buried him on the headland.[cg] I dug a hole in the crevice of the rock, digging for two days from dawn until the going down of the sun, and put him there with some sand flowers and a stick he liked to chase when I threw it, and covered him with pebbles of many colors that I gathered on the shore.

That winter I did not go to the reef at all. I ate the things I had stored and left the house only to get water at the spring. It was a winter of strong winds and rain and wild seas that crashed against the cliffs, so I

would not have gone out much even if Rontu had been there. During that time I made four snares⁹ from notched branches.

In the summer once, when I was on my way to the place where the sea elephants lived, I had seen a young dog that looked like Rontu. He was running with one of the packs of wild dogs, and though I caught only a glimpse of him, I was sure he was Rontu's son.

He was larger than the other dogs and had heavier fur and yellow eyes and he ran with a graceful stride like Rontu's. In the spring I planned to catch him with the snares I was making.

Check the Skills

Understanding the Selection

1. Were the girl and Rontu friends? Why do you think as you do? Why do you think the girl wanted to catch the wild dog she believed was Rontu's son?

Literary Appreciation Skills Figurative Langauge

2. Several idioms from the story are listed below. How can you tell they are idioms? What do they mean?

    night had fallen
    the sun was up
    the going down of the sun

Comprehension Skills Literal Meaning

3. Which event in the following sentence happened first? How do you know?

    He touched my hand with his tongue, but only once
    and then he was quiet and scarcely breathed.

Apply What You Learned in Unit 16

The Theme

Friendship

1. In this unit you read about several examples of friendship. Friends care about each other. They often like the same things. They keep each other company. A friend can make you feel that somebody understands you. An old saying is "To have a friend, be one." Do you think that is true? Why or why not? Do you think having friends is important? Why?

• In this unit you read about people's friendships with plants and animals. Many young children think of a favorite doll or teddy bear as a friend. How are these friendships different from those with people? How are they alike?

The Skills

Literary Appreciation Skills Figurative Language

2. If you come across a phrase in your reading that doesn't seem to make sense, remember that it may be an idiom. An idiom has a different meaning than the words in it usually do. Many idioms are very familiar to you and will give you no trouble. But you will sometimes meet new ones.

3. See if you can figure out an idiom's meaning from the sense of the surrounding words. If not, try checking a dictionary. Look up the word within the idiom that seems to be the most important.

Comprehension Skills Literal Meaning

4. One way to figure out the sequence of events you read about is to watch for certain signal words. Some of these are *first, next, afterwards, then, finally, before, last, while,* and *meanwhile.*

• Sequence is often important in history. And when you're doing an experiment in science, or working a problem in math, it can be crucial! Be sure to watch for words that signal sequence as you read materials in these classes.

Apply the
Literary Appreciation Skills
You Have Learned

Apply the Skills As You Do Your Schoolwork

The literary appreciation skills you have learned in this section will be very useful when you read materials assigned in school. You will see that this is true when you read the following excerpt. It was taken from a textbook used in reading and language arts classes. Read to find out what happened when a famous anthropologist tried to study chimpanzees first hand.

The literary appreciation skills you have learned will help you to get the most enjoyment from this selection. You can see how this works by keeping the following questions in mind as you read. Answer them after you finish.

1. **Nonfiction.** What type of literature is this? Refer back to pages 351 and 352 if you need to recheck literary types.

2. **Characters and setting.** What is the setting? Which sentences help to establish the setting? What kind of person do you think Jane Goodall is? How are these characteristics brought out in the excerpt?

3. **Unusual characters, situations, settings, events.** How does the author develop an entertaining style? Does he use an unusual character, an unusual situation, an unusual setting, unusual events, or all of these?

4. **Idioms.** There are two idioms in the last paragraph of the excerpt. What are they? Refer to pages 431 and 432 if you want to recheck idioms.

Jane Goodall

Gilbert Grail

The rainy season came to the jungle around Lake Tanganyika in central Africa early in 1961. Rain pattered on the thick leaves of the tall trees and dripped on the lush grass below. A young Englishwoman moved silently among the dripping trees. She stopped quickly when she saw a chimpanzee just ahead. Except for the sound of the rain, the jungle was very quiet. Then soft *hoos* came from the right and the left and from behind the young woman.

All at once she was showered with water and twigs. Looking up, she saw a large chimpanzee in the tree above, shaking it angrily. He uttered a loud *wraa,* one of the most savage of jungle sounds, and other chimpanzees echoed it. The chimpanzee in the tree shook it so hard that a branch hit the woman on the head. She fell to the ground and a dark shape charged her, veering to one side at the last moment.

Jane Goodall crounched in the wet grass, expecting her next breath to be her last. Slowly she realized that the jungle had become silent again and cautiously she looked around. She was alone.

A great surge of happiness came over her. For months she had been trying to study the chimpanzees at first hand but with little success. The problem was that they were afraid of her. Every time she would come near, they would disappear. Now they no longer were afraid. She felt this was a giant step toward attaining their confidence and friendship.

Apply the Skills As You Deal with the World

You'll find these literary appreciation skills helpful when you read material outside of school. The following column from a newspaper is something you might read because its headline makes it sound interesting. See how the columnist explains a common error in logical thinking that is made by many people. Again, read the questions first. Then keep them in mind as you read. Answer them after you finish.

1. **Nonfiction.** Why is a newspaper column like this considered to be nonfiction instead of fiction?

2. **Characters and setting.** What was the setting of the problem used in the college course? Is there any other "setting" in the column? How does the author seem to characterize the students who got the problem wrong?

3. **Unusual characters, situations, settings, events.** Which of the following does the author use to develop an entertaining style: an unusual character, situation, setting, or event?

4. **Idioms.** The following sentence from the selection could be considered an idiom. Why do you think this is so?

    Statistics take a terrible beating from people.

Odds are, most people can't figure the intricacies of statistics

Sydney J. Harris

People talk about "averages" and "odds" all the time. But it is simply amazing how few understand them.

A few years ago, a college course in statistics offered the following problem to 95 students. About three-quarters of these college students got it wrong.

A certain town is served by two hospitals. In the larger hospital, about 45 babies are born each day. In the smaller hospital, about 15 are born. As we know, about 50 per cent of all babies are boys. The exact percentage varies from day to day, sometimes higher and sometimes lower.

For a year, each hospital recorded the days on which more than 60 per cent of the babies born were boys. Which hospital do you think recorded more such days? Exactly 21 students chose the larger hospital. Exactly 21 students chose the smaller hospital. Fifty-three replied that the number would be about the same. What is your answer?

Anyone who knows anything about "sample size" would answer "the smaller hospital." This is because the smaller the sample is, the more distorted the result is likely to be. The larger the sample, the truer to absolute probability it should be. Statistics take a terrible beating from people. We should be on guard that our abilities to guess accurately are not reliable guides to "the odds" and use our heads more.

Glossary

Pronunciation Key

After each entry word, letters and symbols in parentheses show you how the word is pronounced. Some symbols that may confuse you are shown below. Pronounce a symbol as you pronounce the spelling in bold, or very dark, type in the words next to the symbol. For example, ô should be pronounced the same way you say the *a* in **all** and the *aw* in **saw**. For your convenience, a shorter list of these symbols is at the bottom of each right hand page of the glossary.

Sometimes a word can be pronounced in different ways. When that is the case, the more common pronunciation is given first.

A syllable that gets the most stress when spoken is followed by a primary accent mark, as the first syllable in **accent** (ak'sent). A syllable spoken with less stress is shown with a secondary accent mark, as the last syllable in **accelerate** (ak sel'ə rāt').

A brief history of a word, called its etymology, is given for some words. It is in brackets at the end of the entry.

a	**a**pple, h**a**t	o	**o**dd, t**o**p	u	**u**p, p**u**ff		
ā	**a**ble, s**ay**	ō	**o**pen, h**o**se	ù	p**u**t, b**oo**k		
ã	**ai**r, c**a**re	ô	**a**ll, s**aw**	ü	b**oo**t, m**o**ve		
ä	**a**rm, f**a**ther	ôr	**or**der, f**or**ce	ū	**u**se, m**u**sic		
e	**e**levator, b**e**st	oi	**oi**l, b**oy**	ə	**a**bout, giv**e**n, penc**i**l, lem**o**n, unt**i**l		
ē	**ea**ch, m**e**	ou	**ou**t, h**ow**				
ér	**ear**th, t**ur**n						
				th	**th**in, boo**th**		
i	**i**tch, p**i**n			ŦH	**th**en, smoo**th**		
ī	**i**vy, n**i**ce			zh	mea**s**ure, sei**z**ure		

ac com plish (ə kom′plish), to complete suc-cessfully. [from Latin *ad-* to + *complere* to fill up or finish]

ac cur ate (ak′yər it), exact; correct.

ac cus tomed (ə kus′təmd), usual. **accus-tomed to,** used to.

a dapt (ə dapt′), to adjust to conditions.

ad jec tive (aj′ik tiv), a word used to modify, or limit the meaning of, a noun or pronoun. The word *green* is used as an adjective in both the following sentences. *Hand me the green book. The book is green.*

ad verb (ad′vėrb), a word used to modify, or limit the meaning of, a verb, adjective, or another adverb. Many adverbs end in the suffix *-ly.* The word *awkwardly* is an adverb in the following sentence. *He smiled awkwardly at the robot.*

af ter math (af′tər math′), the result or con-sequence, especially of violence.

ag gres sive (ə gres′iv), ready to fight or at-tack.

ag o ny (ag′ə nē), extreme pain or suffering.

air tight (ār′tīt′), fitting so closely that air or gas cannot enter or leave.

al der (ôl′dər), a small cone-bearing tree that grows in cool, moist soil.

a lert (ə lėrt′), watchful; on guard.

al ti tude (al′tə tüd), height above the surface of the earth.

am a teur (am′ə chər *or* am′ə tər), a person who performs an activity for pleasure and not for money.

an ces tors (an′ces′tərz), people from whom one is descended; that is, parents, grandpar-ents, and so forth. [from Latin *antecessor* one who goes before]

an chor per son (ang′kər per′sən), 1. the last person to perform on a relay team. 2. the person on a television or radio news show who puts together reports from correspon-dents.

an nu lar (an′yə lər), like a ring. **annular eclipse,** the blocking of the sun′s light by the moon passing between the sun and the earth in such a way that the moon covers all but the thin outer ring of the sun.

an tics (an′tiks), funny or silly actions.

ap pa ri tion (ap′ə rish′ ən), something that seems to be a ghost or phantom. [from Latin *apparitiō* appearance]

a quar i um (ə kwār′ē əm), a show place for living fish, water animals, and plants. [from Latin *aquā* water]

A ra li a Spi no sa (ə rā′liə spī nō′sə), a plant with a very prickly stem. It can grow to 40 feet (12 meters). Also known as the Devil′s Walking Stick.

ar chae ol o gist *or* **ar che ol o gist** (är′kē ol′ə jist), a scientist who studies ancient people and cultures by digging up and analyzing the remains of their settlements.

a ris to crat ic (ə ris′tə krat′ik), being part of the upper class; born into nobility, culture, and wealth. [from Greek *aristokratia* rule by the best (citizens), from *aristos* best]

ar ti fact (är′tə fakt), any object made by a human being, such as a tool or ornament.

as sist ant (ə sis′tənt), a person whose job it is to help another.

as sur ance (ə shür′ əns), 1. a positive state-ment intended to give confidence. 2. confi-dence; certainty.

as tron o my (ə stron′ə mē), the science that deals with the sun, moon, stars, planets, and other heavenly bodies. [from Greek *astron-omos* star-arranger]

at mo sphere (at′mə sfir), 1. the air around the earth. 2. the mood in a particular place. [from Greek *atmó(s)* vapor + *sphaîra* sphere]

bal let (bal′ā *or* ba lā′), a dance accompanied by music and that tells a story.

ban quet (bang′kwit), an elaborate meal, often to honor a person or occasion.

bar ren (bār′ ən), producing little or nothing.

bar ri er (bār′ē ər), something that blocks.

B.C., before Christ. *B.C.* is used with dates be-fore the birth of Christ.

be drag gled (bi drag′əld), wet and dirty.

blub ber (blub′ ər), layer of fat in whales and other sea animals, often melted into oil and burned in lamps.

blue bot tle (blü′bot′l), a large two-winged fly with a blue body.

boil (boil), the movement of water made by a fish swimming near the surface.

bolt (bōlt), large roll of cloth or wallpaper. [from Middle English *bolt* heavy arrow]

box score, a listing, usually in a newspaper, that ranks baseball players according to hits, runs, errors, times at bat, and so forth.

brae (brā), *Scottish.* A hillside.

Braille (brāl), a system of writing for the blind in which raised dots represent letters and can be read by touch. [from Louis Braille, 1809–52, a French educator who invented it.]

bram bles (bram′bəlz), plants or shrubs covered with little thorns.

Brit ish (brit′ish), of or about Great Britain and its people. Great Britain includes England, Scotland, and Wales.

buoy ant (boi′ənt *or* bü′yənt), 1. having the tendency to float. 2. light-hearted.

bur row (bėr′ō), 1. a hole dug in the ground by an animal. 2. the act of digging a hole in the ground.

can yon (kan′yən), a deep valley with steep sides, often with a stream at the bottom. [from Spanish *cañon* pipe, tube]

ca per (kā′pər), to leap or jump about playfully. [short form of Latin *capriole* a leap, from *caper* goat]

cap ti vate (kap′tə vāt), to fascinate; to interest by special beauty or charm.

car bo hy drate (kär′bō hī′drāt), one of the types of foods necessary to the human body, such as sugar and starch.

car ni val (kär′nə vəl), a traveling show featuring games, rides, and displays.

cat a pulted (kat′ə pul təd), hurled, thrown, or launched.

cat e go ry (kat′ə gôr′ē), a group of things or people alike in some way; a division in classification. *Dogs come in two categories: long-haired and short-haired.*

cau tious (kô shəs), careful; trying to avoid danger.

chal lenge (chal′ənj), 1. to call to compete. 2. to object; dare. [from Latin *calumnia* trickery or false statement] **chal leng ing ly** (chal′ ənj ing lē), in a way that demands an answer.

chant ed (chant′id), said with a rhythm, using one tone for several syllables.

Chev vie (shev′ē) shortened form of *Chevrolet*, sometimes used as a nickname for that kind of car.

clan (klan), a group of related families; a group of people closely united by a common interest. [from Scottish Gaelic *clann* children, family]

clat ter ing (klat′ ər ing), making a loud rattling noise.

cleft (kleft), a split; a crack.

co coon (kə kün′), 1. the silky covering spun by larvae of moths and insects to live in while they grow to adulthood. 2. any protective covering.

co in cide (kō′in sīd′), to occur at the same time.

co ma¹ (kō′mə), a loss of consciousness for a long period of time, often caused by sickness or injury. [from Greek *kōma* deep sleep]

co ma² (kō′mə), the part of the head of a comet that appears to be a hazy cloud. [from Greek *komē* hair]

com et (kom′it), a small, bright heavenly body that orbits the sun like a planet. Comets often have cloudy tails. [from Greek *komētēs* long-haired]

com pound (kom′pound) **eye,** the eye of certain insects, arachnids, and crustaceans. It is made up of many tiny units, called *facets,* each of which receives part of the image.

com pute (kəm pūt′), to find out mathematically; to calculate.

con duct (kən dukt′), 1. to behave in a certain way. 2. to carry out or direct.

con serve (kən sėrv′), to keep from being wasted; use wisely.

con sti tu tion (kon′stə tü′shən *or* kon′stə tü′shən), 1. the physical makeup or nature of a person or thing. 2. a person's health.

con tract (kən trakt′), to draw together; make smaller; tighten.

court yard (kôrt′yärd), an open space surrounded by buildings or walls.

cow ard ice (kou′ ər dis), a lack of courage.

cow er (kou′ ər), to draw back in fear; to shrink from someone's anger.

coy o te (kī ō′tē *or* kī′ōt), a small North American, prairie wolf, known for its loud howling at night.

crit i cism (krit′ə siz′ əm), fault finding; unfavorable comment.

cue (kū), a word or action of one actor that serves as a signal to another actor to come on stage or speak.

cul mi nate (kul′mə nāt), to reach the highest point; to end up in.

cul ti vate (kul′tə vāt), 1. to prepare land for raising crops; to till. 2. to tend a crop.

cul vert (kul′vərt), a small drain for water that passes under a road.

cum ber some (kum′bər səm), clumsy; hard to manage.

curl i cue (kér′lə kū), a fancy curl.

daz zle (daz′əl), to impress greatly.

daz zling (daz′ling), magnificent.

de clin ing (di klīn′ing), 1. turning down or refusing. *I am declining your invitation.* 2. moving toward the last part. *She is in her declining years.*

de com pose (dē′kəm pōz′), 1. to break down into basic parts. 2. to decay.

de fense less (di fens′lis), without protection; helpless to resist attack.

de lib e ra tion (di lib′ə rā′shən), thoughtful, careful consideration and debate before a decision.

del ta (del′tə), a triangular deposit of earth at the mouth of a river.

de mon (dē′mən), an evil spirit.

depth (depth), 1. distance from top to bottom. 2. lowness of pitch, as in a voice or musical instrument.

des per ate ly (des′pər it lē), extremely; hopelessly; recklessly.

de spite (di spīt′), in spite of. *She drove the car despite the flat tire.*

de spond en cy (di spon′dən sē), discouragement; loss of hope.

de tect (di tekt′), to discover; find out. (from Latin *dētectus* to uncover)

de test (di test′), to dislike intensely.

de vot ed (di vō′tid), loyal; faithfully attached to someone or something.

di a gram (dī′ə gram), a drawing designed to outline or explain something.

dig (dig), 1. to make a hole in or turn over the ground. 2. an area dug by scientists in search of the remains of ancient peoples and cultures.

dis crim i na tion (dis krim′ə nā′shən), showing a difference in treatment for no logical reason or because of prejudice. [from Latin *discrimināre* to divide, distinguish]

di shev eled (də shev′əld), messy; rumpled. [from French *descheveler* to disarrange the hair]

dis port (dis pôrt′), to amuse oneself. [from French *desporter* to carry away]

doc trine (dok′trən), 1. a belief; the teaching of the beliefs of a church, nation, or group. 2. teachings.

dor mant (dôr′mənt), 1. asleep. 2. not active; in a state of rest.

dor mi to ry (dôr′mə tôr ē), a building with many rooms for sleeping. Some colleges have dormitories for students living away from home.

dra ma tic (drə mat′ik), 1. like something that might appear in a play in a theater. 2. full of emotion or action.

ec cen tric (ek sen′trik), unusual; peculiar; odd. [from Latin *eccentricus* out of center]

e clipse (i klips′), the partial or complete blocking of the light of one heavenly body by another. **solar eclipse,** the blocking out of the sun's light by the moon passing between the earth and the sun.

ed i ble (ed′ə bəl), suitable to eat.

ee rie (ēr′ē), frightening because of seeming strange or weird. *The old swing made eerie noises at night.*

ef fi cient (ə fish′ənt), able to perform well and easily without problems.

em blem (em′bləm), a sign, design or token that represents something else; symbol. *A dove is an emblem of peace.*

e merge (i mérj′), to become known; appear.

e nor mi ty (i nôr′mə tē), 1. the quality of going greatly beyond what was expected. 2. monstrous. 3. greatness.

en thu si asm (en thü′zē az′ əm), active interest or excitement.

e quiv a lent (i kwiv′ə lənt), equal in measure, worth, meaning, and so forth.

es sen tial (ə sen′shəl), absolutely necessary; basic; very important.

e ter ni ty (i tér′nə tē), 1. time without beginning or end. 2. endless time.

---

a **a**pple, ā **a**ble, ã **a**ir, ä **a**rm; e **e**levator, ē **ea**ch, ér **ear**th; i **i**tch, ī **i**vy; o **o**dd, ō **o**pen, ô **a**ll, ôr **or**der; oi **oi**l, ou **ou**t; u **u**p, u̇ **p**ut, ü b**oo**t, ū **u**se; ə **a**bout; th **th**in, ŦH **th**en, zh mea**s**ure

e val u ate (i val'ū āt), to find the value of; to judge what something is worth. *An expert will evaluate the diamonds you want to sell.*

e vap o rate (i vap'ə rāt'), to change from a liquid into steam or a vapor.

ex ceed ing ly (ek sē'ding lē), extremely; unusually.

ex cep tion (ek sep'shən), 1. something left out. 2. a case or situation to which a rule does not apply.

ex pect ant (ek spek'tənt), looking for or thinking something will happen.

ex posed (ek spōzd'), uncovered; left open to.

ex port (ek spôrt' *or* ek'spôrt), to send goods to another country for sale.

ex press way (ek spres'wā'), a highway designed and built so that traffic can travel quickly and directly.

ex ter i or (ek stir'ē ər), 1. the outer surface. 2. the outward appearance.

ex tinct (ek stingkt'), no longer existing.

ex tin guish (ek sting'gwish), 1. to put out a fire or light. 2. to destroy.

fas ci na ting (fas'ə nāt'ing), attractive; enchanting. [from Latin *fascināre* to enchant or bewitch]

fa tal (fā'tl), resulting in death.

feat (fēt), an unusual act, often showing bravery, skill, or strength.

fee bly (fē'blē), weakly; lacking force.

fife (fīf), a high-pitched flute.

Fil i ca les (fil'ə kā'lēz), scientific term for certain flowerless plants, such as ferns.

floes (flōz), 1. sheets or blocks of floating ice. 2. something that resembles sheets of floating ice.

fly (flī), 1. any of a group of insects having two wings. 2. a fish hook decorated to look like one of these insects.

for bid ding (fər bid'ing), looking disagreeable, threatening, or unapproachable.

fore men (fôr'mən), 1. people who guide and speak for juries in law courts. 2. people who organize and direct groups of workers.

for tu nate (fôr'chə nit), lucky.

fos ter (fô'stər), 1. to bring up; to help the growth of or encourage. 2. in the same family but not related by birth. **foster parent,** a person who raises or takes care of a child not related by birth.

foun da tion (foun dā'shən), the base on which a building rests.

freeze-dried (frēz'drīd), preserved by fast freezing and then drying.

frol ic (frol'ik), happy play; a joyful game.

frond (frond), a palm tree or fern leaf.

frus tra tion (fru strā'shən), the feeling that effort is useless; feeling defeated because something gets in the way.

fugue (fūg), a musical composition in which a theme or melody is repeated and varied in a complicated pattern.

gaff (gaf), a strong hook on a handle used to pull large fish out of the water.

gale (gāl), a very strong wind.

gam ble (gam'bəl), 1. an act involving a risk or an uncertain outcome. 2. a bet of money on the outcome of a game.

gang plank (gang'plangk), a temporary bridge used to get on and off a ship.

gar ri son (gar'ə sən), 1. the troops stationed in a fort to protect it. 2. a fort protected by soldiers and weapons.

gor ings (gôr'ingz), wounds made by a horn or tusk.

gram pus (gram'pəs), a large sea animal something like a dolphin.

grim (grim), 1. fierce; cruel. 2. stern looking. 3. unyielding; without let up.

gul ly (gul'ē), a small, narrow ditch made by heavy rains or running water.

har assed (har'əst *or* hə rast'), 1. tormented by repeated attacks. 2. worried; disturbed. *The bus driver was harassed by the angry passengers.*

har poon (här pün'), a barbed spear used to catch large sea animals. It has a rope tied to it and is thrown or shot from a gun.

haugh ty (hô'tē), too proud of oneself. [from French *haut* high]

haz ard (haz'ərd), a risk or danger. [from Spanish *azar* unlucky throw of the dice]

head land (hed'lənd), a point of high land that extends out into water.

hik ing straps (hīk'ing straps), a 2″ nylon webbing that runs the length or width of a sailboat and enables sailors to hike their bodies out (lean out) of the boat to right it when it is heeling (tipping).

ho gan (hō'gän'), a traditional dwelling of the Navajo Indians, made of earth and branches and covered with mud.

ho ri zon tal (hôr'ə zon'tl), 1. level or flat. 2. longer from side to side than from top to bottom. 3. lining up with the horizon.

hos tel (hos'tl), a supervised lodging place where travelers may stay.

hos tile (hos'təl), unfriendly; against.

hu man i tar i an ism (hū man'ə tār'ē ən izm), the practice of being helpful to humanity; the actions of a person who is interested in the well-being of all.

hu mil i ate (hū mil'ē āt'), 1. to lower someone's self-respect or pride. 2. to hurt a person's feelings; to make someone feel ashamed and embarrassed.

hus ky (hus'kē), a dog of the arctic region used to pull sleds. [probably from a shortened form of *Eskimo*]

hy dro e lec tric (hī'drō ə lek'trik), having to do with the production of electricity by water power.

ig loo (ig'lü), a dome-shaped traditional Eskimo house built of blocks of ice or snow. [from Eskimo *iglu* house]

il le gal (i lē'gəl), forbidden by law.

il lu sion (i lü'zhən), something that appears to be real but isn't. *The clown gave the illusion of being ten feet tall.* [from Latin *illūdere* to mock]

im age (im'ij), what is seen.

im ma ture (im'ə chur'), not fully grown.

im mense (i mens'), huge; vast.

im port (im pôrt' *or* im'pôrt), to bring goods for sale in from a foreign country.

in bred (in'bred'), natural; born into. *Her good manners were inbred.*

in con test a bly (in'kən tes'tə blē), without a doubt; unquestionably.

in dex (in'deks) **finger,** the finger next to the thumb, used to point with.

in dif fer ent ly (in dif'ər ənt lē), 1. having no interest; not caring. 2. having no preference.

in dis tinct (in'dis tingkt'), 1. not clearly seen or heard. 2. not clearly separated.

in dus tri al i za tion (in dus'trē ə lə zā'shən), development of industry, manufacturing, and trade.

in fi nite (in'fə nit), endless; without boundaries or limits.

in her it ance (in hār'ə təns), 1. the property that passes at the owner's death to his or her heirs. 2. the physical or mental qualities one receives from parents or ancestors.

in sist ence (in sis'təns), a strong demand; urgency.

in stinct (in'stingkt), an inborn sense to behave in a certain way.

in su late (in'sə lāt), 1. to protect from loss of inside heat by special material or covering. 2. to separate. [from Latin *insulatus* made like an island]

in tel lect (in'tə lekt), 1. power to learn and reason. 2. great mental ability.

in tel li gence (in tel'ə jens), the ability to learn and understand.

in ter sec tion (in'tər sek'shən), the location on a street or highway where traffic going in different directions meets and crosses.

in ter view (in'tər vū), to meet with someone to discuss a particular subject, such as a job. [from French *entre-* each other + *voir* to see]

in vade (in vād'), 1. to enter with force; to attack. 2. to move into.

in vol un tar i ly (in vol'ən tār'ə lē), 1. without choice or will. 2. unintentional.

i so late (ī'sə lāt), to set apart. [from Latin *insula* island]

I van hoe (ī'vən hō'), a character in a novel (1819) of the same name by Sir Walter Scott. Ivanhoe was a Crusader Knight who chose to show mercy to his enemy instead of taking revenge.

jeer (jēr), to make fun of in a rude or unkind way.

jer sey (jér'zē), a close-fitting knitted shirt worn in certain sports.

jug ger naut (jug'ər nôt), something to which one is blindly dedicated or cruelly sacrificed. *The stock market was his juggernaut.*

---

a **a**pple, ā **a**ble, ã **a**ir, ä **a**rm; e **e**levator, ē **ea**ch, ér **ear**th; i **i**tch, ī **i**vy; o **o**dd, ō **o**pen, ô **a**ll, ôr **or**der; oi **oi**l, ou **ou**t; u **u**p, ú **p**ut, ü b**oo**t, ū **u**se; ə **a**bout; th **th**in, ŦH **th**en, zh mea**s**ure

keen (kēn), 1. shaped to cut well, as the edge of a knife. 2. vivid; alert; strong. [from Old English *cēne* wise, bold]

knack (nak), a particular skill.

la bored (lā'bərd), not easy; done with difficulty; forced.

lam i nat ed (lam'ə nā'tid), made up of thin layers stuck together. *The table top was laminated wood.*

lat i tude (lat'ə tüd), 1. the distance north or south from the earth's equator. 2. the region as located in relation to its distance from the equator.

law suit (lô'süt), action in which one party claims something against another in a court of law.

league¹ (lēg), a group of teams that forms an association. [from Latin *ligare* to bind]

league² (lēg), a measure of distance equal to about three miles. [frorn Latin *leuga* a measure of distance]

ledg er (lej'ər), a book in which a record of business accounts is kept.

leg end ar y (lej'ən der'ē), like a legend, which is a story from the past that may or may not have really happened. *King Arthur is a legendary hero.*

lest (lest), for fear that; to prevent the possibility that. *Walk softly lest you wake the baby.*

lev er (lev'ər), a bar used to pry up or lift a weight.

lig a ment (lig'ə mənt), a band of body tissue that connects bones or holds organs in place.

lo tus (lō təs), a type of water lily.

lu di crous (lü'də krəs), laughable; ridiculous. *The dancing monkey looked ludicrous in the ballet costume.*

mar gin (mär'jən), 1. the blank space around the edges of a page. 2. an indefinite number or amount of difference.

mar shal (mär'shəl), to put in order.

mass transit system, transportation of many people on trains or buses provided by a government.

me di an (mē'dē ən), 1. the middle; the average. 2. a divider, such as a painted line or low wall, that separates traffic going in opposite directions.

Med i ter ra ne an (med'ə tə rā'nē ən), characteristic of the Mediterranean Sea and the areas bordering it in Africa, Asia, and Europe. [from Latin *mediterrāneus* from *medius* middle + *terra* land]

mi grate (mī'grāt), 1. to move from one location to settle in another. 2. to move from one climate to another as the seasons change. *Geese migrate south in winter.*

mil i tan cy (mil'ə tən sē), condition of being eager or willing to fight for a cause or idea one believes in.

mir a cle (mir'ə kəl), a happening that is or seems to be outside of, or to go against, the laws of nature. [from Latin *mirari* to wonder at]

mol ly cod dle (mol'ē kod'l), to be overprotective; to spoil or pamper.

monk (mungk), a man who gives up all he owns and joins a religious group living in a monastery. [from Greek *monakhos* solitary, from *monos* alone]

mon soon (mon sün'), a wind of the Indian Ocean and southern Asia that changes direction seasonally.

mood (müd), a feeling or frame of mind. [from Old English *mōd* mind, spirit]

muse (mūz), to consider thoughtfully.

mush (mush), food made from cornmeal boiled in water.

mus ter (mus'tər), to collect or gather up. [from Latin *monstāre* to show]

mys ti fi er (mis'tə fī ər), someone who confuses or puzzles on purpose.

nar whal (när'hwəl), an arctic water mammal. The male has a long, spiral tusk extending from the upper jaw.

nav i ga tion (nav'ə gā'shən), the science of directing the course of a ship or aircraft.

near-sight ed (nir'sī'tid), unable to see clearly at a distance.

nest ling (nest'ling), a young bird not ready to leave the nest.

neu ro tox ic (nü'rō tok'sik), poisonous to the body's nerves. [from Greek *neuron* nerve + *toxikon* poison arrow]

no ble (nō'bəl), 1. important because of birth, rank, or title. 2. splendid, admirable. [from Latin *nōbilis* knowable, famous]

Nor man Con quest (nôr′mən kong′kwest), the invasion and defeat of England by the people of Normandy in 1066. The Normans then united England under one ruler and brought about many changes in the lives of the English.

nos trils (nos′trəlz), the two openings in the nose through which air is breathed.

noun (noun), a word that names a person, place, thing, quality, or event. The words *Pam, books,* and *table* are nouns in the following sentence. *Pam put the books on the table.*

o blit e rat ing (ə blit′ə rāt′ing), wiping out or destroying all traces. *The fog was heavy, obliterating the traffic lights from view.* [from Latin *obliterare* to blot out]

ob serv a to ry (əb zér′və tôr′ē), a place with a telescope for looking at stars, planets, and other heavenly bodies.

ob vi ous (ob′vē əs), easy to see or understand; in plain view. **ob vi ous ly,** openly; easily seen; plainly. *The sick baby obviously needed a doctor.*

om i nous ly (om′ə nəs lē), in a threatening way.

op po nent (ə pō′nənt), one who is on the other side in a struggle.

o rang u tan (ô rang′ü tan′), a large, long-armed ape with reddish-brown hair. [from Malay *orang hutan* man of the woods]

or bit (ôr′bit), the curved path of one heavenly body, planet, or satellite around another body in space.

pan han dle (pan′han′dl), the narrow strip of northwestern Texas bordered on three sides by Oklahoma and New Mexico, so called because on a map it appears to be a handle.

par al lel (pār′ə lel), 1. in the same direction and at an equal distance apart, never meeting, as railway tracks. 2. very similar.

par tic u lar (pər tik′yə lər), 1. separately from others; single. 2. different from the rest; special.

pat ent (pat′nt), a government grant that gives a person the sole right to make, use, or sell a new invention for a certain period of time. **pat ent med i cine,** a medicine, protected by a patent, that can be bought without a doctor's prescription. **Pat ent Of fice,** the United States government agency that issues patents. **pat ent right,** the right to the sole ownership and control of an invention granted by a government patent.

pa tri ot (pā′trē ət), a person who loves and defends her or his country.

pe des tri an (pə des′trē ən), a person who travels on foot; one who walks. [from Latin *pes* foot]

pem mi can (pem′ə kən), cake of dried meat pounded into paste and mixed with berries and fat, first prepared by North American Indians. [from Cree *pimikân* from *pimii* grease, fat]

pen sion (pen′shən), money paid regularly after retirement to a person for a special reason such as time in service, injuries, and so forth.

per cus sion (pər kush′ən), musical instruments played by striking, such as drums, cymbals, xylophones, and pianos.

per pet u al (pər pech′ü əl), 1. lasting forever. 2. occurring continually without interruption.

pet ty (pet′ē), 1. of little importance. 2. mean; unkind. [from French *petit* small]

pi lot (pī′lət) **light,** a small flame that burns continuously and is used to light a main burner when needed.

piñ on (pin′yən *or* pē′nyōn), a certain kind of pine tree that grows in the southern Rocky Mountains. It bears nutlike seeds that can be eaten.

plum age (plü′mij), a bird's feathers.

po lar (pō′lər), referring to the areas near the North or South Pole.

por tal (pôr′tl), a doorway or entrance.

pre cau tion (pri kô′shən), action taken in advance to avoid evil or danger.

pre cise ly (pri sīs′lē), exactly; definitely correct.

pre ci sion (pri sizh′ ən), exactness; accuracy.

---

a **a**pple, ā **a**ble, ã **a**ir, ä **a**rm; e **e**levator, ē **ea**ch, ér **ea**rth; i **i**tch, ī **i**vy; o **o**dd, ō **o**pen, ô **a**ll, ôr **or**der; oi **oi**l, ou **ou**t; u **u**p, u̇ **p**ut, ü **b**oot, ū **u**se; ə **a**bout; th **th**in, ᴛʜ **th**en, zh mea**s**ure

pre dic a ment (pri dik'ə mənt), a situation that is unpleasant, difficult, or dangerous, and hard to get out of.

pre his to ric (prē' hi stôr'ik), referring to the times before history was written.

pre oc cu pied (prē ok'yə pīd), so deep in thought as to be unaware of other happenings.

pre vail (pri vāl'), to exist in a widespread area, to be common or frequent.

prey (prā), an animal hunted as food by another animal. [from Latin *prehendere* to seize]

pri mate (prī'māt), any of the group of mammals that include humans, monkeys, apes, and lemurs.

prime (prīm), 1. first in rank, as prime minister. 2. first in time, as primetime television. 3. highest quality, as prime meat.

pro (prō), shortened form of *professional,* a person who, for money, does something that others do for pleasure.

prob a bil i ty (prob'ə bil'ə tē), the condition of being likely to occur; a likely chance.

pro ceed ings (prə sē'dingz), actions that are taking place; goings-on.

prod i gy (prod'ə jē), a young person having a very rare talent or ability; a marvel or wonder. [from Latin *prodigium* prophetic sign]

pro hib it (prō hib'it), 1. to refuse to permit. 2. to forbid by law.

pro phet i cal ly (prə fet'ik lē), in the way of a prophet, a person who tells what will happen in the future.

pros per i ty (pro sper'ə tē), good fortune; thriving condition.

prowl (proul), to wander about secretly in search for something.

pul ley (pùl'ē), a machine used to lift weights and change the direction of a pulling force. It consists of a wheel with a groove through which a rope or chain is pulled.

punc ture (pungk'chər), to make a hole with a sharp, pointed object.

pun gent (pun'jənt), having a sharp effect on the organs of smell and taste.

quar ry men (kwôr'ē men), men who work with stone, excavating it and cutting it into shapes.

rafts (rafts), floating platforms, or something that resembles them.

rak ish (ra'kish), dashing or jaunty.

ram (ram), 1. a male sheep. 2. to force in by heavy blows; shove.

rash (rash), careless; overly hasty; done without thinking.

re al i ty (rē al'ə tē), the true state of affairs; actual fact.

reap (rēp), 1. to cut or gather a crop. 2. to get a result or reward.

rear ward (rir'wərd), backward.

re as sur ing (rē'ə shùr'ing), comforting; making more confident.

re ject (re ject'), to refuse to accept. [from Latin *rejicere* to throw back]

rem nant (rem'nənt), a small part left over; a scrap.

res in (rez'n), a sticky substance that comes out of certain plants and trees. *Heated pine resin yields turpentine.*

re sist ance (ri zis'təns), 1. strong opposition to something. 2. strength enough to fight off something. 3. opposition to an obstacle.

re treat (ri trēt'), a quiet place where one is away from all worries.

rit u al (rich'ü əl), the form or system of a solemn ceremony.

ro dent (rōd'nt), animal whose teeth are specially made for gnawing or nibbling, such as mice, rabbits, and rats. [from Latin *rodere* to gnaw]

ro tate (rō'tāt), to turn in a circle.

rouse (rouz), to wake up.

row an (rō' ən), a mountain ash tree with white flowers and red berries.

ruck sack (ruk'sak'), a kind of knapsack or backpack.

run (run), 1. a small, swift stream.

sa cred (sā'krid), holy; religious. [from Latin *sacer* dedicated, holy]

salm on (sam' ən), a large fish used for food.

sal u ta tion (sal'yə tā'shən), a polite gesture or expression of greeting.

sa rong (sə rong'), a brightly colored length of cloth wrapped around the body to form a garment something like a skirt.

sa van na (sə van'ə), an open grassland with few or no trees.

Schuyl kill (skül'kil) **River**, a river in Pennsylvania that runs from northwest to southeast to meet the Delaware River at Philadelphia.

scribe (scrīb), a person whose job was to keep records, copy letters, and write for those who could not. [from Latin *scribere* to write]

script (skript), the text for a play, television or radio show, or movie. [from Latin *scribere* to write)

scroll (skrōl), a length of parchment, paper, or silk rolled around a rod at each end.

sculpt (skulpt), to make an art object by carving, modeling, chiseling or casting.

scur ry (skėr'ē), to scamper; run about.

se clud ed (si klü'did), hidden away; set apart from others.

se cure (si kūr') safe; free from danger. [from Latin *sē* without + *cūrus* care]

sen sa tion (sen sā'shən), 1. a response of the senses: seeing, hearing, tasting, feeling, or smelling. 2. a feeling.

shal lows (shal'ōz), an area (in a body of water) where the water is not deep.

shel ter (shel'tər), to take cover; to find protection.

shoul der lift (shōl'dər lift), a dance technique in which a male dancer lifts his female partner into a sitting position on his shoulder.

shriek (shrēk), a loud, shrill sound.

sin ew (sin'ū), a tendon, a band of tissue that joins muscle to bone.

skulk (skulk), 1. to hide to avoid anger or duty. 2. to move in a sneaky way.

smat ter ing (smat'ər ing), a very small amount.

smug gle (smug'əl), 1. to transport something into or out of a country secretly and illegally. 2. to bring, carry, or take secretly.

smug ly (smug'lē), in a self-satisfied way; too pleased with one's own ability.

snare (snār), a noose made to trap small birds and animals.

soc cer (sok'ər), a form of football in which only the goalkeeper is allowed to touch the ball with the hands and arms. [formed from *(as)soc(iation)* + *er*—association football]

sod (sod), a section of ground covered with grass.

som ber (som'bər), gloomy; serious. [from Latin *subombrāre* to shade]

sooth (süŦH), 1. to make quiet or calm. 2. to bring comfort.

sough (suf, sou), to make a rushing, rustling, or murmuring sound.

spe cies (spē'shēz), 1. to group a class of animals or plants that have some basic characteristics or qualities in common. 2. type; sort; kind.

spec i men (spes'ə mən), a sample; one taken from a group to show what the others are like.

spell (spel), a period of unusual behavior or magical happenings.

splen did (splen'did), 1. grand; glorious. 2. fine, excellent.

splen dor (splen'dər), magnificence; grandeur.

stan dard (stan'dərd), something set as a goal to be compared against. **standard of living**, the economic level at which people live; the amount and type of food, clothing, shelter, and so forth.

stoop¹ (stüp), a small porch or raised platform at the door of a house. [from Dutch *stoep* a step in a stair]

stoop² (stüp), to bend one's body forward and downward. [from Middle English *stoupen* to bend]

strat e gy (strat'ə jē), a well thought out plan of action. [from Greek *stratēgos* general of an army]

strik ing (strī'king), very noticeable or impressive; attracting attention.

suc ces sion (sək sesh'ən), the following of one person or thing by another in a sequence or series.

sum mit (sum'it), the highest point, [from Latin *summum* highest part]

su per nat ur al (sü'pər nach'ər əl), 1. beyond the usual experience or knowledge of people. 2. godlike.

sur mount ed (sər moun'tid), topped; rose above.

---

a **a**pple, ā **a**ble, ā **a**ir, ä **a**rm; e **e**levator, ē **ea**ch, ėr **ea**rth; i **i**tch, ī **i**vy; o **o**dd, ō **o**pen, ô **a**ll, ôr **o**rder; oi **oi**l, ou **ou**t; u **u**p, u̇ **p**ut, ü **b**oot, ū **u**se; ə **a**bout; th **th**in, ŦH **th**en, zh mea**s**ure

sur vey ing (sər vā′ing), the science of measuring, with special equipment, the size, shape, location, and boundaries of land, mountains, bodies of water, and so forth. **surveyor**, a person who determines these exact measurements and boundaries.

swel ter ing (swel′tər ing), overwhelmingly hot.

swiv el (swiv′əl), a kind of fastening that allows whatever is attached to it to turn around freely upon it.

tal ly (tal′ē), 1. a stick into which notches are cut to keep score. 2. a count or score. [from Latin *tālea* twig, stick]

tech ni cal (tek′nə kəl), belonging to or having to do with the mechanical or industrial arts or applied science.

tech nol o gy (tek nol′ə jē), a special knowledge of, and skill in using, scientific, mechanical, and industrial resources.

tem per a ment (tem′pər ə mənt), one's nature or disposition. *His gentle temperament was appealing.*

thren o dy thren′ə dē), a funeral song. [from Greek *threnos* lamentation + *ōdē* song]

thrive (thrīv), to do well; prosper, grow.

throb (throb), to beat rapidly; to vibrate.

Ti bet an (ti bet′n), of or about Tibet and its people. Tibet is in southern China.

tide (tīd), the periodic rise and fall of the ocean about every 12 hours.

till er (til′ ər), the bar used to turn the rudder of a boat to steer it.

tran sit (tran′sit *or* tran′zit), 1. a passage. 2. the carrying of people or goods from one place to another.

trench (trench), a long, narrow ditch dug for protection or underground work.

tri umph (trī′umf), 1. a victory or a win. 2. joy over a victory or win.

trough (trôf), a long, narrow container used to hold food or water for animals.

trum pet (trum′pit), to make a sound like a trumpet, which is a brass wind instrument played in bands and orchestras.

ul u la tion (ūl′ū lā′shən), 1. the sound of howling. 2. a wailing or cry of sadness. [from Latin *ululare* to howl]

un dis tin guished (un′dis ting′gwisht), not special; ordinary.

u nique (ū nēk′), 1. being one of a kind. 2. having no equal.

un jus ti fied (un jus′tə fīid), without good cause.

un sus pect ing (un′sə spek′ting), not expecting something to happen.

vac u um (vak′ū əm *or* vak′ūm) **-sealed**, completely sealed with the air removed.

vast ness (vast′nes), great area or size.

venge ful (venj′fəl), having a strong desire for revenge.

vent (vent), opening which serves as an outlet for air, gas, and so on. *The heating vents in the car were all open.*

ver sion (ver′zhən), a report or description of an event giving one point of view; one side of a story. *Each girl gave her version of the movie.*

ver ti cal (ver′tə kəl), 1. in an upright position. 2. longer from top to bottom than from side to side. 3. straight up and down.

vi ol (vī′əl), a stringed musical instrument played with a bow. Viols were common in the 16th and 17th centuries.

vir tu al ly (ver′chü ə lē), for all practical purposes; essentially.

vul ner a ble (vul′nər ə bəl), open to injury or attack. *Mountain climbers are vulnerable to the cold.* [from Latin *vulnerāre* to wound]

wane (wān), 1. to gradually decrease. 2. to draw to a close.

war ren (wôr′ ən *or* wor′ ən), an area filled with burrows where rabbits live.

war y (wār′ē), watchful; cautious; on one's guard against a trick or a danger.

whal ing (hwā′ling), whale fishing.

wiz ard (wiz′ ərd), one who is said to have magic power. [from Middle English *wysard*, from *wys* smart, wise]

year ling (yēr′ling), an animal that is one year old.

yield (yēld), 1. to produce. *The garden will yield a large crop.* 2. To give up one's place. **yield right of way,** to allow another to go first.

Word List

The first time it appears in a selection, a word included in the **glossary** is followed by a^g. Words in the selections for which there are **context clues** to meaning are followed by a^c. These words are listed below in alphabetical order by selection.

Glossary Words	Context Clue Words	Glossary Words	Context Clue Words

Vocabulary Development Skills

Unit 1

Selection 1

amateur	captivated
captivate	constitution
constitution	maneuvers
ligament	technique
succession	trampoline

Selection 2

foster	ASL
foster parent	species
primate	
species	

Selection 3

banquet	(none)
curlicue	
emblem	

Selection 4

eclipse	feat
feat	uncooperative
patriot	
prevail	
surveyor	
tide	

Selection 5

amateur	Carbon 14 dating
archaeologist	technique
artifact	effigy mound
decompose	isolated
prehistoric	
sculpt	
sod	
surveyor	
unique·	

Unit 2

Selection 1

assurance	assurance
Braille	mollycoddling
cumbersome	
declining	
expectant	
fugue	
mollycoddle	
precision	
prodigy	

Selection 2

clattering	cocoon
cocoon	nestled
feebly	pellets
pulley	
stoop	

Selection 3

puncture	nourishment
rouse	punctured
	rousing

Selection 4

hogan	hogan
piñon	piñon

Selection 5

detest	bloodthirsty
exterior	blundered
gamble	detested
inheritance	exterior
lest	last
near-sighted	lest
salutation	
trough	

Glossary Words	Context Clue Words	Glossary Words	Context Clue Words

Unit 3

Selection 1

Selection 4 (continued)

		infinite	panic
blubber	amauts	involuntarily	peril
essential	device	precaution	precaution
igloo	durable	rash	previous
narwhal	essential	remnant	
polar	garments	retreat	
sinew	igloo		
	kamiks		
	modernized	### Selection 2	
	seeping		
	tilugtut	deliberation	bewildered
	ulo	diagram	bleak
		dormant	contraption

Selection 2

		eccentric	fantastic
accurate	accurate	intellect	figure
bolt	commissary	patent	laboratory
delta	"de ducks"	Patent Office	painstaking
illegal	glared	patent right	patent rights
ledger	illegal	reap	reap
patent	settle		
patent medicine		### Selection 3	

Selection 3

		muse	mused
caper	bloated	obvious	obvious
desperately	capered	precisely	prowling
	desperately	prowl	raged
	dribble	smugly	smugly
	peered	striking	unsuspecting
	rooted	triumph	
	steal	unsuspecting	

Selection 4 (none)

Selection 4

Selection 5

		defenseless	brace
cultivate	cultivate	devoted	defenseless
enthusiasm	enthusiasm	essential	essential
export	exports	husky	marooned
import	import	labored	warily
industrialization	industrialization	ominously	
secure	manufactured	wane	
standard	productive	wary	
standard of	secure		
living	standard		

Comprehension Skills

Selection 5

Unit 5

		### Selection 1	
extinguish	extinguished	foundation	scuttled
pemmican	palisade	pilot light	
wary	wary	ram	
		vent	

Unit 4

Selection 1

Selection 2

		discrimination	illegal
aftermath	abruptly	lawsuit	
barrier	barbed-wire	league	
cautious	beam	pro	
dramatic	dramatic	soccer	
eternity	escapees		
indifferently	impulse		

Glossary Words	Context Clue Words	Glossary Words	Context Clue Words

		Unit 7	
Selection 3		*Selection 1*	
adapt	dodo	carnival	authorities
extinct	extinct	harpoon	carcass
	fossils	incontestably	exhibit
		shallows	harpoon
Selection 4			immerse
dazzling	misdirection		kraken
illusion	shell		stranded
miracle	vanished		tentacles
mystifier			
wizard		*Selection 2*	
		gangplank	celebration
Selection 5		mood	embrace
ballet	plié	shriek	murmur
shoulder lift			
		Selection 3	
Unit 6		canyon	burden
Selection 1		chanted	falter
anchorperson	communications	clan	lance
assistant	distributed	haughty	trudged
interview	journalism	jeer	
script	lion's den	league	
technical	minority	mush	
temperament	responsible	portal	
	specialized		
		Selection 4	
Selection 2 (none)		Chevvie	ebbs
Selection 3		juggernaut	embers
carnival	cluster	pension	
eerie	fortunately	pungent	
orangutan	hold	resin	
rowan	inform	somber	
rucksack			
		Selection 5	
Selection 4		lotus	clambered
aquarium	graceful	monk	clucked
fascinating	helmet	monsoon	peering
	pearl divers	ritual	scurried
		sacred	subside
Selection 5		sarong	wrenched
accomplish	criticisms	scurry	
atmosphere	democratic		
box score		**Unit 8**	
challengingly		*Selection 1*	
dazzle		assurance	assurance
depth		cowardice	burden
dramatic		criticism	cowardice
emerge		gorings	criticism
hostile		hazard	fate
inbred		intelligence	functioning
marshal		noble	gruff
militancy		reality	intelligence
swivel		reject	rejected
unjustified			
virtually			

Glossary Words	Context Clue Words	Glossary Words	Context Clue Words

Selection 2

catapulted	catapulted		
compound eye	delicate		
contract	draught		
floes	molt		
frond	opponent		
opponent	predicament		
predicament	sargassum weed		
rafts	toting		
vulnerable	vulnerable		

Selection 3

courtyard	catch
despite	jarred
enormity	throbbed
throb	

Selection 4

agony	crested
exposed	gully
gully	infinitely
illusion	recollect
infinitely	seeped
panhandle	withered
prosperity	
sough	

Selection 5

cue	frantically
fife	splendor
splendor	stage fright

Study and Research Skills
Unit 9

Selection 1

airtight	air pressure
evaporate	thunderhead
	water vapor

Selection 2

image	focusing
index finger	

Selection 3

expressway	octagon
horizontal	
intersection	
median	
pedestrian	
prohibit	
vertical	
yield	
yield right of way	

Selection 4

knack	(none)
soothe	

Selection 5

exception	confident

Unit 10

Selection 1

aggressive	aggressive
alert	burrow
burrow	threatened
fatal	venomous
indistinct	
neurotoxic	
nostrils	
parallel	
prey	
rodent	

Selection 2

conserve	conserving
hydroelectric	industrial
insulate	insulated
mass transit system	per capita basis
standard	
standard of living	
transit	

Selection 3

efficient	clumsy
immature	exquisite
migrate	feature
rearward	rearward
resistance	shield
rotate	

Selection 4

equivalent	accuracy
perpetual	crests
summit	perfected
surveying	

Selection 5

B.C.	coma
coincide	indistinct
coma	
indistinct	
Norman Conquest	

Unit 11

Selection 1 (none)

Glossary Words	Context Clue Words	Glossary Words	Context Clue Words

Selection 2

ancestors	ancestors
barren	continent
exceedingly	enormous
forbidding	population
grim	survivors
lever	
supernatural	

Selection 5

archeologist	feats
feat	mastabas
foremen	
quarrymen	
scribe	

Selection 3

legendary	shelter
obliterating	
shelter	

Literary Appreciation Skills

Unit 13.

Selection 1

| jersey | crimson |

Selection 4

alder	alders
antics	antics
cleft	insistence
insistence	intently
instinct	preoccupied
nestling	prime
plumage	
preoccupied	
prime	
reassuring	
sweltering	
technology	
undistinguished	
vertical	

Selection 2

| altitude | precipitation |
| Mediterranean | |

Selection 3

annular	(none)
annular eclipse	
astronomy	
comet	
compute	
detect	
isolate	
navigation	
observatory	
orbit	
whaling	

Selection 5

| threnody | (none) |
| ululation | |

Selection 4 (none)

Unit 12

Selection 1

extinct	competing
invade	extinct
savanna	
smuggle	

Selection 5

edible	rehydrating
freeze-dried	
laminated	
vacuum-sealed	

Selection 2

conduct	margin of error
margin	poll
probability	pollsters
	population
	random
	researchers
	sample

Unit 14

Selection 1

ancestors	ancestors
dormitory	enrolled
fortunate	hovered
scroll	skimmed
viol	

Selection 3

| carbohydrate | calories |
| latitude | |

Selection 4

garrison	baggataway
version	lacrosse
	overwhelmed

Selection 2

accustomed	clatter
accustomed to	clutter
challenge	embers
coyote	flock
immense	yappings
smattering	
vastness	

479

Glossary Words	Context Clue Words	Glossary Words	Context Clue Words
	Selection 3		*Selection 3 (continued)*
hiking straps	bow	disport	frantically
muster	cleat	frolic	garment
reassuring	desperate	grampus	prey
tiller	experienced	ludicrous	refuge
	gusting	proceedings	romp
	luffing	rakish	sapling
	mainsheet	Schuylkill River	slithered
	obediently	scurry	
	surfaced	secluded	
	tack	surmounted	
	Selection 4		*Selection 4* (none)
(none)	scoff		
	Selection 5		*Selection 5*
category	capable	aristocratic	cowslip
doctrine	portions	bluebottle	delicacy
evaluate	preaches	brambles	oppressive
frustration	professional	buoyant	whimper
humanitarianism	relished	burrow	
humiliate	sensing	cower	
obviously		culvert	
particular		harassed	
splendid		warren	
		yearling	

Unit 15

	Selection 1
British	engineer
hostel	inquiries
keen	lodgings
Tibetan	puckered
	rank
	tongue

	Selection 2
boil	anglers
brae	line
demon	point
fly	strain
gaff	
prophetically	
run	
salmon	
sensation	
skulk	
strategy	

	Selection 3
antics	anxiety
apparition	cur
bedraggled	discern
culminate	donned
despondency	elegant
disheveled	floundering

Unit 16

	Selection 1
spell	(none)
trumpet	

	Selection 2
Aralia Spinosa	*Aralia Spinosa*
Filicales	collectively
percussion	*Filicales*
specimen	scrawny
thrive	

	Selection 3
archeologist	(none)
dig	
gale	
gully	
trench	

	Selection 4
Ivanhoe	petty
petty	vengeful
tally	
vengeful	

	Selection 5
headland	headland
snare	lair

Acknowledgments (continued)

1965 by Jackie Robinson and Alfred Duckett; reprinted by permission of Harper & Row, Publishers, Inc.; New York, and Lester Lewis Associates, Inc., New York. An adaptation of pages 63, 64 from *Buffalo Woman* by Dorothy M. Johnson; copyright © 1977 by Dorothy M. Johnson; reprinted by permission of Dodd, Mead & Company, Inc., New York, and McIntosh and Otis, Inc., New York. An adaptation of "Build a Balloon Barometer" by John Waugh; copyright © 1975 by John C. Waugh all rights reserved; originally adapted by *Cricket* Magazine, October 1975; reprinted by permission of Northeast Literary Agency, Concord, New Hampshire. (continued on page 481)

An adaptation of "The Cake Icing Caper" by Shirley Lee from *Boys' Life* Magazine, June 1977; copyright © 1977 by the Boy Scouts of America, North Brunswick, New Jersey; reprinted by permission of the author. An adaptation of "Cathy Rigby" from *Women in Sports* by Irwin Stambler; copyright © 1975 by Irwin Stambler; originally adapted by *Cricket* Magazine, January 1976; reprinted by permission of Doubleday & Company, Inc., New York, and Paul R. Reynolds, Inc., New York. An excerpt, with illustration, from pages 36–41 of *Charlotte's Web* by E. B. White, illustrated by Garth Williams; copyright © 1952 by E. B. White; reprinted by permission of Harper & Row, Publishers, Inc., New York, and Hamish Hamilton Ltd., London. "Clothes" from *The Secret Brother* by Elizabeth Jennings; reprinted by permission of Macmillan, London and Basingstoke. "Conserving Energy" by Jack Myers from *Highlights for Children*, December 1977; copyright © 1977 by Highlights for Children, Inc., Columbus, Ohio; reprinted by permission of the publisher.

An excerpt from pages 125–128 of *Daughter of the Mountains* by Louise Rankin; copyright 1948 by Louise S. Rankin, renewed © 1976 by Everett H. Rankin; all rights reserved; reprinted by permission of Viking Penguin Inc., New York. "Dawan is Leaving Home," an adaptation of Chapter 13 from *Sing to the Dawn* by Minfong Ho; copyright © 1975 by Minfong Ho; reprinted by permission of Lothrop, Lee & Shepard Company, a Division of William Morrow & Company, New York. An adaptation of "The Day It Rained Cats and Dogs" by Linda Allen; copyright © 1978 by Linda Allen; originally adapted by *Cricket* Magazine, April 1978; reprinted by permission of the author. An adaptation of "Designed for Flight" by George Laycock from *Boys' Life* Magazine, January 1976; copyright © 1976 by the Boy Scouts of America, North Brunswick, New Jersey; reprinted by permission of the author. An adaptation of "Do You Like Spinach?" by John Weiss; copyright © 1976 by John Weiss; originally adapted by *Cricket* Magazine, November 1976; reprinted by permission of the author. An adaptation of *Dodos and Dinosaurs* by Julian May Dikty; text copyright © 1970 by Julian May Dikty; reprinted by permission of Creative Education, Inc., Mankato, Minnesota. An adaptation of pages 33–37 from *Don't Take Teddy* by Babbis Friis-Baastad; translated from the Norwegian by Lise Sømme McKinnon; copyright © 1967 by Babbis Friis-Baastad; reprinted by permission of Charles Scribner's Sons, New York, and American Literary Exchange, New York. An adaptation of pages 32–39 from *Doug Meets the Nutcracker* by William H. Hooks; copyright © 1977 by William H. Hooks; reprinted by permission of Frederick Warne & Company, Inc., New York.

"The Egyptian Pyramids," an excerpt from *Inquiring About Technology—Studies in Economics and Anthropology* by Mindella Schultz; copyright © 1972 by Holt, Rinehart and Winston, Publishers; reprinted by permission. Encyclopedia Articles: "Classification, Scientific" from *The World Book Encyclopedia;* "Climate of Greece," adapted from *Greece* in *The World Book Encyclopedia;* copyright © 1979 by World Book Childcraft International, Inc., Chicago; reprinted by permission of the publisher. "End of a Journey," an adaptation of pages 148–150 from *Journey to America* by Sonia Levitin; copyright © 1970 by Sonia Levitin; reprinted by permission of Atheneum Publishers, Inc., New York. An adaptation of pages 38, 41, and 43 from *Eskimos* by Mary Bringle; copyright © 1973 by Franklin Watts, Inc., reprinted by permission of the publisher. "Eugenie Clark Begins Her Life's Work," an adaptation of pages 7–19 of *Shark Lady, True Adventures of Eugenie Clark,* by Ann McGovern; copyright © 1978 by Ann McGovern, reprinted by permission of Scholastic Book Services, a Division of Scholastic Magazines, Inc., New York.

"Floating Frankfurter" from *Science Puzzlers* by Martin Gardner; copyright © 1960 by Martin Gardner and Anthony Ravielli; originally adapted by *Cricket* Magazine, March 1974; reprinted by permission of Viking Penguin, Inc., New York, and Macmillan, London and Basingstoke. "Focus on the Social Scientist," an adaptation of page 45 from *The Social Sciences: Concepts and Values,* Second Edition (Brown) by Paul F. Brandwein et al; copyright © 1975 by Harcourt Brace Jovanovich, Inc., New York; reprinted by permission of the publisher. "Food for Space" from *Child Life Mystery and Science-Fiction* Magazine; copyright © 1978 by The Saturday Evening Post Company, Indianapolis, Indiana; reprinted by permission of the publisher.

"Getting Information from Graphs," an adaptation of pages 32–34 from *The Social Sciences: Concepts and Values,* Second Edition (Brown) by Paul F. Brandwein et al; copyright © 1975 by Harcourt Brace Jovanovich, Inc., New York; reprinted and reproduced by permission of the publisher. An adaptation of "Giants on the Earth" by Helen Achczynski from *Cricket* Magazine, September 1978; copyright © 1978 by Open Court Publishing Company; reprinted by permission of *Cricket* Magazine, La Salle, Illinois. An adaptation of "The Gift of Reason" by Walter D. Edmonds; copyright © 1977 by Walter D. Edmonds; originally adapted by *Cricket* Magazine, October 1977; reprinted by permission of the author. "Grading the Giant Mountains," adapted from *Mountain Conquest* by Eric Shipton; copyright © 1966 by American Heritage Publishing Company, Inc., New York; reprinted by permission of the publisher. "Growing: For Louis" from *The Way Things Are and Other Poems* by Myra Cohn Livingston (A Margaret E. McElderry Book); copyright © 1974 by Myra Cohn Livingston; reprinted by permission of Atheneum Publishers, Inc., New York, and McIntosh and Otis, Inc., New York.

"Halley's Comet," adapted from *Visitors From Afar, The Comets,* by Willy Ley; copyright © 1969 by Willy Ley; reprinted by permission of McGraw-Hill Book Company, New York. An adaptation of "HaroldandBurtandSueandAmy, etc." by Casey West from *Boys' Life* Magazine, February 1976; copyright © 1976 by the Boy Scouts of America, North Brunswick, New Jersey; reprinted by permission of the author. An adaptation of pages 209–214 from *Honestly, Katie John!* by Mary Calhoun; copyright © 1963 by Mary Calhoun; reprinted by permission of Harper & Row, Publishers, Inc., New York. An adaptation of pages 41–46 from *The House of Sixty Fathers* by Meindert DeJong; copyright © 1956 by Meindert DeJong; reprinted by permission of Harper & Row, Publishers, Inc., New York, and Laurence Pollinger Limited, London. " 'Hurry, Please,' said the Chimpanzees," adapted from *Reading, Writing, Chattering Chimps* by Aline Amon; copyright © 1975 by Aline Amon Goodrich; originally adapted by *Ranger Rick's Nature Magazine,* September 1977; reprinted by permission of Atheneum Publishers, Inc., New York, and Curtis Brown Ltd., New York.

An adaptation on pages 77–79 of pages 108–111 and 114–116 from *India* by T. A. Raman; copyright © 1972 by The Fideler Company, Grand Rapids, Michigan; reprinted by permission of the publisher. An excerpt of pages 158–161 from *Island of the Blue Dolphins* by Scott O'Dell; copyright © 1960 by Scott O'Dell; reprinted by permission of Houghton Mifflin Company, Boston, and Penguin Books Ltd., London. An excerpt from "Jane Goodall" by Gilbert Grail from *Time and Tigers, Reading Basics Plus Sixth Reader;* copyright © 1976 by Harper & Row, Publishers, Inc., New York; reprinted by permission of the publisher. "January—Yas Nilt'ees" from *Alice Yazzie's Year* by Ramona Maher; poems copyright © 1977 by Ramona Maher; reprinted by permission of Coward, McCann & Geoghegan, Inc., New York.

"The Largest Sea Monster in the World," an adaptation of Chapter 1 from *The Greatest Monsters in the World* by Daniel Cohen; copyright © 1975 by Daniel Cohen; originally adapted by *Cricket* Magazine, March 1976; reprinted by permission of Dodd, Mead & Company, Inc., New York, and Henry Morrison Inc., New York. An adaptation of pages 21–25 from *The Loner* by Ester Wier; copyright © 1963 Ester Wier; reprinted by permission of David McKay Co., Inc., New York. "The Long Trail," an excerpt from pages 91–96 of *Sing Down the Moon* by Scott O'Dell; copyright © 1970 by Scott O'Dell; reprinted by permission of Houghton Mifflin Company, Boston, and Hamish Hamilton Ltd., London. "Ludell's Amazing Paper," an adaptation of pages 167–169 from *Ludell* by Brenda Wilkinson; copyright © 1975 by Brenda Scott Wilkinson; reprinted by permission of Harper & Row, Publishers, Inc., New York.

"Maria Mitchell, Astronomer" by Charlene Lundell from *Highlights for Children*, March 1976; copyright © 1976 by Highlights for Children, Inc., Columbus, Ohio; reprinted by permission of the publisher. An adaptation of "Missing Australian pilot feared held by 'people from another planet'," from *Chicago Sun-Times*, October 25, 1978; reprinted by permission of United Press

Illustrations

Editorial Credits

Managing Editor: Kathleen Laya
Assistant Editor: Elizabeth M. Garber
Director of Design: Allen Carr
Design Assistants: Ken Izzi, Marcia Vecchione

Editors: John Hancock, Manya Pleva, Carol Steben